C0-AYK-183

TIME AND ETERNITY IN CHRISTIAN THOUGHT

TIME AND ETERNITY IN CHRISTIAN THOUGHT

BEING EIGHT LECTURES
DELIVERED BEFORE THE UNIVERSITY OF
OXFORD, IN THE YEAR 1936, ON THE FOUNDATION OF
THE REV. JOHN BAMPTON, CANON
OF SALISBURY

by

FRANK HERBERT BRABANT, M.A.
PRINCIPAL OF THE MACKENZIE MEMORIAL COLLEGE,
ZULULAND ; FORMERLY CHAPLAIN AND FELLOW OF
WADHAM COLLEGE, OXFORD

LONGMANS, GREEN AND CO.
LONDON • NEW YORK • TORONTO

LONGMANS, GREEN AND CO. LTD.
39 PATERNOSTER ROW, LONDON, E.C.4
6 OLD COURT HOUSE STREET, CALCUTTA
53 NICOL ROAD, BOMBAY
36A MOUNT ROAD, MADRAS

LONGMANS, GREEN AND CO.
114 FIFTH AVENUE, NEW YORK
221 EAST 20TH STREET, CHICAGO
88 TREMONT STREET, BOSTON

LONGMANS, GREEN AND CO.
215 VICTORIA STREET, TORONTO

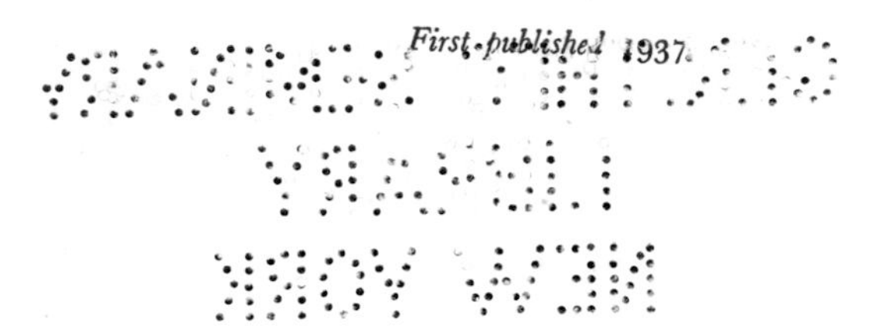

First published 1937

Printed in Great Britain

EXTRACT

FROM THE LAST WILL AND TESTAMENT

OF THE LATE

REV. JOHN BAMPTON

CANON OF SALISBURY

'... I give and bequeath my Lands and Estates to the Chancellor, Masters, and Scholars of the University of Oxford for ever, to have and to hold all and singular the said Lands or Estates upon trust, and to the intents and purposes hereinafter mentioned; that is to say, I will and appoint that the Vice-Chancellor of the University of Oxford for the time being shall take and receive all the rents, issues, and profits thereof, and (after all taxes, reparations, and necessary deductions made) that he pay all the remainder to the endowment of eight Divinity Lecture Sermons, to be established for ever in the said University, and to be performed in the manner following:

'I direct and appoint that, upon the first Tuesday in Easter Term, a Lecturer be yearly chosen by the Heads of Colleges only, and by no others, in the room adjoining to the Printing-House, between the hours of ten in the morning and two in the afternoon, to preach eight Divinity Lecture Sermons, the year following, at St. Mary's in Oxford, between the commencement of the last month in Lent Term and the end of the third week in Act Term.

'Also I direct and appoint, that the eight Divinity Lecture Sermons shall be preached upon either of the following subjects—to confirm and establish the Christian Faith, and to confute all heretics and schismatics—upon the divine authority of the holy Scriptures—upon the authority of the writings of the primitive Fathers, as to the faith and practice of the primitive Church—upon the Divinity of our Lord and Saviour Jesus Christ—upon the Divinity of the Holy Ghost—upon the Articles of the Christian Faith, as comprehended in the Apostles' and Nicene Creeds.

'Also I direct, that thirty copies of the eight Divinity Lecture Sermons shall always be printed, within two months after they are preached ; and one copy shall be given to the Chancellor of the University, and one copy to the Head of Every College, and one copy to the Mayor of the city of Oxford, and one copy to be put into the Bodleian Library ; and the expense of printing them shall be paid out of the revenue of the Land or Estates given for establishing the Divinity Lecture Sermons ; and the Preacher shall not be paid, nor be entitled to the revenue, before they are printed.

'Also I direct and appoint, that no person shall be qualified to preach the Divinity Lecture Sermons, unless he hath taken the degree of Master of Arts at least, in one of the two Universities of Oxford or Cambridge ; and that the same person shall never preach the Divinity Lecture Sermons twice.'

PREFACE

If I venture to remind the reader that these Lectures were, for the most part, written on the Mission Field (in Zululand), it is not with any idea of seeking for an excuse to cover their many imperfections. Bad philosophy is no more to be pardoned at Isandlwana than at Oxford ; indeed, the silence of the veldt and the absence of interruptions should have been a stimulus to meditation.

But the reader may expect references to recent books and recent theories, ignorance of which may perhaps be somewhat condoned in a missionary.

The general subject was not suggested (as has been supposed in some quarters) by 'the great spaces of Africa.' I have really been expanding and following out (sometimes, I fear, with repetition) the line of thought I adopted in an essay called 'God and Time' in *Essays on the Incarnation and the Trinity*.

If the Lectures seem sometimes to assume Christianity rather than prove it, I can only plead that the Bampton Lectures are normally supposed to be addressed to Christians—and also that for some people the attempt to explain what Christianity is may be, in itself, a not unworthy apologetic.

Some, I know, have found these Lectures difficult. I cannot undertake to divide the responsibility between the nature of the subject and the incompetence of the lecturer. I can only hope that those who patiently attended the sermons at St.

Mary's may find the (somewhat larger) book at least not more incomprehensible.

My thanks are due to Dr. Simpson of Oriel College for supplying me with information about the Hebrew words for 'eternal'; to Dr. Lowther Clark for suggestions on the use of *Αἰώνιος*; to Father Ngidi (a Roman Catholic native priest in Zululand) for lending me his copy of St. Thomas Aquinas; to Dr. Darwell Stone for lending me some extracts from the forthcoming Lexicon of Patristic Greek; to Mr. Edwyn Bevan for a private letter, which I found helpful; also to Mr. Tod of Oriel College for help in correcting the Greek quotations, and to the Rev. Philip Hopkinson for aid in compiling the Index. I should also like to thank my publishers and printers for speed and goodwill in getting through the proofs before my return to South Africa.

OXFORD,
July 1936.

CONTENTS

FIRST LECTURE

THE CONCEPTION OF ETERNITY IN GREEK THOUGHT

Hell is naked before Him, and destruction hath no covering. . . .
The pillars of Heaven tremble and are astonished at His reproof. . . .
Lo, these are parts of His ways: but how little a portion is heard of Him? but the thunder of His power who can understand?—JOB xxvi. 6, 11, 14.

THE words of our text, so characteristic of Old Testament theology in their caution and reverence, will help us to keep in mind, from the very first, with what humility and godly fear we should approach the mystery of God's Eternity. There is a well-known story of St. Augustine which tells how he was meditating upon his book—the *De Trinitate*—by the seashore. He saw a child engaged in filling a shell from the ocean, and then pouring it out into a hole he had dug in the sand. Questioned as to what he was doing, the child replied that he meant to empty all the sea into his hole. The theologian gently pointed out the futility of such a task, and the child retorted, 'What I am doing is more likely to be accomplished than what you are trying to do, that is, to understand the Divine Nature.'

The humour of the admonition convinced the saint that he was being entertained by an angel unawares.

When any modern theologian compares his task and equipment with that of the great African doctor, the proportions of the parable inevitably shift and alter. The sea becomes deeper, the shell smaller, and the child weaker. Where St. Augustine hesitated, should we not do well to be silent?

Apart from its obvious and inherent difficulties, it might be felt that the subject of Time and Eternity is too metaphysical for a course of sermons which (even with the latitude allowed to Bampton Lecturers) ought to have some remote connection with the edification of the faithful. The Christian doctrine of God, it might be urged, is a religious doctrine and, as such, distinct from speculations of the philosopher about the Absolute or discussions of the physicist about the nature of Time and Relativity.

Let me say at once that I earnestly hope to avoid turning these sermons into a course of lectures on metaphysics; I also hope to avoid (and I am not competent enough to find much difficulty in avoiding) the technical treatment of isolated problems more fitted for the lecture-room than the pulpit. Theology and philosophy both have their dusty corners which I shall do nothing at all to disturb.

However, nothing is so important for the Christian religion as its doctrine of God. Many errors in thought and hesitations in practice have their roots far back in misunderstandings of the Divine Nature. It may be objected that this is true of His Love or His Holiness, but hardly of such unintelligible attributes as His Eternity. But we cannot really make such separations ; in the doctrine of God's Eternity is involved that of His Perfection, His Power and His relation to finite things, upon which hang further doctrines about Creation and Predestination which have notably affected human life and thought. Sometimes inside Christianity and sometimes outside it (as in Buddhism) a certain conception of God's Eternity has exercised a paralysing effect upon action. On the other hand, in the West we have now for a long time too much neglected to consider the Power and Majesty of God as He is in Himself and too often introduced Him only to play a useful part in our schemes for explaining the universe or improving human society. As Dr. Forsyth says in his remarkable war-book, *The Justification of God* (p. 19), in much modern piety 'God is there but to promote and crown the development of Man. . . . He is there to draw upon to save Man's career at the points where it is most threatened. . . . To that has come the Fatherhood, though for Christ its first claim and the first petition in His prayer was that it should be hallowed, not exploited.' All the deepest thought of our age is at one in demanding return to a Theocentric Religion, which shall find its highest expression in worship and adoration. I need not remind you how impressively one of my predecessors in this pulpit has taught us that not the edification of ourselves nor even the edification of others, but the Vision of God should be the centre of the Christian life. Such an orientation of the devotional life can only be obtained by meditation and adoration, but reflection also has its part to play, and no subject, more than that of God's Eternity, carries our mind to the Divine Nature, not as condescending to our needs but as it is, in its own richness and holiness and perfection.

But we need not shrink from claiming a more directly human interest in our subject. In all literature many of the greatest passages have had for their theme the inevitable passing away of earthly things; many of the sweetest and most solemn notes in our own language are tuned to this thought. We remember Shakespeare's great sonnet:

Since brass, nor stone, nor earth, nor boundless sea,
But sad mortality o'er-sways their power,
How with this rage shall beauty hold a plea,
Whose action is no stronger than a flower?
O, how shall summer's honey breath hold out
Against the wreckful siege of battering days,
When rocks impregnable are not so stout,
Nor gates of steel so strong, but Time decays?
(*Sonnet* 65)

or the gentler lines of Spenser, more philosophic and less personal:

When I bethinke me on that speech whyleare
Of Mutabilitie and well it way,
Me seemes that though she all unworthy were
Of the Heaven's rule, yet very sooth to say
In all things else she beares the greatest sway,
Which makes me loath this state of life so tickle
And love of things so vain to cast away,
Whose flowering pride so fading and so fickle
Short Time shall soon cut down with his consuming sickle.

or those lines from *Adonais*, in which it is so hard to account for the magical charm of the words:

Life, like a dome of many-coloured glass,
Stains the white radiance of eternity,
Until Death tramples it to fragments.

To the same theme is set the organ-roll of Sir Thomas Browne's periods in the *Hydriotaphia :*

Since our longest sunne sets at right descensions, and makes but winter arches, and therefore it cannot be long before we lie down in darkness and have our light in ashes. . . . Diuturnity is a dream and folly of expectation.

Religion has always directed the heart of man to something which endures. The Psalmist cries to his God, 'They (that is, Heaven and earth) shall be changed : but Thou art the same, and Thy years shall have no end.' [1]

So Milton :

Then, all this earthly grossness quit,
Attired with stars, we shall for ever sit,
Triumphing over Death and Chance and thee, O Time.

So Kingsley in a pathetic fragment :

They drift away—ah, God, they drift for ever :
I watch the stream sweep onward to the sea
. . . Ah God, my God, Thou wilt not drift away.

Professor Whitehead has found formulated in the first two lines of a famous hymn the complete problem of Metaphysics,[2] and there, too, the contrast is between the changing and the unchangeable :

'Abide with me;
Fast falls the eventide.'

The problem of Time and Eternity is no problem of mathematical relations but a profound question

[1] Psalm cii. 26, 27. [2] *Process and Reality*, p. 296.

of values. Amid the inescapable flux, can Man find and hold on to anything which abides?

Because the problem goes down so deep into the very meaning of life, it is (as we should expect) a mystery; but a mystery is not something to be hidden away, like a skeleton in a cupboard, or to be ashamed of, like a sum that won't work out right. True, there may be no answer; the journey may have no 'end,' but we pass many interesting things on our way, for the attempt to understand the universe is not the search after some dry formula, but a voyage of the mind. The true traveller will not grumble because there are new countries for him to discover; it would surely be the height of vanity and self-centredness to be abashed by our failure to understand rather than exalted by the richness and subtlety of life.

Plato

May I now dispense with further preface and ask you to plunge *in medias res* by considering the first defined conception of Eternity in the history of Greek Philosophy—I mean Plato's doctrine of Ideas or Forms?

The word 'eternal' may be used in three distinct senses: (1) what is everlasting and never ends; (2) what is unchanging and never alters; (3) what is perfect, so that nothing can be added to or taken away from it. In early Greek thought (dealing largely with the problems of the material universe) these meanings were rather separate; the Flux of Heracleitus was everlasting, but the reverse of unchanging ; Parmenides' unchanging One was probably a closed sphere and had no claims to perfection ; while from the point of view of the artist a perfect statue was neither everlasting nor unchanging, for it might be smashed to pieces. But in Plato's spiritual world of Forms the three meanings are inextricably interfused.

First of all, the Forms are *unchanging* ; the conception of an unchanging element in the universe seems to have come from Parmenides' criticism of the perpetual movement of Heracleitus' Flux. Movement implies empty space, for the arrow cannot move unless there is empty space for it to occupy. But empty space is an impossibility ; therefore motion is an illusion and the real world is one and unchanging. One at least of the origins of the idea of Eternity is physical speculation about the void.

Plato, of course, admitted the Flux at the low stage of sense-perception, of which the objects are and are not, as in a dream. But the world which geometry studied was spaceless and motionless ; thought must have an eternal object.

Socrates says to Cratylus, who is bitten with the Heracleitan virus, 'Can we rightly speak of true Beauty, which is always passing away and is first this and then that ; must not the same thing be born and retire and vanish while the word is in our mouths ?' There must not only be stable objects but also a stable subject to know them. 'Knowledge,' he says, 'cannot continue to be knowledge unless continuing always to abide and exist. But if the very nature of knowledge changes, at the time when the change occurs, there will be no knowledge . . . there will be no one to know and nothing to be known.' [1]

Secondly, the Forms must be eternal in the sense of *perfect*. The Forms of true beauty and justice cannot be increased or diminished without losing their character. The most famous passage on this point, from the *Republic*, is concerned with God rather than with the Forms, but we may be excused a reference to it, as by many it is regarded as the very *fons et origo mali*, the source of the so-called static character of Greek thought. 'Things which are at their best are also least liable to be altered or discomposed; when healthiest and strongest, the human frame is least liable to be affected by meats and drinks. . . . Everything which is good . . . is least liable to suffer change from without . . . God therefore can hardly be compelled by external influence to take many shapes. . . . If He change at all, He can only change for the worse, for we cannot suppose Him to be deficient either in virtue or beauty' (as would be the case if He could change for the better).[2]

Thirdly, the Forms are *everlasting* as being the real causes of things; they must always be there for anything to exist, at least to exist as we know it; they are creative. 'To my simple mind,' says Socrates (mindful of the high-brow art critics of the day), 'a thing is beautiful, because the Form of beauty is present to it.' [3] The Forms give reality

[1] *Cratylus* (Jowett, i. p. 388). [2] *Republic* (Jowett, iii. p. 64).
[3] *Phaedo*, 100 (Jowett, ii. p. 246). I have paraphrased the words a little.

to the particulars of sense-perception in three ways, by παρουσία (presencc with them), by κοινωνία (by which the particulars participate in the Forms), and by μίμησις (according to which the Forms are models which the particulars imitate).

There is something else which is eternal in Platonism, and that is the ψυχή, or Soul. Before birth the human ψυχή has been familiar with the Forms (carried round in a chariot to view them),[1] and it remembers them by ἀνάμνησις, the recall of thought. It is this recollection which proves it immortal, for in the *Phaedo* it is rather the non-beginning than the non-ending of the soul which is demonstrated. It is not that the soul *will* be immortal, but rather that it *is* already immortal and cannot really be affected by what happens in this life. This is the true meaning of the doctrine that Vice is Ignorance; the inner principle of knowledge may be clouded but cannot really be contaminated by the tumult of bodily passions; if, therefore, a man really lives an evil life, it must be because the reasonable element is wanting or dormant.

In the earlier part of Plato's thought the ψυχή is slightly in the background; the Forms are supreme, ruled by the Form of the Good; the ψυχή has eternity only because of its communion with the Forms. In Plato's later thought the Forms have receded and Soul has come to the front. There is a personal and creative God, while in man and in the cosmos Soul is the very source of order and harmony.

Whether the change is a real transformation of

[1] *Phaedrus*, 247 (Jowett, i. p. 453).

Plato's philosophy or whether it is merely a change in the order of exposition is a matter of much controversy: with such disputes we have nothing to do; for our purpose the *Timaeus* is of central importance, not because it is a truer or deeper Platonism, but because it gave to succeeding generations a story of Creation and a cosmology. It was probably because of the *Timaeus* that one of the early Fathers called Plato 'Moses talking Attic Greek,' and in the Middle Ages, which hardly knew Plato save through fragments of a Latin version of the *Timaeus*, it had marked effects on doctrines of Creation.

The *Timaeus* makes strange reading. It is like the fairy tale of a scientist with its diagonals and demigods, part mysticism, part mathematics. It is curious to pass from such poetic phrases as 'The Creator Who is jealous of none,' or 'Time the moving image of eternity,' to the fantastic machinery of respiration or the gigantic, geometrical shapes of the four elements. The work has been called a hymn of the universe; perhaps it is more like a sacred masque, in which ambiguous figures, stately and grotesque, move to their appointed measures. It is easy to lose one's way, fascinated or perplexed by details; we must keep sternly to our task, which is to disentangle from the story the four different 'natures' and ask how far Eternity is predicated of each.

These are, first, the nature of the Demiourgos (the Artist and Artificer rather than Creator) by whose initiative the world, as we know it, has been brought into being.

Secondly, the nature of the intelligible Paradeigmata or Models, to which as examples or patterns the Demiourgos ' looked,' when He made the world.

Thirdly, the Matter or Stuff (χώρα Plato calls it) within which the process of world-becoming takes place.

Fourthly, the World Soul with its World Body, which includes the gods—that is, the fixed stars (their divine souls and bodies of fire made by the Demiourgos), and human beings, whose souls were made by the Demiourgos and their bodies by lesser gods.

One general remark we shall find to have its importance ; questions of interpretation were constantly exercising the Platonic school of commentators. If God is (as Plato held) the true Source of movement, why does He delegate part of His creative power to demigods ? Why is He bound to regulate His action by the independent Paradeigmata or Models ? Why is Matter or χώρα spoken of as if it existed before the Creation ? Again, how is it that, after saying expressly that ' Time came into being along with the visible Heaven ' (38 *b*, 6), Timaeus professes to be able to tell us about the state of things before God made the visible Heaven ? [1] Again, what is the relation between the eternal and temporal in the world ? Plato seems to speak of one of the circles of the visible Heaven as standing for Eternity, and yet he lays down the principle that nothing which is perceived by the senses can be eternal.

[1] A. E. Taylor, *Commentary on the Timaeus*, p. 69.

To all these questions and all questions of this kind the proper answer seems to be that the description of the Creation is mythical; Plato himself tells us in 29 *b*, 'In speaking of the original (that is, the eternal Paradeigma or exemplar of our world) and the copy (that is, the perceived world modelled upon the Paradeigma), we may assume that words are akin to the matter which they describe; when they relate to the lasting and permanent and intelligible (that is, eternal things), they ought to be lasting and unalterable, and (as far as their nature allows) irrefutable and immovable—nothing less. But when they express only the copy or likeness, not the eternal things themselves, they need to be only likely and analogous.' For Plato the eternal is the intelligible; such timeless sciences as logic and mathematics are also faultless and intelligible. No cloud of incense (neo-Platonic or Christian) has yet begun to blur their sharp outlines. Mystery and mythology only begin with the world of sense-perception; here we are in the world of τὸ ἄπειρον, the Infinite (the opposite, notice, of the Eternal); we are in the sphere of δόξα or guess-work, and any exposition of how things began or how they continue to work must take the form of a 'likely tale' [1]; the *Timaeus* itself is much less an account of the origin of everything than a series of pictures showing from different points of view the elements of which the world consists. But if that was the standpoint of Plato, it was not that of Christian Theology.

[1] 'The appropriate vehicle for half-truths of this kind is myth, and . . . myth expresses something lower than science, and not something higher' (Burnet, *Greek Philosophy*, i. p. 340).

It had to face the same problem as Plato. Was God bound to create when and as He did? What was the Matter which seemed to lie ready to His creating hand? Had the world a beginning in Time? How does the eternal impinge upon the temporal, by means of what Divine intervention or angelic ministrations? But it was not prepared to meet such a problem by telling myths; in contrast to the reckless speculation of philosophers, had it not the truth soberly and plainly revealed in the Scriptures? All that was needed was to interpret them. More than this, history was the record of something God had done, whereas for the true Platonist it is largely a story invented to teach us what to think; to Christianity, devoted to faith in a personal God Who had revealed Himself, everything He had done was of importance because it showed His nature; it asked eagerly, When did God create? why did God create? how did God create? Does He still intervene? Plato, interested in the universe as a revelation of eternal law, not as a revelation of the purpose or action of a Person, did not much care to ask how things happened to become what they now are. Both points of view needed correction. Platonism had to be reminded that because the ultimate beginning of things could not be understood, it did not follow that the whole course of history or process was irrational. Christianity had to be reminded that, although the course of history was a revelation of God's continued purpose in the realm of fact, yet (as has been said) we can only be taught about the ultimate beginning and end of things by means of stories.

Thus, if we start from the Demiourgos, we are struck at once by the difference (if we take it as theology) between His Nature and that of the Christian Creator. Doubtless the representation of Him in the *Timaeus* put into concrete form a conception which had been haunting Greek thought since Anaxagoras—that of Mind 'arranging all things.' But at first sight the Demiourgos seems not to be in any full sense a Creator. In making the world He 'looks towards' the intelligible Paradeigmata for guidance, and we have no hint that these Paradeigmata are thoughts of God or in any sense caused by Him.[1] He creates the World Soul from the Intelligible (already found in the Paradeigmata) and what Plato calls the Other, which is infected with Ananke or Necessity, an element which is spoken of as if it were independent of Him.[2] The Body of the World is made from Matter, which is spoken of as though it already existed in a disordered state[3]; the bodies of men (having a tendency to evil) are not made by Him at all. In a word, He unites Harmony and Disorder so as to make a Cosmos. He is less the Creator of the World than (in the phrase of the *Philebus*) the 'Cause of the mixture.'

He designs the world because, 'being free from

[1] Dr. Adam argues from 28 *c* that the Demiourgos, as 'Father and maker of all,' exercises all-creative functions. The words are τὸν ποιητὴν καὶ πατέρα τοῦδε τοῦ παντός. But τοῦδε τοῦ παντός seems to refer not to all things but to this actual World Soul; the phrase 'Father of becoming' is used, later, of the Paradeigmata.

[2] 'He had to compress by force' τὴν θατέρου φύσιν δύσμεικτον οὖσαν (35 *a*).

[3] In the primitive state of chaos, the four elements had as yet 'only faint traces of themselves,' ὥσπερ εἰκὸς ἔχειν ἅπαν, ὅταν ἀπῇ τινος θεός (53 *b*).

jealousy,' He wishes to extend the realm of order and reason. When human bodies are to be made He leaves the work to demigods and His Majestic Figure, 'hard to be spoken of,' withdraws to 'its accustomed nature.' This is Allegory, not Theology; Plato seems to be describing (and perhaps separating for purposes of description) three elements in the universe as we know it. There is the element of Necessity, something irrational (the problem of evil, as the Jews called it, looking at it from the moral point of view).[1] There is the element of Intelligence, or rather the Intelligible, represented by the eternal Paradeigmata. But these two have no connection without the intervention of a third element—the creative element of Life, the source of all good and orderly movement, Who almost by an act of will brings chaos under the dominion of intelligible laws. The relation of the Demiourgos to the eternal Paradeigmata therefore represents what in Christian thought we call the relation between God's Will and His Intelligence or Moral Nature. He creates the world of His own free will, and yet if the world must be created and if God would not be supreme wisdom unless He were 'essentially creative,' then He is bound to create it; Leibnitz tried to meet the problem by the paradoxical phrase about 'God's choice of the Best.'[2]

[1] Plutarch from a phrase in the *Laws* conjectured that Ananke was caused by an Evil Soul, but there seems no real foundation for this (see Burnet, *op. cit.*, i. 342).

[2] It might be urged that, although the Demiourgos is eternal, yet (in spite of the principle laid down on p. 12) Plato allows Him to be the subject of a myth. But the myth only refers to His creation of the world in Time; Plato sternly denies himself any myth about God's own Nature; there is no Heaven nor any Vision of God in the *Timaeus*.

We pass to the second point—the eternal nature of the Paradeigmata. In 29*a* Plato proves their existence from the perfection of the world: 'If the world be indeed fair and the Artificer good, He must have looked to that which is eternal.'

But why (we ask) should the world be a 'copy' of some pre-existing and intelligible pattern? Why is the intelligible to be regarded as perfect, and how can what is heard and seen 'imitate' the inaudible and invisible objects of the mind? Plato tries in the *Timaeus* to answer these questions by his theory of Perfect and Imperfect Motions, to which (difficult as it is) we must now address ourselves.

Readers of the *Republic* will remember the feeling of astonishment with which they first read the statement that the visible Heavens should be regarded only as an 'orrery' from which we can deduce the invisible lines traced by the movements of the stars. In the *Timaeus* Plato is a little more indulgent to what is visible; he speaks of the brightness of the fiery bodies which the fixed stars, the eternal deities of Heaven, assume; he praises sight as the best of divine gifts by which we are able to lift up our eyes to the sky, but it is to admire the 'circlings of Intelligence' (τὰς ἐν τῷ οὐρανῷ τοῦ νοῦ περιόδους). I suppose that a modern astronomer might agree with him in preferring the intricate intellectual problems raised by the stellar movements to their romantic charm. In any case for Plato they stood for the 'perfect motions,' for that idea of harmony which, applicable alike to shape and sound, suited his Pythagorean association of Geometry and Music.

The highest, because the most regular,[1] movement was that in a circle ; this is represented in the *Timaeus* by the motion of the fixed stars, what is called the Circle of the Same, while the Circle of the Other stands for Change or Becoming.

The movement of the Circle of the Same is 'single and undivided' ; it includes the fixed stars, which are fastened like nails in the circle, which carries them round. The movement is circular, because that implies the least change, always forward, always returning on itself. Left to themselves, these stars would move in a straight line ; their circular motion, therefore, is due to the influence of the gods, who in them 'think consistently of the same things at the same time.'[2]

Time, 'the moving image of Eternity,' is caused by the planets, the Sun and the Moon, the 'instruments

[1] The Circle of the Same declares Intelligence (τὸ λογιστικόν) by running smoothly (εὐτρόχως).

[2] In the *Laws*, 897–9, the Athenian stranger says, 'Both Mind and the Motion which is in one place (*i.e.* round a fixed centre) move in the same and like manner.' In the case of the Sun, for instance, either the Soul that guides it is in the body of the Sun or the Soul provides 'itself with an external body of fire or air (as some affirm) and violently propels body by body' (*i.e.* the body of the Sun by means of this external body) or 'without such a body the Soul guides the Sun by some extraordinary and wonderful power.' In the *Epinomis*, 983, it is argued that only a god and no mortal could move such vast masses as the stars. From this doctrine comes the mediaeval view of the stars as guided by Angels ; *cp.* Dante, *Par.* ii. 127–129 :

> 'Lo moto e la virtù dei santi giri,
> Come dal fabbro l'arte del martello,
> Dai beati motor convien che spiri.'

('The movement and the virtue of the sacred wheelings, as the hammer's art from the smith, must needs be an effluence from the sacred movers.') Calvin (*Institut.*, 1, 5. 11) treats Platonic Astronomy with contempt. 'Plato inter omnes (philosophos) religiosissimus, et maxime sobrius, ipse quoque in rotundo suo globo evanescit.'

by which Time is caused' (ὄργανα τῶν χρόνων); they have a double motion, partly caused by the Circle of the Same and partly by the Circle of the Other; by their relative positions they mark the seasons and years; their motion is not uniform, but it is fixed and predictable (κατ' ἀριθμὸν ἰοῦσα); beneath this comes the Flux of Becoming in the world of Growth and Decay, where movement is irregular and unpredictable, where circlings are 'confused and wandering' (τεταραγμένοι καὶ πεπλανημένοι) as opposed to the heavenly calm and order, where the 'periods' of human history swing from progress to decay according to the rhythm, not of the stars but of Ananke.[1]

There are therefore three kinds of movement in the *Timaeus*—the highest and best, that of the fixed stars, is uniform and unchanging and stands for eternity; there is the movement of the Flux, changing and irregular, as for instance in the periods of the lives and deaths of individuals. Between the two comes the movement of the planets, not uniform (that is, not circular) but changing according to predictable laws. This represents the real Time of the universe.

It is important to notice the distinction Plato draws between the movement of the Flux and real Time. What impresses Plato about Time is not the element of change but the element of unchangeability. Time is not here treated (as in Neo-Platonism) as itself evil and decadent. Rather

[1] 'Seeing that everything which has a beginning has also an end, even a (perfect) Constitution such as yours will not last for ever, but will, in time, be dissolved' (*Republic*, Jowett, iii. p. 250).

it is that which confers the highest dignity on the universe by making it most like the Eternal.[1] Doubtless this separation between Time and change can be adapted to terms of modern thought; to the modern Relativist also the real change or 'passage' of events is to be distinguished from our systems of temporal measurement which vary with the position of the observer. But it must not be forgotten that, for Plato, Time, just because it is more uniform, is higher and more divine than change; the glorification of change as in itself a good thing would have seemed to him the height of paradox.

Even in the case of the Flux all is not sheer change; even here Plato finds an element called χώρα, which is stable and is a kind of caricature of true Eternity. He remembers the saying that you cannot step into the same river even once; you cannot say 'This is a hot thing,' or 'This is a cold thing,' for these are only points through which the elements pass and repass. We can only predicate the 'such' of quality—'Here it is hot,' 'There it is cold.' But thisness and thatness cannot be completely abolished. Even if only for a moment, heat seems to be here rather than there; the colour does seem associated closely (if not permanently) with the rose. Therefore Plato posits a lasting element, χώρα, which probably means space—the position through which the changing elements

[1] 'The Time of *Timaeus* is thus precisely the "true, absolute, or mathematical Time" of Newton. . . . The *temporality* of Becoming . . . is dwelt upon not as the character which distinguishes what "becomes" from what "is," but as the point of closest resemblance' (A. E. Taylor, *Faith of a Moralist*, ii. 335 (Macmillan)).

pass ; χώρα and the four elements which move through it are the realm of Ananke, what Professor Taylor calls ' the given element in things ' ; if the *Timaeus* were theology, this would introduce a certain dualism into Plato's thought. It is spoken of as having a quasi-eternity just as it is apprehended by a quasi-Reason. God is said to find or ' receive ' it as existing in a state of primitive confusion due to ' the absence of God.' One last word as to the eternity of the animals in the universe ; the world itself and the gods are deathless, not by nature but by Grace from the Demiourgos. ' Since ye are but creatures,' so He addresses them, ' ye are not altogether immortal and indissoluble, but ye shall certainly not be dissolved, having in my Will a greater and mightier bond than those in which ye were bound at the time of your birth.' This conception of a conferred or derived Eternity we shall find of importance in the Christian doctrine of the angels.

The souls of men are sown by God in the planets, the sphere of Time ; but only after they have been shown the universe and its laws in the fixed stars, which are to be the eternal home of the wise. Only that part of the soul which is worthy to be called Divine, the directing and commanding Nous, is sown by God [1] ; the lower part of the soul, which

[1] Even this is not pure like the World Soul but ' diluted to the second and third degree.' Professor Taylor says, ' We may certainly take the meaning to be that in our case the resulting compound is always more or less unstable. In the World Soul, he means to say, eternity and temporality are together, in permanent interpenetration and equilibrium ; in our human spiritual life there is a tension between them, more or less acute according to the quality of the individual life ' (*Faith of a Moralist*, i. 69).

is mortal, was made by the gods and placed below the neck ; this is the region of passion and desire. The human body was created by the gods, ' not with the indissoluble chains by which they were themselves bound but with little pegs too small to be visible.' The Demiourgos will take no part in the creation of the mortal body nor of the mortal part of the soul, that He may not be ' the author of future evil to any of them.' [1]

How far the rush and tumult of the passions are bound to obscure the Circle of Wisdom in man's soul it is hard to say ; certainly they do so in infancy ; the human soul is not of ' first-rate quality ' ; the human body is partly under the sway of Ananke. But there is the possibility for Wisdom to triumph over passion ; the philosopher by making the movement of his soul resemble the motion of the heavens can hope to claim the starry chariot which ' swings low ' for him. As always in Plato, the doctrine of Recollection makes the best human life not so much a learning of something new as the holding fast of what is dimly recognised already.

Plato's general conception of Eternity, then, is clear—changelessness and order, best symbolised by the regular movements of the fixed stars, best exemplified by the tranquil contemplation of the sage ; Plato crowns his system by what he loves best—Stability and Harmony.

[1] In the Myth of Er (*Republic*, 617 *e*), the words of the prophet are that responsibility rests with the chooser ; God is free from blame and the choice results from formed habit ; Plato's view seems to have darkened in the *Timaeus*.

Aristotle

In the particular problem we are considering—Time and Eternity—we may select three important contributions made by Aristotle—a distinction, a definition and a metaphor.

The distinction is an important one, as one would expect from Aristotle's scholastic mind ; it is drawn between Movement (*Κίνησις*) and Activity (*'Ενέργεια*).

In a famous passage from the Tenth Book of the *Ethics* he seeks to show that pleasure is not a movement ; all movement, he says, is incomplete at one moment and complete at another ; the building of a house gradually approaches and finally attains its end, or Telos, but pleasure, like seeing, is complete 'at any moment you like to choose.' Movement can be fast or slow, but there can be no rates of pleasure ; I can become pleased more quickly at one time than another, but the state of being pleased is a spiritual activity which while it lasts has nothing to do with change or movement ; it is complete in itself (a ὅλον τι).

This conception of an Activity without Change is of the utmost importance in the Christian idea of Eternity ; it has been well expounded by Dr. Schiller in his *Humanism* (pp. 204–227). The nearest modern equivalent to Aristotle's Energeia seems to be a state of equilibrium, in which there is complete adaptation to environment ; there would be no Change, but it would be the reverse of rest or death. 'Could we once attain an object of contemplation which was wholly satisfying, should we not seek to retain it in consciousness for ever? If he had achieved the Best, could any one be mad enough to wish to change it, for the worse?'; [1] because of our imperfection, we shift our attention; our pleasures pall; our desires become dim; our highest activity is the contemplation of eternal things by the wise man, but God alone has unchanging activity and therefore enjoys unbroken pleasure (μονόχρονος ἡδονή).

Aristotle's definition attempts to describe the content of God's eternal activity; it is the contemplation of His own intellectual Being (νόησις νοήσεως), the thinking of thought. It is a type of self-consciousness, in which 'mind and its object have an identical character, and to know an object is to know one's mind as it is in knowing the object.' [2] Unfortunately, Aristotle is so anxious to keep this Divine knowledge 'perfect' that he does not include in it any contact with the world of becoming. 'The result of the wish to exclude from the divine life any relation to evil and any "shadow of turning" is the impossible and barren ideal of a knowledge with no object but itself.' [3]

The metaphor concerns God's function as the First Mover; He is Himself unchanging; how then can He cause Motion and Change? [4] Aristotle's answer is that God influences the world quite unconsciously by His desirableness; He attracts the universe *ὡς ἐρώμενόν τι*, as a beautiful face or statue attracts the observer. This phrase

[1] Schiller, *Humanism*, p. 217. [2] Ross, *Aristotle*, p. 182.

[3] *Ibid.*, p. 183.

[4] Compare the Christian hymn 'Thyself unmoved, all motion's source.'

has important echoes in mediaeval poetry and philosophy ; all readers of Dante will remember the kind of spiritual gravitation by which in the *Paradiso* heavenly things draw the kindred soul up to themselves. Aristotle himself is not thinking of 'up' or 'down,' 'near' or 'far' ; the *πρῶτος οὐρανός* or Outer Circle of heaven is not trying to get nearer to God but to imitate, as far as it can, the Divine Eternity by its ceaseless circular motion. While, therefore, in Plato God sets the world in motion, in Aristotle the world sets itself in motion to imitate God.

Plotinus

If it is true that Plotinus turned Platonism into a religion, we should expect that in him the idea of Eternity should begin to assume a more numinous and supernatural meaning.

St. Augustine says that when he read Plotinus he thought that Plato was alive again. We know, of course, that a historical revival is never a mere resurrection ; much that is new comes from the new context and setting ; much that is old is self-conscious and archaic. Six hundred years separated Plotinus from Plato ; Plato lived in a city passionately Greek, devoted to culture, politics, athletics ; he was revived in a city packed with Orientals and foreigners, as un-Greek as can be imagined. Plato lived in a rather self-centred City State ; he was revived in a world that was cosmopolitan. He lived in an atmosphere of clear thought and remarkably secular interests ; he was revived in an atmosphere where everyone was seeking for a religion that would give him purification and salvation.

I am far from wishing to expound Plotinus' system and still farther from being able to do so : I only wish to say a few words as to the idea of Eternity and Time in connection with his three Hypostases, the One, Mind and Soul.

The first of these, the One, recalls Plato's Demiourgos and, like Him, remains rather aloof and obscure : the second and third Hypostases flow from it ; they are not really directed or governed by it. Greek thought even when sincerely monotheistic seems always to have found difficulty in expressing in imaginative language all that the Divine sovereignty involves ; the Greeks had not the Hebrew gift of transforming polytheistic stories.

The second Hypostasis, Mind or Intelligence, represents the old Platonic world of ideas, but whereas in Plato it was mostly an intelligible world, in Plotinus it also includes intelligences ; there are persons to think as well as things to be thought. Dr. Inge has rightly said that the doctrine of a complete correspondence of the subject and object in eternal life is ' the most precious part of Neoplatonism.' [1] Their mystical fusion goes far to change the rather frigid abstractness of the Platonic Forms into the Christian conception of Heaven. Thus for the first time the temporal and the eternal come to be thought of less as abstract types of movement and more as concrete types of experience. This ' personalising ' of the problem has far-reaching results for religion.

[1] *God and the Astronomers*, p. 48.

Let us take, for example, the definition of Eternity in the Third *Ennead*: 'such a life possesses everything as present, not this at one time and afterwards another . . . that which neither was nor will be, but alone is, stable, possessing its being, total and full . . . a life infinite because it is all, nothing of which is consumed . . . all things at once. . . . It now possesses that which it ought to be.' Plotinus speaks of the World of Intelligence in the plural: 'intelligible things quietly energising' . . . 'everything in the intelligible world is many, because of the never-failing resources of infinite power.' [1]

Yet this world is also one, for the real source of separation is not that things are many, but either the fact of Succession (things following one after another) or the fact of Finitude (one thing not being able to know another fully); neither of these barriers exists in the intelligible world; 'permanency suffers no change of its nature, because it is not mingled with the unstable . . . there is no weariness of vision; whatever is there possesses an untamed and unwearied power.' We might compare the words of the Christian hymn,

> There dawns no Sabbath; no Sabbath is o'er;
> Those Sabbath-keepers have one evermore.

Also all natures interpenetrate; 'all things there are diaphanous . . . all things are everywhere and all is all. Each star is the sun and all the stars.' [2]

[1] Taylor, *Select Works of Plotinus*, pp. 119, 122, 124.

[2] Taylor, p. lxxiii. Compare the use made in Christian theology of the text 'One star differeth from another in glory,' used (though it was not St. Paul's meaning) of the different degrees of glory enjoyed by the saints in Heaven.

Subject and Object are united. 'The being which sees itself is not separated from its essence. . . . It thinks in the highest sense, because it possesses what it thinks.' This world is (as in Plato) the Paradeigma, of which our world is a copy. 'This sensible world is admired for its grandeur, its beauty, the order of its eternal movements and the gods who are in it. . . . But turn back to its model which contains in it all immortal beings, all gods and souls in an eternal changelessness.' [1]

Nothing that is good in this world is lost there; even sensation has a richer equivalent. 'A sweetness which will be a smell at the same time. . . . It has all the qualities perceived by touch and hearing, for it is all harmony and rhythm.' [2]

Such words remind us again of Christian hymnology:

> There cinnamon, there sugar grows,
> There nard and balm abound.

And

> The Lamb's Apostles there
> I might with joy behold;
> The harpers I might hear
> Harping on harps of gold.

But there is a subtle difference. The Christian symbolism is an attempt to express what 'eye hath not seen nor ear heard,' faint analogies from our earthly experience used with conscious inefficacy for a new and untried state of being, while for Plotinus the World above is a reproduction, though in

[1] *Enneads*, V, 6. 1 (quoted Bréhier, *La philosophie de Plotin*, p. 96).
[2] *Enneads*, V, 1. 4 (quoted Bréhier, p. 91).

perfect form, of the universe we know, raised to a higher state. Again, in the Christian Heaven, the Love of God comes first ; for Plotinus the first place is given to that illumination of mind and spirit which we call Intelligence and which is the right (and indeed the reality) of every philosophic soul. 'The life there is Wisdom.'

Do the denizens of Plotinus' Heaven know the eternal One ? Can we ascribe to them, too, the Vision of God ? This is one of the thorniest questions of interpretation.

His second Hypostasis is in some rather undefined way inferior to the first, from which it emanates. Therefore (again in a sense) its eternity and joy come from the One, but the One always seems rather distant and transcendent. One must not say that Intelligence sees the One, but it lives turned towards it ; it depends upon it ; it moves towards it. It sees things in God rather than sees God. This is because Thought, however unified, always perceives distinctions ; it knows the difference between itself and others, even in the act of transcending that difference. Plunged into the One where there are no distinctions, how could it continue to be Thought at all ? Yet Plotinus did believe in a supra-rational experience he called Ecstasy, where the soul goes beyond all differences and is 'alone with the alone.' [1]

We may if we please call one tendency Greek and the other Oriental ; in any case, there seem the

[1] 'There is no barrier left ; the Soul and God are completely one ; as long as this Presence endures, no distinction of any kind is possible' (VI, 7. 34, *cit.* Bréhier, *La philosophie de Plotin*, p. 162).

two ideas of eternal life—one where minds, though one, are also distinct and God is not directly present ; the other a mystical way, in which all distinction between the soul and God is lost. The Christian Heaven lies somewhere between the two ; God is directly known, but there is no absorption in Him or in one another.

What then is Time ? and how does Experience in Time begin ? Here we come to the third Hypostasis—the World Soul of the *Timaeus*.

In the Third *Ennead* we have two statements as to the beginning of Time—in the abstract and the concrete ; one a definition, the other a story. 'In the case of generated beings, to remove the future is to destroy them. But in the case of eternal things, if you add a future, then a departure from the seat of existence results,' or (in more pictorial form) 'A certain Nature, much conversant with action and wishing to govern, was moved and tended to the hereafter.' In plainer words, certain souls in the intelligible world got tired of contemplating all things together ; they lusted for the active life, where things happen one after another.[1]

Time, then, is a moral fall—from the contemplative to the practical life—and yet it is only an imaginary fall. 'According to Plotinus our salvation is not to be achieved ; it has been eternally

[1] An admirable contrast between Time and Eternity is given in the tenth section. 'Instead of permanency of substance, we have that which always has another and another energy ; instead of an essence which is one and without interval, we have an image of the One which possesses unity in continuity of succession ; instead of that which is now infinite and a whole, we have that which proceeds *ad infinitum* and is always about to be a whole.'

achieved, since it is part of the order of things. Passion, suffering, sin have never touched more than the lower part of the soul.'[1] How different such an illusory fall is from the real Fall of the Bible! For Neo-Platonism, the life of Time is degradation from Eternity; for the Christian, life is a preparation for Eternity.

Plotinus, however, is not perfectly happy on the subject; he had inherited two rather different traditions from Plato: in the *Phaedrus* myth it is only the soul which has lost its wings that falls into the life of the body[2]; while in the *Timaeus* the animation of the World Body by the World Soul is spoken of as part of God's excellent purpose. Plotinus, therefore, rather tends to distinguish the Soul of the World, which 'has dominion over its body' and is as perfect as it can be, from *our* souls, bound to the body and capable of corruption.[3]

Plotinus does not identify Time and Motion; even if Time stopped, the movement of the universe, that is the Circle of the Same, would continue to energise; motion in the World Order itself is good and right; Time is in our souls, a certain restlessness, a fever in the blood, for which Heaven was too monotonous and unexciting, a desire to live separate and independent lives, an ambition like that of Lucifer, followed by a Fall like his.

[1] *Enneads*, ed. Bréhier, p. 215. [2] 246 *c*.

[3] The contrast between the two is put in a humorous simile: 'Just as in a great dance which is conducted in a becoming manner, a tortoise, being caught in the middle of the progression, should be trod upon, not being able to escape the order of the dance; though if the tortoise had arranged itself with the dance, it would not have suffered from those that composed it.' So we must 'arrange ourselves' with the World Order (Taylor, pp. 56, 57).

Here we leave the study of Greek thought. I should like to close with a few words (to remind myself and you that this *is* a sermon) on the religious value of this Greek attitude of mind.

Some people object that the term 'Greek thought' should not be used only of the school of philosophers we have been considering; were they really representative of Greece at its best? or were they not disillusioned decadents of the post-Periclean age?

It might be enough to answer that, whether Plato and his school were decadents or not, it was their thought which descended to Christianity in what the Schoolmen called 'the great tradition.' But there is a little more than that to be said.

It is an obvious remark that great men are great not only because they embody but also because they correct what is characteristic of their age. Shakespeare was a typical Elizabethan dramatist; he could rant and rave with the best of them; he could toss about words as though they were jewels or push a fancy to extravagance. Yet when the occasion called, he could correct all this by a directness and 'centrality' that makes him universal. So Plato shared the intellectual daring, the passion for argument, the thirst for new experiences of the younger generation; otherwise he could not have written the *Symposium* or the *Phaedrus* (to the unending scandal of Puritans). But he corrected this by an austerity that seems excessive, the restraint of a rich and complex nature.

The Greeks were not naturally lovers of contemplation; they adored the active life and the moderation we associate with the Delphic oracle and Greek statues, and Plato was admired precisely because it was found so difficult. So (as has often been pointed out) the passionate mediaevalists admired the patience and calm of Our Lord's character, while our quieter age loves His activity and energy. But the matter is more complicated than that; the Greeks for all their joy in life were easily depressed and very often disappointed. 'The κόσμος of the Greeks is . . . a world without a history, an eternal order in which Time counts for nothing, whether because it leaves that order always self-identical, or because it produces a series of events which always reverts to the same point through an indefinite repetition of cyclical changes.' [1] They did not seem able to grasp the idea of a purpose behind history; Fate, Nemesis, Destiny rather than Providence seemed what life proclaimed. This discontent did not lead to quietism and mysticism—at least not till the Hellenistic age. But it led philosophers to seek for what is rational outside and beyond history.

This was profoundly true of their religion; beautiful and exhilarating in times of happiness, it had not the deep seriousness needed for times of trouble. Just because the Greeks were not frivolous, that want was felt. In face of the vivid, all too

[1] Professor Taylor, quoting from Laberthonnière (*Faith of a Moralist*, ii. 325). He adds himself: 'Even the divine Plato has not yet the clear conviction that the play (of history) is working out to an end in which its author-spectator takes a supreme interest; nor does Thucydides see the struggle of which he is the historian as an act in a drama which has significance as a whole, a stage in the "education of humanity"' (*ibid.*, 327).

human deities of Olympus, Plato (when he is serious) often shrinks from speaking of a personal God at all ; in face of the varied history and shifting persons of the deities, he insists that God is unchangeable.[1] It was the greatness, not the littleness of the Greeks that made them feel that history and the Time process had a tragedy at the heart. It is often said that they separated Time and eternity so as to split the world in two. So Gentile says[2] : 'The Ideas belong to a world that is eternal and infinite but placed side by side with the temporal world. Nature is thus torn into two irreconcilable parts.' This is exaggerated ; the Platonic doctrine that the sensible world *imitates* the eternal at once admits close relation between them. It may not be the deepest description of their relation, but it is a description. In any case Greek thought took the first step and the right step when it separated the temporal from the eternal ; no one who does not see clearly the separation between the Divine and the human can hope to understand how they are connected.

[1] In the famous passage in the *Republic*, ii. 381, the unchangeability of the Deity is especially insisted upon as against stories of Protean transformations.

[2] *Logica*, i. 24.

SECOND LECTURE

ETERNITY IN CHRISTIAN THOUGHT

Thus saith the high and lofty One that inhabiteth eternity, Whose Name is holy ; I dwell in the high and holy place.—ISAIAH lvii. 15.

IN the last sermon we were considering how Greek thought arrived at the idea of eternity ; how it was impelled partly by an intellectual desire for abiding certainty, partly by an aesthetic admiration for repose, partly by an ethical striving after perfection. We saw how Plato's doctrine of the changeless Divine nature led to Plotinus' conception of the Divine life as a Totum Simul.

When we pass to the Hebraic conception of God, we are in a different atmosphere—not that we must press too far Matthew Arnold's famous antithesis between the Hellenic love of Culture and the Hebraic passion for Conduct. The Greeks may have been men of sweetness and light, but in many of the Socratic dialogues there is an intense preoccupation with the urgent issues of moral choice. The Hebrews may have been primarily concerned with righteousness in action, but that did not deter them from deep rumination on the problems of life ; it would be a very rigid definition of philosophy which denied the name to the book of Job.

What is true is that the Hebrews of the Old Testament were not interested in Metaphysics ;

they did not care for definitions. The prophets would have had little sympathy with the attempts to define piety in the *Euthyphro* ; they were too busy with the problem of getting it done ; nor were the Hebrews accustomed to the dialectical method of question and answer ; they arrived at truth by immediate moral and spiritual intuitions ; no Hebrew would have offered up the prayer which introduces the cosmological part of the *Timaeus*. 'We must pray the gods and goddesses that we may speak what is most pleasing to them and most consistent with itself from our point of view.'[1] We were considering in our last lecture how the Greeks failed to acquire a sense of the Divine purpose in history. Perhaps we hardly emphasised enough that it was the great disappointment of the Peloponnesian War which shook the Athenian faith in life and heralded the change to mysticism and mystery-cults which marked the Hellenistic world. Professor Bury in a well-known phrase has called this growth of other-worldliness a 'failure of nerve.' The nerve of the Jewish people did not fail ; persecution and oppression seemed only to purify the conviction that they were God's chosen people and that the course of history (however troubled) must lead to their vindication in the eyes of the world.[2]

The conception of Eternity in the Bible.[3]—The Jewish 'sense of history' is perhaps illustrated by

[1] *Tim.*, 27 *c.*

[2] It is true that in the later Apocalyptic the hope of the Messianic Kingdom on this earth recedes, but still the Day of the Lord is a historical intervention of God and all history is a preparation for it.

[3] For detailed treatment, see Appendix I.

the fact that the most important Hebrew word for 'eternal,' *olam*, can be used for 'times past' and 'days of old.'

It is used in the Second Isaiah of the wanderings in the wilderness [1]; in Micah v. 2 the future ruler of Davidic ancestry is spoken of as one 'whose goings forth are from everlasting' (A.V. mg. 'days of eternity,' R.V. mg. 'from ancient days'), the reference being to the far-off origin of his family.[2] As an adjective, it is used of 'ancient peoples' such as the Babylonians,[3] of the gates of Zion of immemorial antiquity,[4] of God, Whose Throne is established 'of old' and Who Himself is 'from everlasting.'[5]

Olam can also be used of the remote time in the indefinite future; in this sense it means 'for ever,' whether it refers to the lifetime of the individual [6] or to the perpetual duration of the earth [7] or sky.[8]

In connection with the Divine Nature, we find

[1] 'He bare them and carried them all the days of old,' Isa. lxiii. 9.

[2] 'Goings forth' means 'origin'; Vulgate has 'a diebus aeternitatis.'

[3] Jer. v. 15, 'It is a mighty (mg. enduring) nation, it is an ancient nation.'

[4] Ps. xxiv. 7, 'Be ye lift up, ye everlasting (mg. ancient) doors' (Vulg. 'portae aeternales').

[5] Ps. xciii. 2, 'Thy Throne is established of old (LXX, ἀπὸ τότε; Vulg. 'ex tunc'): Thou art from everlasting' (LXX, ἀπὸ τοῦ αἰῶνος; Vulg. 'a saeculo').

[6] Deut. xv. 17, 'He shall be thy servant for ever.'

[7] Eccles. i. 4, 'The earth abideth for ever'; as in most of the Old Testament there is no idea of the end of the world, the phrase means 'always'; *cp.* the curious case of 1 Cor. viii. 13, where St. Paul says rhetorically, 'I will eat no flesh for evermore,' and the A.V., for some unknown reason but quite in accordance with Hebrew idiom, has 'while the world standeth.'

[8] 'He hath also stablished them (the heavens) for ever and ever' (Ps. cxlviii. 6).

the word once used as a title for God—*El Olam*.[1] The thought is rather moral than metaphysical; it describes God's faithfulness either in contrast with human infirmity[2] or with special reference to His covenant relationship to Israel.[3]

The beginning of Ps. xc. is perhaps the clearest exposition of the eternity of God in the Old Testament. 'Before the mountains were brought forth, or ever Thou hadst formed the earth and the world, even from everlasting to everlasting, Thou art God.' The use of the present tense to cover the *olam* of the past and future (the two everlastings) sounds metaphysical and might seem to imply the changeless perfection of the Totum Simul, but probably it means little more than 'Thou continuest.'

'A thousand years in Thy sight are but as yesterday when it is past, and as a watch in the night.' Dr. Kirkpatrick[4] comments: 'Time no more exists for God than it does for the unconscious sleeper.' This is too Augustinian; the only point stressed is the smallness of the millennium in the

[1] Gen. xxi. 33.

[2] Isa. xl. 28; while the young men faint 'the everlasting God fainteth not.'

[3] The prayer 'Let Thy Name be magnified for ever' (2 Sam. vii. 26) finds its fulfilment in the praises of the Temple; 'In Jerusalem will I put My Name for ever' (2 Chron. xxxiii. 7). So in the case of Exod. iii. 14, the phrase 'I am that I am' is less a revelation of God's essential nature than of His readiness to perform His promises; it should be 'I will be that I will be.' 'The early Hebrew mind was essentially practical, not metaphysical . . . the verb does not mean "to be" essentially or ontologically, but phenomenally. . . . He will be with them, helper, strengthener, deliverer; the word is explained by the "I will be with thee" of verse 12' (McNeile, *Exodus*, p. 22).

[4] *Psalms*, p. 550.

sight of God ; Watts hits the right sense in his famous version :

> Short as the watch that ends the night
> Before the rising sun.

The same contrast is set up between God's abidingness and the swift flow of human generations in verse 5, 'Thou carriest them away as with a flood.'

The use of the word *olam* in the plural seems to be intensitive, a plural of majesty to heighten the effect, as in the well-known translation of Is. xxvi. 4, 'Rock of Ages.'[1] There seems as yet no idea of the division of history into definite periods or ages ; the word denotes vast ranges of indefinite time ; for more defined periods the Old Testament has 'generations,' 'years'[2] and 'time,' in the sense of life,[3] season of prosperity,[4] accident,[5] opportunity[6] or epoch of power.[7]

The translators of the Septuagint chose the Greek word Aion to render the Hebrew *Olam* ; the Greek word is used in Homer of human life,

[1] A.V. has 'In the Lord Jehovah is everlasting strength' (mg. Rock of Ages) ; R.V. has 'In the Lord Jehovah is an everlasting Rock' ; LXX has ὁ θεὸς ὁ μέγας ὁ αἰώνιος ; Vulgate has 'Dominus Deus, fortis in perpetuum' ; the idea is that of a castle rather than of a refuge as in Toplady's hymn.

[2] Used of God in Ps. cii. 27, 'Thy years shall have no end' ; in Hab. iii. 2, 'Revive Thy work in the midst of the years,' where it is said to mean 'without any long postponement' (*New Commentary*, p. 597), 'in the present era, without waiting for the final judgment' (Peake, *Commentary*, p. 567).

[3] Ps. lxxxix. 47, 'Remember how short my time is.'

[4] Ps. lxxxi. 15, 'Their time (of the godly) should endure for ever.'

[5] Eccles. ix. 11, 'Time and chance happeneth to them all.'

[6] Jer. xlvi. 21, 'The time of their visitation.'

[7] 'It shall be the time of the heathen' (Ezek. xxx. 3).

regarded as the span allotted to each individual; Plato uses it for eternity (as we have seen) in the *Timaeus*,[1] and Plotinus has it in the same technical sense; Aion was a god worshipped in Alexandria from 200 B.C., and a Mithraic inscription celebrates the deity as ἀρχήν, μεσότητα, τέλος οὐκ ἔχων.[2]

The duration of human life cannot be measured beforehand and the duration of eternity cannot be measured by past, present and future tenses; the common idea is that of indefiniteness; the Aion is not usually regarded as divisible into Aiones, but rather into χρόνοι or περίοδοι. In more popular literature, Aion is used (as was the case with *olam*) for infinite ranges of time in the past (Longinus speaks of τοὺς ἀπ' αἰῶνος ῥήτορας 'orators of old')[3] or in the future (at a public meeting the loyal cry is Ἄγουστοι κύριοι εἰς τὸν αἰῶνα, 'the Emperors for ever').[4]

As adjectives αἰώνιος and ἀΐδιος are used by the philosophers for 'timeless'; Aristotle prefers the latter and Plato the former, but it is probably over-subtle to attempt to distinguish them.[5] Both have the looser popular sense; an inscription has τιμὰς ἀϊδίους as voted to Berenice[6]; Josephus has ἐφυλάχθη ὁ Ἰωάννης δεσμοῖς αἰωνίοις, 'John was condemned to perpetual imprisonment.'[7] While, therefore, the words are professionally used for 'timeless' by the philosophers, in the popular and literary usage,

[1] 37 *d*. [2] *Syll.*[3] 1125. [3] *De Subl.* 34. [4] *Pap. Oxy.* 41. 30.

[5] Moulton and Milligan, *Vocabulary of the G.T.*, p. 13, commenting on the dubious occurrence of ἀΐδιος in the papyri, say, 'Possibly the word was only appropriate to the stiffer language of inscriptions.'

[6] Moulton and Milligan, *loc. cit.*

[7] *B.J.*, 6. 9. 4.

αἰώνιος 'depicts that of which the horizon is not in view, whether the horizon be at an infinite distance . . . or whether it lies no farther than the span of a Cæsar's life.' [1]

Without going into details, which will be studied in Appendix I, I would suggest that the definition of the words in Hellenistic Greek adequately covers the Biblical usage.

In the Septuagint, *olam* used adjectivally is generally rendered by αἰώνιος,[2] or (τοῦ) αἰῶνος [3]; we also notice that among the many renderings of 'for ever,' εἰς τοὺς αἰῶνας occurs [4]; in the Hebrew the plural was merely intensive, but Greek had no such idiom and it is probable that the use of the definite article in Greek (*the* Age, *the* Ages) helped to strengthen the idea that history was divided into two distinct ages—a tendency helped by Apocalyptic speculation about the Messianic Age.[5]

As is well known,[6] the second century Apocalyptists still believe in the Messianic Age as coming on earth after the Day of Judgment [7]; so in Daniel εἰς τοὺς αἰῶνας means the life of the coming Kingdom, but, while the Kingdom is itself perpetual, the

[1] Moulton and Milligan, *op. cit.*, p. 16.

[2] Isa. lxiii. 11, ἐμνήσθη ἡμερῶν αἰωνίων (days of old).

[3] Deut. xxxii. 7, ἡμέρας αἰῶνος (days of old).

[4] In 1 Kings viii. 13, 'A place for Thee to dwell in for ever.'

[5] Notice also Isa. ix. 6, where the LXX has πατὴρ αἰώνιος (A.V. 'everlasting Father'; R.V. mg. 'Father of Eternity'); the Greek has an alternative reading: πατὴρ τοῦ μέλλοντος αἰῶνος (Vulg. 'futuri saeculi').

[6] See Charles, *Between the Old and New Testaments*.

[7] Enoch xvi. 1, μέχρις ἡμέρας τελειώσεως τῆς κρίσεως τῆς μεγάλης, ἐν ᾗ ὁ αἰὼν ὁ μέγας τελεσθήσεται, 'Till the Day of the accomplishment of the Great Judgment in which the Great Age shall be accomplished.'

individuals in it do not necessarily live for ever; in Enoch i–xxxvi the righteous eat of the tree of life and live as long as the patriarchs, and have a thousand children.[1]

In Enoch x. 10 *εἰς τὸν αἰῶνα* is 500 years, and in x. 5, 70 generations; in Enoch xx. 9–13 sinners who have not been punished on earth are 'in great pain till the Great Day of Judgment . . . for ever'; in Jubilees also (v. 10) 'for ever' seems to refer to a period before the Day of Judgment.

First-century writers (B.C. and A.D.), feeling that the earth is unfit for God's Kingdom, suppose a temporary Messianic Age on earth followed by the Day of Judgment and the coming of the heavenly Kingdom; in 2 Baruch xl. 3 the 'principate (of the Messiah) will stand for ever, until the world of corruption is at an end'; in the Sibylline Oracles (3. 50) the Messianic Kingdom stands 'for all ages,' that is till the Universal Judgment; in 4 Esdras the Messianic Kingdom only lasts 400 years.

It seems, therefore, that, although the contrast is clear between this Age and 'the Great Age,' yet *εἰς αἰῶνας* refers to an undefined period before the Judgment Day; there seems no evidence of Aion used by itself for a definite length of time, and Aionios means neither 'belonging to the Messianic Age' nor 'lasting for an Aion,' but 'lasting through the Aions,' that is, age-long. A word should be added as to the Millennium. The conception first occurs in the Slavonic book of Enoch, which dates from A.D. 1 to 50; it arose from a combination of Gen. ii. 2 ('God rested on the seventh day') with

[1] Charles, *op. cit.*, p. 54.

Ps. xc. 4 (' A thousand years in Thy sight are but as yesterday ') ; ' Six millennia of toil were to be succeeded by a millennium of rest.' [1] St. John of Damascus, in giving the various uses of Aion, says, ' It means also a period of a thousand years,' [2] and Leontius of Byzantium tells us that ' the followers of Origen regard Aion as a name for a defined period of time ; when the Bible speaks of Aionian punishment, it only refers to such a defined period.' [3]

This is theological rather than etymological exegesis ; never in the New Testament are the words Aion or Aionian used of limited periods of time. In the sixth verse of the Epistle of Jude we have the curious phrase ἀπολιπόντας τὸ ἴδιον οἰκητήριον [ἀγγέλους] εἰς κρίσιν μεγάλης ἡμέρας δεσμοῖς ἀϊδίοις ὑπὸ ζόφον τετήρηκεν, ' The angels, which . . . left their own habitation He hath reserved in everlasting chains under darkness unto the judgment of the Great Day.' [4]

We note (*a*) that the passage seems influenced by the phrase quoted above (p. 40) from Enoch ; in

[1] Peake, *Commentary*, p. 941.

[2] *de fid. Orth.*, II. 1 (Migne, 861 *b*). The earliest (? second century A.D.) example of such a use seems to come in *The Testament of Abraham* (A), c. 19 (James, *Texts and Studies*, ii. 2. 101), τοὺς ἑπτὰ αἰῶνας ἐγὼ λυμαίνω τὸν κόσμον : Death is speaking to Abraham—after 7000 years (corresponding to the Days of Creation) the world will end : but *cp.* (B), c. 7 (James, 112), ἕως ἂν πληρωθῶσιν ἑπτακισχίλιοι αἰῶνες, where the word means ' years ' (*Vario lectio* τὰ ἔτη). The use of αἰών in the sense of 1000 years (known to Origen) may have existed among some chronological Christian Apocalyptists ; it seems quite alien to the atmosphere of the New Testament.

[3] I. 1265 *d*.

[4] In the parallel passage in 2 Pet. ii. 4 we have, instead of ' everlasting chains,' σειροῖς ζόφου (pits of darkness) ; σειραῖς (chains) is also read.

no other passage in the New Testament is 'everlasting' used of a period *before* the Day of Judgment; (*b*) the word used is not Aionios but Aidios, which cannot possibly mean 'lasting for an Aion'; the word must mean 'age-long.' The Book of Revelation admits a Millennium, but this does not affect its use of the words we are considering; on the contrary, in xxii. 5 the words *βασιλεύσουσιν εἰς τοὺς αἰῶνας τῶν αἰώνων* ('they shall reign for ever and ever') are probably chosen 'in contrast with the "thousand years" of the earlier visions.' [1]

In the New Testament Aion is used of this life in opposition to the Age of the Kingdom, which is called *ὁ μέλλων* or *ἐκεῖνος ὁ αἰών* [2]; from this it comes to mean this World Order, under the rule (St. Paul tells us) of an evil angel, the 'ruler' or even 'the god' of this Aion.[3] We notice that the adjective Aionios has already diverged from the varied meanings of its noun; if it followed them strictly, Aionios could mean 'belonging to this world,' which it never does. In 2 Pet. iii. 18 we have the only New Testament use of Aion in

[1] *New Com., ad loc.*; Mr. Emmet says (*Immortality*, p. 193), 'Let it be noted that (the plural) in itself implies that anything belonging to a single "aeon" was not necessarily unending'; this is hardly cogent, as the singular *εἰς αἰῶνα* is used in the same sense (see Appendix I.). Dr. Charles asserts (Rev. ii. p. 120) that in xix. 3 the expression *εἰς τοὺς αἰῶνας τῶν αἰώνων* is 'equivalent here to a thousand years,' but this is only because of the context: the ruins of Rome cannot go on smoking after the world has been destroyed; this seems to me interpreting poetry rather prosaically; he adds that 'in xxii. 5 . . . (the phrase) denotes eternity.'

[2] See Appendix I.

[3] For the word (in the plural) in a good sense, see Heb. i. 2, where Aiones means the ages of history; cp. 1 Tim. i. 17, 'King of the Ages.'

the strict Platonic sense of eternity: νῦν καὶ εἰς ἡμέραν αἰῶνος (' unto the day which consists of Eternity ').

' Aiones ' is used of vast ranges of indefinite time; sometimes they stretch out beyond the history of the world; in Eph. ii. 7 God by sending Christ shows the riches of His Grace ἐν τοῖς αἰῶσι ἐπερχομένοις (' in the Ages to come '); St. Paul could hardly have believed in many future ages *on earth* before the Parousia. In iii. 9 the mystery of God is said to have been hid in Him ἀπὸ τῶν αἰώνων (' from the beginning '); the words ' hid in God ' perhaps suggest that the Apostle is thinking back even beyond Creation.[1] In 1 Cor. ii. 7 πρὸ τῶν αἰώνων seems to mean ' before created history.'[2]

In St. John's Gospel εἰς τὸν αἰῶνα is used in a clearly eschatological sense seven times.[3]

Aionios means age-long, ' lasting through the Aions,' and in some contexts must mean lasting for ever,[4] as when it is used of God,[5] of the Gospel,[6] or of ' eternal things ' in contrast with τὰ πρόσκαιρα.[7]

[1] In Eph. iii. 21 the ἅπαξ λεγόμενον occurs—εἰς πάσας τὰς γενεὰς τοῦ αἰῶνος τῶν αἰώνων. This has been taken to mean ' unto all generations of the Aion, which itself is made up of shorter Aions.' Such a definite subdivision of an Aion into Aions nowhere else occurs and it seems better to regard the phrase as a rhetorical variation of ' to the Ages of the Ages.'

[2] The rulers of this Aion could not see beyond the Aions to God's pre-temporal counsel.

[3] *E.g.* xi. 26, ὁ πιστεύων εἰς ἐμὲ οὐ μὴ ἀποθάνῃ εἰς τὸν αἰῶνα.

[4] The only tinge of difference between the New Testament and Hellenistic usage seems to be that the Jews had the picture of ages one following another, while to the Greeks, more prone to the idea of recurring ' periods,' the phrase is more negative and indefinite.

[5] Rom. xvi. 26. [6] Rev. xiv. 6.

[7] 2 Cor. iv. 18; πρόσκαιρα means ' temporary ' rather than ' temporal.'

We must say the same of the eternal fire,[1] the eternal punishment,[2] and the eternal sin [3] of the Synoptists. The doctrinal question involved will never be settled by etymology ; our generation will not seek to determine the fate of the sinner with the aid of lexicons or grammars. It is enough that Our Lord was using the language of His time ; if ' fire ' is a spatial metaphor, ' everlasting ' may well be a temporal one.

To sum up, we see that the Biblical use of the phrases under discussion implies *duration*, of whatever length ; there seems no reference to the Totum Simul, the changeless perfection of the philosophers.[4]

St. Augustine

Many of my predecessors in this pulpit have adorned their lectures with scholarly dissertations on the historical development of the doctrines which they have chosen for their subjects ; my incompetence in this field is fortunately the less important because the conception of eternity was neither the subject of conciliar decisions nor of heretical attacks. It was taken by St. Augustine from Plotinus and Christianised ; Boethius gave it its most famous formula and Aquinas gave it its final definitions.

We start with St. Augustine.

[1] Matt. xviii. 8 and xxv. 41. [2] Matt. xxv. 46.

[3] In Mark iii. 29 *ἔνοχος αἰωνίου ἁμαρτήματος* seems to be a mere restatement (in positive form) of the negative clause just before *οὐκ ἔχει ἄφεσιν εἰς τὸν αἰῶνα* (the last three words meaning ' never ').

[4] If 2 Pet. iii. 18 is Platonic, it might be an exception.

The names of St. Augustine and Plotinus are associated in somewhat the same way as those of Socrates and Plato or of Dr. Johnson and James Boswell. This was not the result of upbringing or tradition ; Augustine was brought up as a Christian, but he never seems to have grasped at the time that Christianity was a system of philosophy at all ; it appeared to him a collection of unintelligible doctrines drawn from a book written in barbarous Latin ; adrift in a sea of scepticism and superstition, he sought in vain for a great constructive system amid the decadent mediocrity of contemporary academic life. When he came in sight of Neo-Platonism, a theory of the universe based upon reason and on a rational definition of the spiritual life, he felt that thrill of discovery with which we may imagine that in nineteenth-century Oxford a weary sceptic came across the all-embracing speculations of Hegel.

But Neo-Platonism did not touch closely enough his rich emotional and moral nature ; the crisis of his conversion took the form of a passionate humility and penitence which is so often the sign of spiritual change in one who has been over-proud of his intellect. From that moment his heart and his soul were Christ's. We must not think of him as a detached critic coldly neo-platonising Christianity ; for him the Church and the Bible came first. As he says himself in an early work, 'There is no doubt that we are impelled to learn by two forces, authority and reason. With me it stands fast never to depart from Christian authority, for I find no stronger. But as for those matters which it is possible to seek out by subtle reasoning, . . . I am confident that I shall find among the Neo-Platonists that which does not conflict with our religion.' [1] If he brought a contribution to theology from Greek thought, he also brought much from his close study of the Scriptures and his own twice-born experience.[2]

How little, for instance, his Neo-Platonic theory that evil was non-existent weighed against his experience of the power of sin!

If we start with the problem of Creation, we find at once two important points on which his Christian faith opened up new aspects on the problems of the *Enneads*.

The first problem that confronted him was that of the beginning of the world. Plotinus had taught dogmatically that the world was everlasting and its history composed of recurring periods reproducing the same events.[3] He asserted [4] 'that this world never began nor will ever cease to be'; he sneered at the Gnostics for supposing that 'there is a beginning of perpetuity,' as though 'the Demiourgos became the cause of the fabrication of the world through changing his mind.' [5] In the *Timaeus*, Plato had seemed to speak of a creation in Time, and while his heathen interpreters main-

[1] *Contra academicos*, 3. 43 (quoted Montgomery, *St. Augustine*, p. 49).

[2] 'He had . . . the advantage of an undoubted and solid ground of Scripture (*i.e.* in the Predestination controversy); an advantage which his deep and full knowledge of the sacred text, and wonderful skill and readiness in the application of it, enabled him to use with the greatest effect' (Mozley, *Predestination*, p. 233).

[3] Bréhier, p. 36.

[4] *Enneads*, ii. 9 (Taylor, p. 55).

[5] *Ibid.* p. 57; the 'Gnostics' are supposed to have been a Christian sect.

tained that the story was an allegory, the Christians regarded the *Timaeus*, at least on this point, as a literal account, like that in Genesis.[1] In any case, Plato's speculations about the Perfect Year [2] gave his authority to the doctrine of recurring periods, 'circuitus' as they were called in Latin philosophy.

How far could these speculations be admitted into Christianity? St. Augustine begins by rejecting the Plotinian view that the world is eternal; such a doctrine seems to encroach upon the unique eternity of God and to be inconsistent with the account of Creation in Genesis.[3] Of course, he sees at once that we cannot strictly say that God's eternity precedes the existence of Time; 'Nec Tu tempore tempora praecedis . . . sed celsitudine semper praesentis aeternitatis.' 'Thou dost not precede Time in Time, but by the height of Thine

[1] The dispute turned on the question 'whether . . . Plato, in recounting the origin of the world, had meant to give it an origin in time, or whether . . . he had only given to his Cosmogony the form of a story for purposes of exposition' (Bréhier, p. 36).

[2] *Tim.*, 39*d*; this was supposed to last 18,000 years, after which the stars returned to the positions they occupied at Creation; Virgil refers to it in the passage in the Fourth Eclogue beginning:

'Magnus ab integro saeclorum nascitur ordo.'

St. Augustine tells us that some people quoted in favour of the theory Eccles. i. 9, 10, 'The thing, that hath been, it is that which shall be; and that which is done is that which shall be done: and there is no new thing under the sun. Is there any thing whereof it may be said, See, this is new? It hath been already of old time, which was before us' (*De Civitate Dei*, Bk. 12, c. 14).

[3] 'Il ne saurait consentir un seul instant à concevoir un monde éternel' (Guiton, *Le Temps et l'Eternité chez Plotin et Saint Augustin*, p. 160); M. Guiton points out (p. 165) that, before his Platonic period, Augustine had believed in infinite space; on reading Plotinus, he abandoned not only infinite space but (unlike Plotinus) infinite Time also.

eternity which is always present.'[1] In *Conf.* 12. 29 he expressly distinguishes the sense in which God's eternity is 'before' all things (which he says is very hard to grasp) from the sense in which the flower comes 'before' the fruit; so in *D.C.D.*, 12. 16 he sees that in the question 'Has God always created?' there is an ambiguity in the 'always'; if it means 'during the whole of Time' the answer 'Yes' is obvious, as Time and Creation always occur together. One of the difficulties of language is that we cannot speak of the beginning of Time without seeming to imply a 'before.' But the idea of Time and God's eternity as always running side by side, concurrently, is equally temporal; it is as much a figure of speech to speak of God's eternity being 'with' Time as to speak of it being 'before' Time; the relation between the temporal and eternal cannot itself be temporal.

To those who ask what God was doing before Creation, he answers that Time began at Creation[2] and therefore there was no long and empty period during which God did nothing.

'If there was no Time before Heaven and earth, how can you raise the question what God did then? There was no "then," for there was no

[1] *Conf.*, 11. 13.

[2] Everyone knows St. Augustine's story of the answer to the question 'What was God doing before He made Heaven and earth?' namely, 'Preparing hell for the over-curious'; he treats it as a joke meant to evade the point and refuses to make use of it ('aliud est videre, aliud ridere') or to praise the speaker (*Conf.*, 11. 12). On the other hand, the story commended itself to Calvin's gloomy mind; he calls it 'haec non minus gravis quam severa admonitio' and ascribes it (I do not know on what authority) to a 'pius senex' (*Inst.*, 1. 14. 1).

Time,'[1] or (in the more famous words of the *De Civitate Dei*),[2] 'Beyond doubt, the world was made not in Time but together with Time.'

He has also to deal with the question of 'periods' and of the supposed change in God's mind; certain philosophers argued in the following ingenious way[3]: God must have been creating for infinite time, for we cannot suppose that His goodness was ever 'idle'; now Infinity cannot be grasped by any mind, even the mind of God, and therefore God must go on repeating Himself in endless periods.[4]

St. Augustine dismisses the periods with the reflection that, if they exist, then the liberation of the philosopher from his body, preached by the Neo-Platonists, is illusory, for the sage will have to return to earth when his 'period' recurs; the

[1] In *Paradiso*, xxix. 16–21, Beatrice says of God's Eternity:

> 'In sua eternità, di tempo fuore,
> Fuor d'ogni altro comprender, come i piacque,
> S'aperse in nuovi amor l'eterno amore.
> Nè prima quasi torpente si giacque;
> Chè nè prima nè poscia procedette
> Lo discorrer di Dio sopra quest' acque.'

'In his eternity beyond time, beyond all other comprehension, as was His pleasure, the eternal love revealed Him in new loves. Nor did He lie, as slumbering, before (creation)'; the last two lines would be simple and Augustinian if we could read 'precedette,' *i.e.* 'No "before" or "after" came before the outflowing of God over these waters' (that is, the act of creation). But the Temple Classics Editor (p. 360) says that the MS. authority is against the reading. So we must suppose it to mean 'God's act of Creation was not successive (having "before" and "after")'; He first created Matter and the Angels; Time and Succession came later.

[2] 11. 6.

[3] 'acutissimum argumentum putatur' (*D.C.D.*, 12. 18).

[4] In modern language we should say, I suppose, that there are not an infinite number of infinite events to fill infinite Time.

idea that God cannot understand Infinity is based on a comparison of Him with human minds [1]; God can grasp both infinite Time and infinite Number.

Tainted with the same anthropomorphism is the idea that Creation involves a change in God's Will. God's purpose is not in Time, although its accomplishment may be; 'He knows Time without any notion of Time in Himself. . . . Therefore, when He saw that it was good for something to be done, He sees that it is good, which He hath done.' [2] To suppose that He changed His mind is to commit the old fallacy of asking what He was doing before Creation; the fool and the philosopher are in the same boat; there was no 'before' when He could have had different plans.

A more formidable difficulty than that of Creation was lying in wait for St. Augustine in the Plotinian metaphysics; in the *Enneads*, the first two Hypostases—The One and Intelligence—are both eternal. It was true that the Second in some sense eternally 'flowed from' the First, but they were co-eternal, and in the popular mind the beings of the Second Hypostasis were regarded as daimones to be worshipped as mediators between men and the Absolute.[3] Christianity also spoke of an eternal life now enjoyed in Heaven by the angels

[1] With his usual happy ingenuity in Scriptural exegesis he quotes 2 Cor. x. 12; the defenders of the circuitus 'compare not God to God, but themselves to themselves.'

[2] *D.C.D.*, 11. 21.

[3] Proclus had fenced off the One from the Second Hypostasis by calling it Pro-Aionian (pre-eternal); 'Deus dicitur esse ante aeternitatem, prout participatur a substantiis immaterialibus' (Aquinas, *Summa*, 1. 10. 2).

and one day to be shared by all the blessed; St. Augustine, up to a point, was prepared to identify the Christian Heaven and the Nous or Second Hypostasis of Plotinus.[1] But he shrank from the danger of seeming to make it co-eternal with God; a Second Hypostasis ever flowing from the first would seem too like the Only Begotten Word and might lead to the worship of saints and angels.

How does St. Augustine face the problem? In the Twelfth Book of the *Confessions* he describes the Heaven of Heavens (Ps. cxv. 16), so called in contrast to the visible sky, which we call the heaven; it is closely allied to the Second Hypostasis of Plotinus; he even calls it 'creatura intellectualis' (a Latin rendering of Noeton). 'Here it is the property of Intelligence to know all at once, not in part, not darkly nor through a glass, but as a whole, clearly, face to face, not this thing now and that anon, but all at once without any succession of times.'[2]

He even calls it Sapientia (Wisdom, the Plotinian name), while carefully distinguishing it from the uncreated Wisdom, the Word through Whom all things were made. Heaven is spoken of as a city, 'our mother which is above,' 'a spiritual house of God.'[3] At the same time it is repeatedly stressed that its nature is essentially mutable and that it is only by the constant vision of God that it gains its

[1] With this difference, of course, that Plotinus held that the intellectual part of us is already 'in heaven,' while to St. Augustine it was destined for Heaven.

[2] *Conf.*, 12. 13.

[3] 'Mens pura concordissime una stabilimento pacis sanctorum spirituum, civium civitatis Tuae' (*Conf.*, 12. 11); the singular recalls the fact that in Plotinus all the minds are one.

eternity (Plotinus would have admitted the second point, but not, I think, the first). 'Although no way co-eternal with Thee, the Trinity, yet being partaker of Thy eternity, it doth through the sweetness of that most happy contemplation of Thyself, strongly restrain its own mutability and, without any fall since its first creation, cleaving close unto Thee, hath set itself beyond all rolling interchange of times.'[1] Again: 'It does in no place and at no time put off its natural mutability, but, Thyself being ever present with it, . . . it having neither anything in future to expect nor conveying anything it remembereth into past time, is neither altered by any change nor distracted into any times. . . . By continually and inseparably cleaving unto Thee, it suffers not the least changeableness of times.'[2]

But now there presses upon him the no less delicate question—When was this Heaven of Heavens created? If in Time (or with Time) like the world, how can an eternal being have a beginning in Time? Yet if created in eternity, might it not seem to encroach upon the Divine prerogatives?

St. Augustine wavers; in the *Confessions* he inclines to the view that the Heaven of Heavens

[1] c. 9.

[2] c. 12: 'Sine ullo defectu contemplationis, sine ullo intervallo mutationis, quamvis mutabile, tamen non mutatum, tua aeternitate atque inconmutabilitate perfruatur'; c. 15: 'Quamvis Ei coaeterna non sit, in nullam tamen temporum varietatem et vicissitudinem ab illo se resolvat et defluat, sed in eius solius veracissima contemplatione requiescat. . . . Statuisti enim eam in saeculum et in saeculum saeculi . . . nec tamen tibi coaeterna, quoniam non sine initio: facta est enim.' 'Unde ita est abs Te, Deo nostro, ut aliud sit plane quam Tu et non id ipsum. . . . Inest ei tamen ipsa mutabilitas, unde tenebresceret et frigesceret, nisi amore grandi Tibi cohaerens, tamquam semper meridies luceret et ferveret ex Te.'

was made before Time. He takes the text 'In the beginning God created Heaven and earth,' not as a summary of the story of Creation which follows, but as a pre-temporal act by which He made the Heaven of Heavens and the formless matter out of which the universe as we know it was made.[1] 'Ante illam . . . est ipsius Creatoris aeternitas, a quo facta sumpsit exordium, quamvis non temporis, quia nondum erat tempus, ipsius tamen conditionis suae' ('Before it (the Heaven of Heavens) is the eternity of the Creator Himself, from Whose creative act it took the beginning, not of its time (for time was not yet created) but of its own condition.'[2] In the *City of God* he seems afraid that he has gone too far; he rejects, on the whole,[3] the pre-temporal meaning of 'In the beginning' and regards the angels as included in the Fiat Lux of the first day.[4] He is even prepared to admit that, in some mysterious sense, they are 'in Time'; in a remarkable passage[5] he considers the fact that, even if the angels were created on the first day, there were as yet no signs of Time—no sky, no sun, no stars; yet there might be 'Angelical movements by which Time was begun,' for Time is the measure of the movements of creatures. These 'movements' cannot, of course, be bodily (for angels have

[1] *Conf.*, 12. 12: 'Duo reperio quae fecisti carentia temporibus, cum Tibi neutrum coaeternum sit'; and c. 13: 'illud caelum, sed caelum caeli, hoc vero terram, sed terram invisibilem et inconpositam, propter duo haec . . . sentio sine commemoratione dierum dicere Scripturam Tuam.'

[2] c. 12. 15.

[3] But he says of the view that the angels were made before Creation, 'Non e contrario referam contentionem' (*D.C.D.*, 11. 32).

[4] 11. 9.

[5] 12. 16.

no bodies) and can only be movements of their minds.[1]

He goes on to say 'Although the immortality of the angels has no passage in time, though it is not past so as to seem ended nor future so as to seem not yet begun, yet their movements which are the cause of time pass from the future to the past.'[2]

He also regarded as pre-temporally created the formless matter[3] which has some affinities to Plato's χώρα in the *Timaeus* ; Plotinus regarded matter as an evil : 'It is the want of Wisdom, Virtue, Beauty, Strength, Form . . . how is it possible it should not be perfectly evil ?'[4]

St. Augustine regarded it as good, as having been made by God, and allowed it an infinitesimal speck

[1] Plotinus had said that thought itself was a kind of movement.

[2] This mysterious passage should perhaps be read in connection with *D.C.D.*, 11. 29 : 'Ipsam quoque creaturam (angeli) melius . . . in sapientia Dei, tanquam in arte, qua facta est, quam in ea ipsa sciunt ; ac per hoc et se ipsos ibi melius quam in se ipsis' ; he adds : 'verum tamen et in se ipsis. Facti sunt enim et aliud sunt quam Ille Qui fecit,' *i.e.* their knowledge of themselves cannot be the same as their knowledge of God ; they must be conscious of themselves as different from him ; 'Multum differt, utrum in ea ratione cognoscatur aliquid, secundum quam factum est, an in se ipso ; . . . aliter iustitia in veritate incommutabili (the Platonic idea of Justice), aliter in anima justi. . . . Omnia haec (*i.e.* created things) aliter in Verbo Dei cognoscuntur ab angelis, ubi habent causas rationesque . . . aliter in se ipsis, illa clariore, hac obscuriore cognitione, velut artis atque operum.' He compares these two kinds of knowledge to the morning and evening of the days of creation ; there is a double movement of the angelic mind—one directed to themselves and created things (the 'evening knowledge') and the other directed to the Creator ('morning knowledge') ; these two movements perhaps correspond to the 'temporal' movement of the angels and the 'non-temporal' immortality.

[3] The word 'matter' suggests something solid and tangible, whereas the *prima materia* could not be perceived at all.

[4] *Enneads*, 2. 4. 16.

of reality : ' Fecisti de nulla re paene nullam rem '[1] (' Thou hast made, from nothing, what itself is practically nothing '). This matter (' quaedam informitas ') was in a sense ' before ' Creation ; in the *Confessions* he regards it as ' the earth ' made in the pre-temporal ' beginning ' and to be distinguished from ' the dry land ' of the third day. It is the ' earth without form and void,' the deep (' abyssus '), the waters of Gen. i. 2 ; he says of it : ' Est, non est,' ' Quo inferius nihil est.'[2]

This matter, which in some sense existed first, so that form might be imposed upon it, cannot have existed in Time, for Motion (and Time its measure) cannot have been given till it had acquired form. But in a remarkable chapter (c. 29) St. Augustinc defines the sense in which matter came first. There are four different ways in which we can use the word ' first ' : (1) of Eternity, used of God in relation to His creatures ; (2) of Time, as the flower precedes the fruit ; (3) of Choice, as we prefer the fruit to the flower ; (4) of Origin, as the sound precedes the music ; matter cannot be ' before ' in the sense of eternity, for it cannot be co-eternal with God ; nor in the sense of Time (for it is not in Time) ; nor in the order of choice, for everyone prefers the ordered to the formless world. There remains, therefore, the fourth kind—

[1] *Conf.*, 12. 8.

[2] It cannot be in Time. ' Ubi nulla species, nullus ordo, nec venit quicquam nec praeterit, et ubi hoc non fit, non sunt utique dies nec vicissitudo spatiorum temporalium ' (*Conf.*, 12. 9). ' Sine varietate motionum non sunt tempora ' (*ibid.*, c. 11). ' Ita informe erat, ut ex qua forma in quam formam vel motionis vel stationis mutaretur, quo tempori subderetur, non haberet (c. 12).

order of origin. He gives the example of the sound (the matter) and the song by which the sound is given beauty, order and rhythm. The bare sound does not exist 'before' the song, for it is only heard in its formed state as music.

St. Augustine is clearly trying to express the Aristotelian idea of potential existence; matter exists as a possibility of form, sound as the possibility of song.[1] The pre-temporal existence of something which 'is nearly nothing,' and only exists as the possibility of something else, is clearly not a serious rival to the eternity of the Creator.

We now come to St. Augustine's teaching as to the nature of Time in Book 11 of the *Confessions*; no analysis can do justice to the triumphant march of the argument, interrupted by constant supplications and prayers for light to the Giver of Life, from the famous epigram 'If no one asks me what time is, I know; if I want to explain it to a questioner, I do not know,'[2] to the cry of joy as the solution glimmers on the horizon: 'See where the truth dawns.'[3]

[1] Augustine practically admits this in the important phrase 'Cantus . . . est sonus verus.'

[2] Cp. *Enneads*, 3. 7, 'We think that we have a certain clear perception of these (time and eternity) . . . when, however, we endeavour to . . . approach nearer to them, we are involved in doubt.' Berkeley (*Principles*, 97) puts this in his popular style, 'Bid your servant meet you at such a time, in such a place, and he shall never stay to deliberate on the meaning of those words. In conceiving that particular time and place, or the motion by which he is to get thither, he finds not the least difficulty. But if Time be taken exclusive of all those particular actions and ideas that diversify the day, merely for the continuation of existence or duration in abstract, then it will perhaps gravel even a philosopher to comprehend it.'

[3] *Conf.*, 11. 27.

It must be read in the original by those readers who are wise enough to know that the interest of the *Confessions* does not end with the close of the narrative portion at the death of Monica.

Like the discussion on Memory in Book 10, the discussion on Time is made memorable by St. Augustine's great psychological gifts. He brings out forcibly the fact that Time is always passing and never is ; the past is no more ; the future is not yet ; the present is never at a stay but flows continually from what is not yet to what has been ; we might almost say that Time only exists in so far as it hurries towards non-existence.[1] Yet we have knowledge of the past, as is shown by history, and of the future, as is shown by prophecy.[2] Again, we can measure Time, as in verse we say that the long quantity has twice the value of the short syllable we said half an hour ago and half the value of the spondee we are going to say in a few moments. Therefore, though Time never is, yet in some sense past, present and future 'stay' or linger for our knowledge.

The solution is that they are known and measured by the mind.[3] By memory we know the past, by perception ('contuitus') the present, by anticipation ('expectatio') the future[4] ; Time itself

[1] c. 27, *cp.* c. 15, 'Praesens . . . ita raptim a futuro in praeteritum transvolat, ut nulla morula extendatur. Nam, si extenditur, dividitur in praeteritum et futurum.'

[2] c. 17, 'Ubi ea viderunt qui futura cecinerunt, si nondum sunt? . . . et qui narrant praeterita, non utique vera narrarent, si animo illa non cernerent.'

[3] c. 27.

[4] c. 20. In this way past and future exist in God's mind.

is a lengthening out 'of what I know not unless it be of the mind itself.' [1]

We must not suppose, however, that St. Augustine was a Berkeleian idealist, who held that everything happened 'in the mind'; he is rather a Representationalist, that is, he believes that external things leave 'tracks' ('vestigia') on the mind, and these are the objects of knowledge.[2] 'When past things are truly related, there are brought out of the memory not the actual things, which have passed, but words formed from the images of these past things which in their passing have, through the senses, left, as it were, tracks in the mind. . . . When we say that future things are seen, it is not the things themselves that are seen (for they are not yet), but perhaps their causes or signs which exist now.' [3]

He clearly distinguishes Time from Motion; he says in the case of Joshua's successful prayer, 'The sun stood still, but Time went on.' [4] Time cannot be the same as the movement of the heavens, for if the stars stopped and 'only a potter's wheel

[1] c. 26; the example he takes is that of a short syllable pronounced slowly so as to take more 'time' than a short one; Time arrests the flux, and what has disappeared in the past remains 'lengthened out' in the memory (like the after-echo of a sound); in c. 29 he plays on these words; the mind is 'distentus,' drawn out like elastic to past and future; and so distracted. In Christ, the soul rises above temporal things, 'non distentus sed extentus' (stretching up; *cp.* Philippians iii. 12–14), 'non secundum distentionem, sed secundum intentionem (eagerly).'

[2] Montgomery, *St. Augustine*, p. 116, 'What is perceived in sense, is not the object directly but its impress on the sense.'

[3] 11. 18; *cp.* c. 27, 'Affectionem (impression), quam res praetereuntes in te faciunt . . . ipsam metior praesentem, non ea quae praeterierunt, ut fieret.'

[4] c. 23.

went round,' Time would continue [1]; again, if the sun performed its circuit in twelve hours, we should say (from our own independent measure of Time) 'It has done it in half its usual time.' [2] Nor can Time be the motion of bodies; for I cannot measure the movement of a body by looking at it; I must know when it began,[3] and, again, bodies rest as well as move; now rest can also be measured in Time.[4] His view is, therefore, quite Bergsonian; there is an external motion (Space, Bergson would call it) and a Time which is in consciousness.[5]

When we turn to St. Augustine's conception of God's eternity, we find the Plotinian conception of the eternal Present. 'Thy years stand together at the same time . . . nor are some pushed aside by those that follow, for they pass not. . . . Thy years are one Day and Thy Day is not like our sequence of days but is To-day. . . . Thy To-day is eternity.' [6] God knows Time but not in any temporal manner,[7] for it is already spread before Him like a map.

So in the famous chapter six of the First Book of

[1] c. 23.

[2] *Ibid.*; cp. *Enneads* 3. 7. The example is used by Bergson.

[3] c. 24.

[4] *Ibid.*

[5] 'It is impossible to conceive a bond of union between a Before and an After without an element of memory and therefore of consciousness' (*Durée et Simultanéité*, p. 60). Aristotle had defined Time as 'the measure of motion'; Plotinus (and Augustine with him) prefers to say that Motion measures Time. 'It was not possible for Time itself to be measured by us, since it is invisible and incomprehensible; hence the Demiourgos made day and night' (Taylor, p. 137; *cp.* Lucretius, 1. 459–63):

> 'Tempus item per se non est, sed rebus ab ipsis
> Consequitur sensus, transactum quid sit in aevo,
> Tum quae res instet, quid porro deinde sequatur.
> Nec per se quemquam tempus sentire fatendumst
> Semotum ab rerum motu placidaque quiete.'

[6] *Conf.*, 11. 13.

[7] *D.C.D.*, 11. 21.

the *Confessions* : 'Summus enim es et non mutaris, neque peragitur in Te hodiernus dies, et tamen in Te peragitur, quia in Te sunt et ista omnia : non enim haberent vias transeundi nisi contineres ea. . . . Quam multi jam dies nostri et patrum nostrorum per hodiernum Tuum transierunt et ex illo acceperunt modos et utcumque extiterunt, et transibunt adhuc alii et accipient et utcumque existent. Tu autem Idem Ipse es et omnia crastina atque ultra omniaque hesterna et retro hodie facies, hodie fecisti.' We notice the skill, if we may use so secular a word in connection with so splendid a passage, with which St. Augustine joins together the Greek view of God as changeless and the Hebrew view of history as purposeful.[1]

[1] 'Thou art the Highest and Thou art not changed ; neither is this present day spent in Thee ; yet it is spent in Thee, because even all these times are in Thee, nor could (they) have their ways of passing on unless Thou containedst them . . . and how many soever our days and our fathers' days have been, they have all passed through this one Day of Thine ; from that Day have they received their measures and manners of being ; and those to come shall so also pass away and so also receive their measures and manners of being. But Thou art the same still and all to-morrows and so forward and all yesterdays and so backward Thou shalt make present in this Day of Thine ; yea and hast made present' (Watts' translation, p. 19).

'Pure poetry,' it might be objected, 'in which high-sounding words are jingled one against another.' We shall try to see, later, whether they mean anything ; for the moment let us notice that Augustine's antithetical style is not merely the sword-play of an African Professor of Rhetoric. It comes from a profoundly Christian mind dwelling in two worlds (Nature and Grace, as Aquinas afterwards distinguished them) ; for Plotinus the world 'here' was far from God and the world 'yonder' was near Him, but for Augustine, the Incarnation has bridged the gulf between ; God is at work in both, and the paradox (so dear to Augustine's type of mind) is the sign of a soul moving happily in both ; *cp.* what is almost a caricature of his own method in *D.C.D.*, 12. 19, 'Cuius Sapientia simpliciter multiplex et uniformiter multiformis tam inconprehensibili conprehensione omnia inconprehensibilia conprehendit.'

But he is far from content with the view of God as a Super-historian with the course of events spread out before Him; God's eternity is not merely knowing together what we know successively; it is far deeper and richer than the Time process which is merely a broken expression of its creative perfection. 'With Thee stand the causes of things that here are so unstable; with Thee abide the origins of all things that here abide not; with Thee live the eternal reasons of all which is here unreasonable and temporal.'[1]

As to St. Augustine's treatment of human immortality, we need only here note the classical attempt to represent it in the ecstatic vision he had by the side of his dying mother. 'If God were to speak Himself, not through created things but through Himself and we were to hear His Word . . . so that life should be for ever as it was at that moment of understanding, . . . would not that be Enter into the joy of Thy Lord?'[2] This idea of eternal life as the prolongation of a moment of perfect bliss or insight will often be in our minds during the more constructive part of these lectures.

[1] *Conf.*, 1. 6. In *D.C.D.*, 12. 20, discussing the meaning of 'saecula saeculorum,' he asks whether it means 'saecula in Sapientia Dei inconcussa stabilitate manentia istorum quae cum tempore transeunt, tamquam efficientia saeculorum . . . aeterna . . . temporalium tamquam dominantia subditorum.' Dr. Welldon comments *ad loc.*, '(They are) in the same relation to the *saecula* of human history as the Platonic ἰδέαι to the objects of Nature and Art' (ii. 30). The point is that the eternity of God is no mere unifying or synthesising of the Time-process but something different in kind, to which the moments of the time-series stand as 'subjects' (subdita).

[2] *Conf.*, 9. 10.

THIRD LECTURE

ETERNITY IN CHRISTIAN THOUGHT

(*Continued*)

Bless the Lord, ye His angels, that excel in strength, that do His commandments, hearkening unto the voice of His word.—Ps. ciii. 20.

I HAVE chosen this text because in this sermon we shall be largely concerned with Aquinas' teaching about the nature of the angels; but first we must say a few words about Boethius.

BOETHIUS

However imperfect our presentation of St. Augustine's thought in the last sermon may have been, it can hardly have failed to give some impression of his penetrating and dominating mind. Yet it fell to Boethius, over a century later, to give to the mediaeval schools a precise formula for eternity which was more congenial to their taste than the diffuse eloquence of the African doctor. The passage occurs in the *De Consolatione Philosophiae*, that stately combination of verse and prose which Boethius wrote during his unjust imprisonment. The philosopher is overwhelmed by the problem of reconciling God's foreknowledge with man's free will. 'What heavenly power,' he cries, 'has set such strife between two truths? Thus though, apart, each brings no doubt, they cannot be linked together.'[1] The Lady Philosophy replies that 'a

[1] Bk. 5, Met. 3 (Temple Classics Edition, p. 150).

result does not come to pass, for the reason that Providence has foreseen it, but the opposite rather —because it is about to come to pass, therefore it cannot be hidden from God's Providence.'[1] Clearly freewill is intact, if there is no foreknowledge ; how then is it fettered by a foreknowledge which 'brings no necessity to bear on events'? You say 'God's foreknowledge is a sign that the future is certain.' Well, but is the future certain? 'We can see many actions developing before our eyes, just as chariot drivers see the development of their actions as they control and guide their chariots. . . . Does any necessity compel any of those things to occur as they do? Of course not.'[2] The confusion is due to the difference between human and divine knowledge, which is far greater than that between the senses and understanding in man. 'Let us, therefore, raise ourselves, if so be that we can, to that height of the loftiest intelligence'[3]; let us consider what eternity is.

'Eternity is the simultaneous and complete possession of infinite life,' so the famous definition runs: 'Interminabilis vitae tota simul et perfecta possessio.' All time is in motion ; even though it were true that the universe had no beginning and will have no end, 'yet it does not embrace the whole simultaneously ; it has not yet experienced the future.' But eternity 'lacks nought of the future and has lost nought of the fleeting past.' God is not older than His creation 'by any period of Time' ; 'the infinite changing of temporal things

[1] 5 Prose 3. [2] 5 Prose 4. [3] 5 Prose 5.

tries to imitate the ever simultaneously present immutability of God's life. It cannot succeed, . . . but inasmuch as the temporal present bears a certain appearance of that abiding present, it somehow makes those to whom it comes seem to be in truth what they imitate.'[1] 'God views everything as though it were taking place in the present.' This is a far better definition of Providence than 'foreknowledge of the future'; it is 'a looking forth rather than a looking forward.'

We see 'present things' without 'putting on them any necessity'; why should they become necessary in the light of God's eternal present? He discerns 'all that shall come to pass, whether (it be) of necessity or not. . . . When you see, at the same time, a man walking on the earth and the sun rising in the heavens, you see each sight simultaneously, yet you distinguish between them and decide that one is moving voluntarily and one of necessity. In like manner the perception of God looks down upon all things without disturbing at all their nature.' If it is answered, 'I will disregard Providence, since I (being free) can change what Providence foresees,' the answer is, 'You cannot escape that Divine foreknowledge, just as you cannot avoid the glance of a present eye, though you may by your free will turn yourself to all kinds of different actions.'[2]

Two things are to be noted: First, the definition

[1] The idea seems to be that the fact that we are always confronted with a *present* (though it is always changing) gives us a faint idea of God's eternal present; Aquinas quotes as from Boethius (v. 6) the phrase 'Nunc fluens facit tempus; nunc stans facit aeternitatem' (I. 10. 2). [2] 5 Prose 6.

of eternity in terms of spiritual life appealed to the mystical side of the Middle Ages, and the fact that Boethius seemed like the last of the Roman philosophers speaking from his dungeon gave him a place side by side with Cicero and Aristotle.

Secondly, we should observe the close connection between the definition of eternity and the problem of Divine foreknowledge. Whatever be thought of the success of Boethius' treatment of this intricate problem, it must be admitted to be a gallant attempt, especially remarkable in its correction of the misleading time-reference in the phrases 'Foreknowledge' and 'Predestination.' St. Augustine, while sharing Boethius' definition of eternity, drew different conclusions from it, for he did not allow much, if any, place for free will or accident in human affairs [1]; the struggle between Calvinist and Arminian reflects the difference between Boethius' Foreknowledge (which allows freedom) and St. Augustine's Predestination. Does God only foreknow or does He also foreordain human action? We shall have to return to the question later; for the moment we must be content with having seen the issue clearly defined in history.

Aquinas

We now come to Aquinas, and in considering the leading master of method it becomes us too to be methodical. We shall discuss:

[1] Dr. Mozley says (and Dr. Williams supports him with his more recent authority), 'St. Augustine held . . . that God by an eternal decree, prior to any difference of desert, separated one portion of mankind from another, ordaining one to eternal life and the other to eternal punishment' (*Predestination*, p. 131).

(*a*) The duration of God—Eternity.

(*b*) The duration of the angels—Perpetuity (to borrow a phrase from Hooker).

(*c*) The duration of the universe—Everlastingness.

(*d*) The duration of human beings—Immortality.

(*a*) *The Eternity of God.*

St. Thomas begins by accepting the Totum Simul of Boethius as against the Scotists who defined eternity simply as 'that which lacks a beginning and an end,' but rejected the idea of simultaneity. He urges that Time is a measurement of motion,[1] implying a Before and After, but God cannot move and therefore there can be no succession in Him. Eternity is different from Time in kind and not merely in degree ; if the only difference was the lack of a beginning and end, then those who held that the world had always existed would have to regard the world as equal to God in duration.[2]

Eternity is the property of God alone[3] ; here Aquinas gets into some verbal difficulties ; Proclus had said that God existed 'before eternity' ; St. Thomas rightly takes 'eternity' here to mean the eternal life shared by the angels and saints ; he

[1] Pars I, Quaestio 10, Art. 1 ; in his definition of Time Aquinas accepts Boethius' idea of the Nunc which 'imitates' the eternal Present of God, 'In tempore est duo considerare ; scilicet ipsum tempus, quod est successivum ; et nunc temporis quod est imperfectum' (1. 10. 1). (Commentator's note : 'Nunc temporis est instans indivisibile, quod, licet sit totum simul, nec habeat partes, non est tamen quid perfectum in ratione durationis, cum statim evanescat ac in illo nihil perfecte possideatur.') Again, in 1. 10. 4, 'Nunc temporis est idem subjecto in toto tempore, sed differens ratione ; . . . inquantum est hic et ibi et ista alternatio est motus.'

[2] 1. 10. 4.

[3] 1. 10. 2.

is also somewhat perplexed by the vagaries of the Vulgate Latin ; he has to explain the apparent bull in Exod. xv. 18, 'Dominus regnabit in aeternum et ultra,' 'God shall reign to all eternity and beyond,' by saying that eternity here means 'some kind of given duration.'

Three questions emerge from the further consideration of the Totum Simul : (1) Why can there be no successiveness in the life of God ? (2) What are the 'all things' which God's mind 'holds together' in the one experience ? (3) What is the mode or manner of this Divine knowledge ?

(1) St. Thomas gives three reasons for denying succession to the Divine life : *first*, God is pure Act, *i.e.* whatever He is, He is not potentially but actually. As there are no unrealised capacities in Him, there is nothing He could become ; *secondly*, God's Nature is absolutely simple ; there are no distinct parts in Him ; He is always and everywhere Himself.[1] Now change and motion imply differences of parts, because they mean that a thing is partly different and partly the same ; *thirdly*, Motion is an attempt to gain something we have not had before, but 'God, being infinite and comprehending in Himself all the fulness of the perfection of every creature, cannot acquire anything new.'[2] Creation was always from eternity in His mind ; the changes of history do not affect the unchangeable Purpose which has already willed and grasped them all[3] ; God's Will is constant ;

[1] I. 3. 7.
[2] I. 9. I.
[3] I. 14. 15 : 'Res creatae sunt in Deo invariabiliter,' and 'Non sequitur (from the change of history) quod scientia Ejus sit variabilis, sed quod cognoscat rerum variabilitatem.'

He never changes His mind ; here St. Thomas gives us the useful formula, 'It is one thing to change one's will ; quite another to will change in things.' [1]

(2) The 'all things' in God's knowledge include not only what has existed or will exist, but all the possible things God might have created and did not ; His knowledge of actual history is called 'scientia visionis' ; His understanding of what is possible but will never occur in the time series is part of His 'intelligentia simplex.' [2]

Boethius had compared the Divine knowledge to an eye ever present and watching all things ; Aquinas uses another and not less famous comparison : 'He who walks on a road does not see those who come after him' (such is human knowledge, which cannot read the future), 'but he who looks at the whole road from some height, sees at once all those who are walking on the road.' [3] Such is God's knowledge ; the future and the past are within His simultaneous present [4] ; but (we ask) if, from His point of view, they have already happened, is not the future as irrevocable as the past ? Is there room for freedom, accident, contingency ?

Like Boethius, Aquinas makes a distinction between the foreknowledge and the foredecrees of God, but, unlike him, he is much hampered

[1] I. 19. 7. So he expounds Gen. vi. 7, 'Etiam aliquis homo absque mutatione voluntatis interdum velit aliquid facere, simul intendens postea illud destruere.'

[2] I. 14. 13. [3] I. 14. 13.

[4] I. 14. 13 : 'prout sunt in Sua praesentialitate' ; in this section St. Thomas rejects as inadequate the view that God only knows the future 'quia habet rationes rerum apud Se praesentes,' *i.e.* that He sees the future in its present causes.

by Augustinian speculation about the nature of sin.

In 1. 19. 8 Aquinas asks himself 'whether the Will of God imposes necessity upon the things willed by it.' His answer is that it does in some cases, and not in others; 'to some things God has fitted (*aptavit*) necessary causes, but to contingent things He has fitted contingent causes'; if all things followed from necessity, then free will and all planning for the future and everything else of this kind would perish. Necessary causes cannot fail; but contingent causes are 'defectible'; to the argument 'What God wills must happen,' St. Thomas replies, 'What is done by God's will has just that kind of necessity which He wills it to have.' The certain movement of the sun cannot make the plants grow without proximate and 'uncertain' causes like the rain and the soil; so God's activity is supplemented by contingent causes, which might have failed, but of course (in so far as they belong to the future known to God) are effective.[1] This seems to preserve some kind of contingency in the world of Nature; certain causes (such as man's will) may fail; then God, foreseeing the fall, provides a remedy in the sphere of Grace. In this second sphere it is intensely difficult to say what Aquinas teaches; he says, on the one hand, 'Deus, movendo causas voluntarias, non aufert quin actiones earum sint voluntariae.'[2] 'Sic Deus voluntatem movet . . . sed remanet motus ejus contingens, et non necessarius'[3]; on the other hand, he regards as Pelagianism the assertion

[1] 1. 14. 13. [2] 1. 83. 1. [3] 2. 10. 4.

that God chose the elect because he foresaw their good deeds : 'id, quod est gratiae, est praedestinationis *effectus*.'[1] Dr. Williams regards the whole of Aquinas' theory of freedom as little more than verbal[2] ; in any case it is worth noticing that he tried to distinguish clearly (and seems to have thought he had done it) between the free and the necessary.[3]

It is also important to notice that St. Thomas does not believe (except possibly in the case of the elect) that the future is known to God, because it is inevitable ; there is no question of God calculating from the present state of the world what it will be hereafter ; the future is not bound to be this rather than that, but as a matter of fact it *is* this or that in the eternal present of the Divine mind.[4]

(3) The last point—and it is far from being the least important—is that of the mode of God's knowledge. When we say that He knows all things together, we cannot mean anything in the nature of sense-perception ; we cannot suppose that in

[1] I. 23. 5. [2] *Fall and Original Sin*, p. 404.

[3] I cannot, however, see the force of Dr. Mozley's contention in *Predestination*, p. 243, 'The will, as a link in a chain of causes and effects, is not freewill, in the common and true understanding of that term, according to which it means an original source of action . . . To reconcile freewill with the Divine Power is to destroy it.' Surely no one, unless (as Aristotle says) to defend a thesis, would regard freedom of the will as meaning a complete independence of all external influences ; the influence of a friend upon me may be a powerful contributing cause to my free choice. May not God's grace work like that ? One can even imagine cases where the influence of love or gratitude might be so overwhelming as to be 'irresistible' without thereby destroying the reality of the ensuing action as veritably my own.

[4] We must distinguish things as they are in themselves and as they are in God's mind ; they are necessary in the second case, not in the first (I. 14. 13).

some cosmic tableau God sees the murder of Julius Caesar side by side with the battle of Waterloo or that, in some symphony of the universe, He hears, at one and the same moment, the Dies Irae and the Marseillaise. Yet if He has no sense-perception, how can He have any knowledge of particulars which the abstractive intellect cannot grasp?

This was one of the difficulties in which Aristotle had entangled himself; Aquinas meets it skilfully by his use of the Ideae—the old Aristotelian Eidê; for Aristotle every separate type had its eidos, the perfect example it was trying to realise—the finished specimen of the animal, in Man Eudaimonia, in Society the Ariste Politeia. But whereas (for Aristotle) the type is merely the quasi-purpose of a semi-personified Nature (φύσις), the Christian doctrine of the Creator gives far fuller content to the idea.

Just as the builder or artificer has in his mind the form or idea of the house he is to build or the statue he is to make, so, before God creates anything, He has in His mind the idea—the special type of perfection,[1] different for each different thing,[2] which

[1] 'Cum omnia sint a Deo, non a casu facta, necessarium est in Ejus mente omnium ideas preexistere objective, ad quarum similitudinem omnia condita sunt' (I. 15. 1). M. Maritain (*Trois Réformateurs*, p. 111) says, 'Les idées divines . . . sont des idées factives ou opératives, des idées d'artiste : exemplaires à l'imitation desquels une chose est faite.' We must not allow the word 'artiste' to suggest aesthetic associations; it is here the rational purpose of the artifex or workman; M. Gilson (rather boldly, I should have felt) says he prefers St. Thomas to St. Augustine because he (Aquinas) has the idea of creation not as a necessary emanation but as a work of art.

[2] 'Cum in mente divina sint omnium rerum propriae rationes, plures ideas in Ejus mente esse necesse est . . . aedificator speciem domus concipere non posset, nisi apud ipsum esset propria ratio cujuslibet partium ejus' (I. 15. 2).

is meant to be realised. This is the very meaning of creative purpose ; God does not know the whole course of things as a historian surveys a period from without, but as a general watches the movements of an army, all planned by him.

How without perception does God know particulars ? Our human intelligences abstract from particulars, but God's creative intelligence knows the work He has planned through and through.[1] According to St. Thomas' very complicated theory of knowledge, our minds can only know forms, *i.e.* universals, directly ; particulars being material, we can only know ' indirecte secundum quandam reflexionem ' ; this is because our minds are passive, not creative. We can only receive, and purely material things cannot (in a sense) enter our intelligences. But God's mind is active and creative ; the particular colours or sounds do not come *into* His mind ; they come *from* it. While God cannot perceive a colour or imagine it after some pattern He has seen, He can have the creative plan of it in His mind, just as (in a lower sense) a musician can ' hear ' a symphony before writing it. As we should put it, perception and understanding are mutilations of reality ; God grasps things by an immediate and complete intuition which is far higher and truer than our partial and divided faculties ; Aquinas is rather puzzled as to how God in His universal knowledge can know evil. He contents himself with saying that as evil is a

[1] ' Intellectus noster speciem intelligibilem abstrahit a principiis individuantibus. . . . Sed species intelligibilis Divini intellectus, quae est Dei essentia, non est immaterialis per abstractionem, sed per seipsam ' (I. 14. 11).

privation of good, it is known by whoever knows good—as one who knows light would know (without needing direct experience) what darkness is.[1]

(*b*) *The Perpetuity of the Angels*

It cannot be denied that the Thomist Angelology has its grotesque side, and we feel some sympathy with Calvin's crude description of it as made up of *ματαιώματα*[2] when we read such questions solemnly discussed as 'Can several angels be in the same place?' or 'Can one angel talk to another?'[3] We ask what such enquiries have to do with religion, and we forget that in the Middle Ages theology, the queen of the sciences, included what we call metaphysics and science. For us, the angels are poetical representations of the principle of worship; St. Thomas hardly ever mentions their worship; for him they represent natural knowledge and will at their highest, disembodied and perfect, instructive (by the very contrast of their perfection) as to the limitations of human knowledge and will.[4] The universe, to be perfect, must include specimens of every conceivable reality; as there is body without soul (matter), as there is soul attached to body (humanity), so there must be souls without

[1] I. 14. 10.

[2] Calvin says (*Inst.* I. 14): 'Si rite sapere volumus, relinquenda sunt nobis illa *ματαιώματα*, quae et ab otiosis hominibus de angelorum natura, ordinibus, multitudine, absque Dei verbo, traduntur.' But Calvin had little interest in metaphysics.

[3] I. 52. 3 and I. 106. I.

[4] M. Maritain has ingeniously called his study of Descartes (*Trois Réformateurs*, II) 'L'Incarnation de l'Ange'; his thesis is that Descartes, forgetting the limitations of the human mind, has described it in just the terms in which Aquinas described the Angelic mind.

bodies; the well-known scholastic problem 'How many angels could stand on the point of a needle?' is simply what we should call the problem of the mind's relation to space. We are not, of course, concerned with St. Thomas' Angelology from any such point of view. But his treatment of the subject demands some attention as elaborating the idea of a blessed life, in some sense eternal yet distinguished from the Eternity of God as well as from the temporal experience of Man.

Aquinas calls this angelic duration by the untranslatable word 'Aevum,' which is really a translation of the Greek Aion. As we have seen above, the ordinary Greek words for time and eternity were originally the same; Aion began by meaning an undefined period and so came to the sense of eternity; for this sense of eternity, Latin theology had the separate word Aeternitas,[1] and therefore it was able to use Aevum in a new and special sense of the heavenly life; St. Thomas, however, is not able to find much ancient authority for it; he quotes from the Vulgate (Ecclus. i. 1): 'Omnis sapientia a Domino Deo est, et cum Illo fuit semper, et est ante aevum,'[2] and from Boethius, 'Qui tempus ab aevo Ire jubes,' where, however, the word is probably a metrical equivalent for 'eternity.'[3]

He defines Aevum as 'medium inter aeternitatem et tempus, utroque participans'; 'some things

[1] See Appendix I.

[2] I. 10. 5*a*; it probably means 'before the ages,' as Aquinas himself translates it in Esdras iii. 4, 'Potestas aevorum est apud Te, Domine'; he says 'Accipitur pro saeculo' (I. 10. 6).

[3] So in the Temple Classics Edition, p. 80, 'Who hast bidden Time stand forth from eternity.'

recede from permanence so as to become subject to change or to consist in change, and such things are measured by time . . . but other things recede less from permanence, because their being does not consist in change, nor is it subject to change, but it has change joined with it (adjunctam), either actually or as a possibility . . . This is the condition of the angels ; they have an unchangeable being as far as concerns their nature and they have the possibility of change as regards their choice,[1] their acts of intelligence, their affections and local movements. . . . Time has a Before and After ; Aevum has no Before and After in itself but they can be joined with it '[2]; and again, 'Spiritual creatures, as far as concerns their affections and acts of intelligence, which are successive, are measured by time ; as far as concerns their natural being, they are measured by Aevum, but as far as concerns their Vision of Glory, they participate in eternity.'[3]

This is the rather difficult conception which I propose to examine, as representing a very important theological attempt to define the part which Time plays in created natures at their highest.

St. Thomas holds that the human mind consists of two parts : (*a*) the Anima sensitiva, which is subject to Time ; (*b*) the Anima intellectiva, which is above Time but which has to work through the

[1] This refers to the initial act of election, by which the evil angels fell and the good angels stood fast.

[2] I. 10. 5 : *cp.* 'Aevum est totum simul, non tamen est aeternitas, quia compatitur secum (it is compatible with) prius et posterius.'

[3] *Ibid.*

temporal appearances: 'adjacet tempori.'[1] It depends, therefore, up to a point, upon Time and change for its functioning; the angelic nature is independent of Time and succession, although it can experience them; if we take the sensitive soul as something in Time, we see that it is not only aware of change but also experiences it; the changes it perceives penetrate deep into its nature; the eye becomes tired of seeing and the ear of listening. Even in the case of the 'anima intellectiva' it is hard to exclude change; by learning we become wiser; by doing good deeds we become better; for good or evil, actions mould habit and character. The angels, free from the body, pure intelligences, may experience change, but change cannot really penetrate to the angelic nature. The angel can pass from one act of understanding or affection to another, but he neither grows nor decays in himself; the acts remain external (conjunctae); he can distinguish before and after, but he never grows older. It would be true of him (in a limited sense)

Tempora mutantur

but in no sense true

et nos mutamur in illis.

This conception of the angelic nature, unmoved by succession as the sea is only ruffled on its surface, is illustrated by two of St. Thomas'

[1] 'Mens humana . . . secundum se quidem est supra tempus, sed per accidens subditur tempori, inquantum scilicet intelligit cum continuo et tempore secundum phantasmata, in quibus species intelligibiles considerat' (2. 113. 7).

doctrines. First, there can be no progress or growth in their experience. Progress 'belongs to the condition of Wayfarers, but the angels are not Wayfarers but understanders (comprehensores).'[1] Angels know God in infinitely varied degrees, some more, some less; but when an angel has attained the rank appointed him 'he cannot pass on to a higher rank.'[2]

Secondly, the succession of angelic experiences is quite different from ours; for us Time is ever flowing from one moment to another and is the very symbol of transitoriness. The angelic moment does not pass away; it remains as a moment of fixed contemplation, lasting till it is replaced by another, and these moments are discontinuous[3]; thus Aquinas holds it probable that the Devil sinned 'statim post primum instans suae creationis'; to the objection that he cannot have sinned 'at once,' because there must have been an interval between the instant of his creation as a perfect being and his fall, he replies that this would be true of human

[1] 'Non viatores, sed comprehensores' (1. 62. 9); *cp.* the prayer of St. Thomas, 'Concede mihi dilectum Filium Tuum, Quem nunc velatum *in Via* suscipere propono, revelata tandem facie perpetuo *contemplari.*'

[2] *Ibid.* St. Luke xv. 10, compels Aquinas to admit that the conversion of a sinner adds a new joy to the angels: 'Sed hoc gaudium ad praemium accidentale pertinet; quod quidem augeri potest usque ad diem judicii'; in the same way he admits that at the Resurrection the joy of the saints is increased by having their bodies, although before that joy was infinite; he explains this by saying that it is an increase of the *extension* of joy (non respicit majus sed plus), but it also 'co-operates' to increase the intensiveness of the joy (3 Suppl. 93. 1).

[3] 'Selon la discontinuité d'un temps tout spirituel qui . . . (est) la permanence d'un stable instant qui dure, immobile, tant qu'il ne fait place à un autre immobile instant de contemplation' (Maritain, *Trois Réformateurs*, p. 85).

time which is continuous; but no time separates one angelic instant from another.[1] Aevum then stands for a state of existence in which all progress, growth and change are excluded, but there are acts in it which have a before and after. He distinguishes four kinds of such acts.

(*a*) Acts of election or choice; such was the act of free will by which (at the very beginning of their being) the angels chose the good or the bad.[2] But the consequences are now irrevocable; the good angels cannot fall from Grace; the evil angels are for ever obdurate in sin.

(*b*) Acts of understanding or intelligence; here we must grasp the distinction between the *natural* capacities of the angels (good and bad angels alike) and the *supernatural* capacities which belong only to the blessed angels.

Angels are not omniscient in the sphere of natural knowledge; they know all that will happen so far as it is necessarily contained in its cause[3]; when the future is contingent, they con-

[1] The objection 'habet veritatem, inquantum est tempus continuum,' but it does not apply to the Angels 'qui non sunt subjecti caelesti motui qui primo per tempus continuum mensuratur' (1. 63. 6). Dante (*Paradiso*, xxix. 49–51) has the curious version that Satan fell 'before you could count twenty' from the moment of his creation. 'Nè giugneriesi numerando al venti Sì tosto, come . . .'

[2] 'In primo instanti omnes fuerunt boni, sed in secundo fuerunt boni a malis distincti' (1. 63. 6).

[3] On the question whether angels know the secrets of human hearts (1. 57. 4), St. Thomas answers that they do, as far as these secrets can be seen in outward effects; 'etiam medici aliquas affectiones animi per pulsum cognoscere possunt; et multo magis angeli, vel etiam daemones'; but only God can know 'cogitationes, prout sunt in intellectu, et affectiones, prout sunt in voluntate.' 'Ea quae ex voluntate sola dependent, vel quae in voluntate sola sunt, soli Deo sunt nota.'

jecture, but their guesses are much more inspired than ours, 'as in the case of a doctor who sees more deeply into causes than others do'; where the future is a matter of complete accident, they are completely ignorant.[1]

In the case of supernatural knowledge, they can only find out the truth by special revelation; the good angels see the mysteries of Grace in the Vision of God, 'non quidem omnia, nec aequaliter omnes.'[2] The evil angels, deprived of Divine Wisdom, may fall into error. 'Seeing a man dead, they may judge that he will not rise again; or seeing Christ as man, they may judge that He is not God.'[3]

In the sphere of natural knowledge they do not know things (as we do) by impressions from without, but from within themselves, by means of innate ideas ('species diversas eis inditas')[4]; they know the Word of God 'per ejus similitudinem in sua natura relucentem'[5]; they know God by contemplating themselves as made in His image[6]; so they know 'things' by the copies of God's creative 'ideas' which He has placed in them.[7] But this

[1] I. 57. 3.

[2] I. 57. 5: 'Et horum etiam mysteriorum quaedam a principio suae creationis cognoverunt; quaedam vero postmodum, secundum quod eorum officiis congruit, edocentur.' This would seem to admit progress in supernatural knowledge, but we must remember that the mysteries of human salvation are 'external' to them; they are not intimately concerned, for they are saved already.

[3] I. 58. 5. [4] I. 12. 10. [5] I. 62. I.

[6] 'Ipsa natura angelica est quoddam speculum divinam similitudinem repraesentans' (I. 56. 3).

[7] 'Dieu, selon le mot d'Augustin, ayant produit les choses intelligiblement dans la connaissance des esprits, avant de les produire réellement dans leur être propre' (Maritain, p. 95).

natural knowledge, though far superior to ours, is still imperfect.[1]

Our reasoning is abstract, but the angelic knowledge, following the track of God's creative plan, grasps things 'secundum earum singularitatem,'[2] in the freshness of their individuality; 'the universality of the angelic ideas is not due to any process of abstraction, but to the universality of Causation or Activity, the property of the creative "ideas" of God, from which things descend into concrete being—ideas, of which the angelic conceptions are a created resemblance.'[3]

(*c*) Acts of will and feeling; like the acts of the understanding they can be successive, but like them they express a nature that cannot grow nor decay but is always full to the brim of goodness and joy.[4]

(*d*) Local movements in space; the faculty the angels possess of appearing in bodies 'made of air which they condense by a divine power'[5] would carry us too far from our subject; two points only are to be noted.

First, St. Thomas will not admit that angels, when they assume bodies, move from one place to another instantaneously. This would destroy the nature of movement in space. Therefore they move in Time, though not in a Time measured by the movements of the heavens.[6]

[1] 'Cognoscit res in Verbo . . . naturali cognitione, imperfecte' (I. 62. I).

[2] I. 57. 2.

[3] Maritain, pp. 95–6.

[4] 'Non distinguitur in eis aliqua virtus irascibilis, vel concupiscibilis; sed indivisus in eis appetitus, qui dicitur Voluntas, manet' (I. 59. 4).

[5] I. 51. 2.

[6] 'Cum angelus proprie moveatur motu . . . non in instanti, sed in tempore ipsum moveri necesse est' (I. 53. 3).

Secondly, all bodies are moved by angels [1]; Aquinas quotes Dionysius, 'Divina Sapientia conjungit fines primorum principiis secundorum,' *i.e.* the inferior nature at its highest point touches the superior nature; movement in space is the highest point of corporeal natures and therefore it is governed by superior natures.[2] So while angels are not themselves in terrestrial Time, they cause terrestrial Time by moving the heavenly bodies which regulate the course of Time.

Beyond the sphere of what can be understood lies the sphere of faith,[3] and here the angels rely on the knowledge revealed by the Beatific Vision, the knowledge of God's essence, 'seeing all things in God' [4] or 'knowing things in their first cause.' [5] Aquinas makes use of the Augustinian conception of 'morning and evening knowledge' [6]; 'morning knowledge' is of God, the beginning and source of all; 'evening knowledge' is of the 'things' in which the creative work ends as the day closes at sunset.[7]

In the supernatural Vision of God the angels see all things 'at once' [8]; they participate in the

[1] 'Corporalis creatura per angelos administratur' (I. 110. 1).

[2] I. 110. 3. 'Ils peuvent . . . jouer de la nature comme d'une guitare' (Maritain, p. 81).

[3] This clear distinction between the spheres of faith and understanding is, of course, one of the most important features of the Thomist system.

[4] I. 12. 10.

[5] I. 58. 6.

[6] *Vide supra*, p. 55 note 2.

[7] I. 58. 6.

[8] 'Secundum quod vident res in Deo, simul eas vident' (I. 12. 10). Aquinas quotes St. Augustine (*De Trinitate*, 15. 16), 'Non erunt volubiles nostrae cogitationes ab aliis in alia euntes atque redeuntes; sed omnem scientiam nostram simul uno conspectu videbimus' (I. 58. 2).

Divine eternity, but their natural knowledge is successive, though in a far higher sense than is true of our human knowledge.

Our knowledge is successive, because we learn new things; the angel has all his knowledge in his mind already, but he turns from one thought to another.[1] The unity of these separate acts of thought is determined by the 'species' or subject-matter; they can know 'simul' whatever can be brought under one species.[2]

Our reasoning is discursive; we labour slowly from point to point; the angel sees the truth intuitively in a moment; 'at the very first grasp of the principle they see all the consequent conclusions as already known.'[3]

On the question of the creation of the angels, which St. Augustine had left doubtful, St. Thomas inclines to the view that they were created with the rest of the universe. They cannot, of course, have been 'from eternity,' for God only is eternal[4];

[1] I. 58. I: 'Utrum intellectus angeli quandoque sit in potentia, quandoque in actu'; St. Thomas decides that in natural knowledge the angelic mind can be 'in potentia,' not in the sense of not yet knowing but of not now considering.

[2] I. 58. 2: '(Les idées sont distribuées) selon la capacité des esprits créés, sous certains grands points de vue, d'après l'unité du rapport des choses à telle ou telle fin' (Maritain, p. 96). '. . . connaissant la force et les actions du feu, de l'eau, de l'air, des astres, des cieux, et de tous les autres corps, aussi distinctement que nous connaissons les divers métiers de nos artisans' (*ibid.* p. 80).

[3] I. 58. 3. For this reason the angelic reasoning is rightly called 'intellectual' and ours 'rational'; they understand, we have to reason; Aquinas adds, 'Angeli syllogizare possunt, tanquam syllogismum cognoscentes; et in causis effectus vident et in effectibus causas; non tamen ita quod cognitionem veritatis ignotae acquirant.' The similarity of this to Descartes' description of *human* reasoning is striking.

[4] I. 61. 2.

he rejects the Greek view, expressed by St. Jerome, that they were created long before the universe.[1] He regards as ' conveniens ' the view that they were created in and with the empyrean heaven, because the angels, as rulers of all corporeal natures, would fittingly make their first appearance ' in the highest created corporeal nature.' [2] But we are running on to our third subject.

[1] ' Sunt quaedam pars universi. . . . Nulla autem pars perfecta est a suo toto separata ' (I. 61. 3). So Dante in *Paradiso*, xxix. 31–45 :

' Concreato fu ordine e costrutto
Alle sustanzie, e quelle furon cima
Nel mondo, in che puro atto fu produtto . . .
Jeronimo vi scrisse lungo tratto
Di secoli degli Angeli creati
Anzi che l'altro mondo fosse fatto ;
Ma questo vero è scritto in molti lati
Dagli scrittor dello Spirito Santo ;
E tu ten'avvedrai, se bene agguati ;
Ed anche la ragione il vede alquanto
Che non concederebbe che i motori
Senza sua perfezion fosser cotanto.'

' Co-created was order and co-woven with the substances and those were the summit in the universe wherein pure act (*i.e.* the angels) was produced. . . . Jerome wrote to you of a long stretch of ages wherein the angels were created ere aught else of the universe was made, but the truth I tell you is writ on many a page of the writers of the Holy Spirit, and thou shalt be aware of it if well thou look ; and also reason seeth it some little, which would not grant that the movers (*i.e.* the angels) should so long abide without their perfecting (*i.e.* their function of moving corporeal bodies).' Milton refers to St. Jerome's view in the Argument to the First Book of *Paradise Lost*, ' That Angels were long before this visible creation was the opinion of many ancient Fathers.'

[2] I. 61. 4. Aquinas quotes St. Augustine's view that the angels are meant by ' Heaven ' in Gen. i. I or ' Light ' in verse 3. ' Nominibus rerum corporalium significati, quia Moyses rudi populo loquebatur, qui nondum capere poterat incorpoream naturam. Et si eis fuisset expressum aliquas res esse super omnem naturam corpoream, fuisset eis occasio idololatriae ' (I. 61. 1).

(*c*) *Creation of the World*

On the question whether the world had a beginning St. Thomas is less precise than one would have expected. Reason cannot decide the matter [1]; the arguments for and against are equally balanced and therefore we have to fall back on faith,[2] which tells us explicitly through the Scriptures that the world has *not* existed from everlasting.[3]

The arguments that the world must be eternal are unconvincing [4]; it is true that the angels have the power of existing for ever, but they did not have it before the moment of their creation. It is true that Aristotle says that Heaven and earth are 'ingeniti [5]; the Christian agrees; they were not 'engendered but created'; St. Thomas rejects as absurd the idea of an empty space or vacuum before Creation or an empty time during which the Creator was 'doing nothing'; but when we speak of God existing before Creation, we no more

[1] I. 46. 2: 'Novitas mundi non potest demonstrationem recipere ex parte ipsius mundi. Demonstrationis enim principium est quod quid est (*i.e.* the definition of a thing). . . . Unde demonstrari non potest quod homo, aut caelum, aut lapis non semper fuit.'

[2] *Ibid.*: 'Mundum incepisse sola fide tenetur.' In a matter where God is not bound (as far as we can see) to act in one way rather than in another, we have to ascertain from revelation how He has acted.

[3] He quotes John xvii. 5: 'Claritate quam habui priusquam mundus fieret,' and Prov. viii. 22: 'Dominus possedit me (sapientiam) . . . antequam quidquam faceret a principio' (I. 46. I), and Gen. i. I: 'In principio creavit Deus caelum et terram.'

[4] I. 46. I.

[5] Aristotle was only attacking certain views of the 'generation' of the universe 'secundum quosdam modos in veritate impossibiles.' Nevertheless it is probable that the language of Aristotle, his favourite philosopher, made Aquinas more apt to hesitate as to the possibility of demonstration on the point.

mean to speak of a real time than we mean to speak of a real space when we say 'There is nothing above the sky.'

On the other hand, the arguments which seek to prove that the world must have had a beginning seem to him equally inconclusive.[1] It is true that God created all things 'ex nihilo,' but it does not follow that He created them 'post nihilum'; even if the world had no beginning, it would not be 'made equal' to God, for God's Eternity would always have the special quality of the Totum Simul; an indefinite regress would not ruin causality, for a cause is not less of a cause because it is 'accidentally' accompanied by an endless number of conditions.[2]

The matter therefore depends upon God's Will, and He has revealed that the world *had* a beginning. One reason for God's action is suggested. Though a cause need not precede its effect ('sicut in illuminatione'), still the nature of the cause is more evident to us if it does so; so the fact that God existed 'before' the world is a witness to His creative power.[3] However, reason or no reason, the matter is settled for faith by the opening words of Genesis.[4]

[1] I. 46. 2.

[2] 'Accidit huic homini inquantum generat, quod sit generatus ab alio. Generat enim inquantum homo, et non inquantum est filius alterius hominis' (*ibid.*).

[3] 'Manifestius enim mundus ducit in cognitionem divinae potentiae creantis, si mundus non semper fuit. . . . Omne enim quod non semper fuit, manifestum est habere causam' (I. 46. I).

[4] The words 'In principio' are meant to exclude three heresies: (i) that the world always existed; (ii) that the world was partly created by an evil power (here 'Principium' means Wisdom or the Logos); (iii) that God was assisted by the angels ('In principio' meaning 'ante omnia') (I. 46. 3).

At the primal act of creation, four entities were made. (*a*) Formless matter ; Aquinas (with St. Augustine) rejects the view that matter could ever have existed without any form ; matter precedes form only 'origine' ; it was at first rude matter not yet sculptured into fair shape.[1] (*b*) The angelic nature, of which we have already spoken. (*c*) The empyrean heaven, created as a habitation for the angels. St. Thomas thus explains it : 'A double glory is expected as our future reward—one spiritual and the other bodily, that is not only the glorification of the human body but the renovation of the entire world. Now a beginning was made of the spiritual glory by the creation of the bliss of the angels, in which the saints are promised an equal share.[2] Therefore it was fitting that a beginning should be made from the very first of the bodily glory in a certain corporeal nature that should be free from the bondage of corruption and change and wholly bright.'[3] The empyrean heaven is a kind of specimen, pledge or firstfruits of the

[1] I. 66. I. 'Informitas materiae non praecessit duratione ejus formationem aut distinctionem, sed natura ; praecessit autem informitas materiae ejus formationem, id est, pulchritudinem et ornatum.' That matter could not have been formless in the sense of 'without any distinction' Aquinas shows by shrewdly pointing out that Heaven is already spoken of as separate from the earth and the earth from the water ; again, the earth is under the waters and the darkness above them. What was still lacking was (i) the beauty of transparency : 'darkness was on the face of the deep'; (ii) the beauty of being seen, for the earth was covered by the waters : 'The earth was without form' ('inanis seu invisibilis') ; (iii) the beauty of flowers, grass and trees : the earth was void ('vacua seu incomposita').—*Ibid.*

[2] 'They are equal unto the angels . . . being the children of the Resurrection' (Luke xx. 36).

[3] I. 66. 3.

glorious condition of the corporeal world after the Resurrection. (*d*) Time ; still ' informe ' (for days and nights had not yet been created), and perhaps only measured as yet by the ' succession of thoughts and affections in the angelic mind.' [1]

(*d*) *Eternal Life*

The life of the blessed after death is like that of the angels ; both share in the Aevum and in the Vision of God's Eternity.[2] The chief difference, of course, is that after their resurrection the faithful enjoy their glorified bodies. St. Thomas' great strength here is that he does not separate the risen body from the renovated universe ; he does not make it move about like a semi-solid phantom in an otherwise spiritual world ; our bodies and the terrestrial world will be glorified together.[3] As to the nature of the risen body, Aquinas holds with much common sense—though one rather wonders what common sense has to do with such a matter—that ' since their bodies are still bodies,' and move from one place to another, they must do so in time and not instantaneously : ' It is not possible that the glorified body should be in two places at once, that is at the final goal and also in all the intermediate stages. . . . But it is probable that the time in which the glorified body moves is imper-

[1] 1. 66. 4.

[2] 2. 180. 8. ' Vita contemplativa . . . competit nobis secundum actionem incorruptibilis partis animae, . . . unde potest post hanc vitam durare.'

[3] ' Gloria . . . corporalis, non solum in corporibus humanis glorificandis, sed etiam in toto mundo innovando ' (1. 66. 3).

ceptible on account of its swiftness, and that one body can pass through the same space more quickly than another, because Time, however small we suppose it, is always infinitely divisible.' [1]

What that Time is, Aquinas is rather embarrassed to say; it cannot be the motion of the sky, for at the Last Day its movement has stopped; he can only say 'erit tempus (post resurrectionem) consurgens ex numero prioris et posterioris in quocumque motu.' [2]

Aquinas' reasons for believing that the motions of the heavens (and therefore Time as measured by them) will stop at the Last Day are interesting.[3] He does not accept the Greek view that rest is necessarily better than movement, and that therefore the heavenly bodies of the sky find their 'completion' in rest; he says it depends on circumstances; God enjoys perpetual rest, but so does the earth, 'the lowest of the elements.' The heavenly bodies at present minister best to man by moving; again, they move in circles and therefore have no natural place at which to stop as though completing their movement.[4] 'Non est magis

[1] 3 (Supp.), 84. 3. [2] *Ibid.* [3] *Ibid.*, 91. 2.

[4] This creates a difficulty; when, at the Last Day, the sun stops, where will it stop? All places are alike indifferent to it. St. Thomas says: 'Probabile est . . . quod caelum habeat nobilissimum situm, qui est possibilis in respectu ad nostram habitationem'—that is, it is more likely to be midday than midnight; to the objection that certain parts of the earth will be left in perpetual darkness, he answers: 'Omnia corpora elementorum habebunt in seipsis quamdam gloriae claritatem' (after the Resurrection); he rejects the view that the Heavens will stop at the position in which they were created (the Platonic year), because such a revolution takes 36,000 years, and therefore astronomers would be able to calculate the date of the Last Day.

naturalis solis accessio ad punctum orientis quam recessus ab eo.'

Therefore the movement of the heavens will stop, not naturally but by a special decree of God. At present they perform two functions; they sustain man's bodily life by causing the growth of plants and the diversity of the seasons; this will no longer be necessary after the Resurrection [1]; their second function—to show forth God's glory—they can perform as well when they are stationary. The souls that are lost are still in Time,[2] as is shown by the fact that their punishments change from cold to heat.[3] This punishment (according to his teaching) lasts for ever; to the objection that it is unjust to inflict an everlasting punishment for a temporal sin, he replies that the time-length of the sin has nothing to do with the sentence, which only considers the disposition of the sinner. 'Adultery, which is committed in a moment of time, is not punished by a momentary penalty.[4] Even in human society, perpetual banishment is pronounced against certain offenders; hell is an endless exile from Heaven for those who have broken the bond of charity which is the test and essence of its citizenship; they have despised an

[1] 'Oportet quod generatio hominum non in perpetuum duret (because there is a fixed number of elect), et eadem ratione nec alia quae ad generationem hominum ordinantur.'

[2] I. 10. 3: 'In inferno non est vera aeternitas, sed magis tempus.'

[3] He quotes Job xxiv. 19, 'Ad nimium calorem transibunt ab aquis nivium' (R.V. has 'Drought and heat consume the snow waters: so doth Sheol those which have sinned'); and Ps. lxxxi. 15. 'Erit tempus eorum in saecula' (which he incorrectly takes to refer to the 'haters of the Lord' in the first part of the verse).

[4] 3 (Supp.). 99. I.

eternal good, rejected an eternal life and offended the Eternal God. They cannot suffer the infinite torment they deserve as regard its *quality* ; human infirmity could not stand the pain ; therefore the infinity is transferred to the duration, which is endless.' [1]

Hooker

From the twelfth century to the fifteenth is an era of theologians ; from the sixteenth to the nineteenth is the era of philosophers. As our next sermon will concern the philosophers, let us take our farewell of the theologians by considering a passage from Hooker.

No contrast could well be greater than that between the Italian doctor and the English divine ; the one a builder of comprehensive systems, the other a master of caution and restraint ; the one seeking for no ornament but the lucidity of reasoning and the bare construction of an argument, as it swings backwards and forwards from a ' Videtur ' to a ' Respondendum ' ; the other possessed of the rich imagination and metrical eloquence of Elizabethan prose ; the one calm and collected, with no nearer opponent than an ancient philosopher or a distant Arabian ; the other plunged in contemporary controversy, in which he achieves the marvellous distinction of being always charitable without being ever dull.

The passage about Time is in the introduction

[1] The apparent callousness is seen to be the result of human laws ; the idea of an offence against the King or against society is simply transferred (with the necessary intensification) to a realm of endless consequences.

to a defence of Festivals against the Puritans.[1] 'Only God hath true immortality or eternity, . . . wherein there groweth no difference by addition of hereafter unto now, whereas the noblest and perfectest of all things besides have continually through continuance the time of former continuance lengthened, so that they could not heretofore be said to have continued so long as now, neither now so long as hereafter.' (This has not the clarity of the *Summa*, but it appears to deny the changeless Aevum of the angels.)

'God's own eternity is the hand which leadeth Angels in the course of their perpetuity; their perpetuity the hand that draweth out celestial motion, the line of which motion and the thread of time are spun together,' *i.e.* they cause Time by moving the stars. Following Plotinus, Hooker argues that, though Time is not an effect of Motion,[2] yet 'to define without motion how long or how short such continuance is were impossible.'

Finally, Hooker protests against the poetical and popular personification of Time—'Time doth but measure other things, and neither worketh in them any real effect nor is itself ever capable of any. And therefore, when commonly we use to say that Time doth eat or fret out all things, that Time is the wisest thing in the world because it bringeth forth all knowledge,[3] and that nothing is more foolish

[1] *Ecclesiastical Polity*, Bk. 5, c. 69.

[2] 'We may also consider in rest (as well as in the case of motion) both that which is past, and that which is present, and that which is future.'

[3] Hooker himself slips into the common use in the Preface, 8. 12. 'What will grow out of such errors . . . impossible it is that ever the wit of man should imagine, *till Time have brought forth the fruits of them*.'

than Time which never holdeth anything long, but whatsoever one day learneth the same another day forgetteth again, that some men see prosperous and happy days, and that some men's days are miserable, in all these and the like speeches, that which is uttered of the Time is not verified of Time itself, but agreeth unto those things which are in Time, and do by means of so near conjunction either lay their burden upon the back, or set their crown upon the head of Time. Yea the very opportunities which we ascribe to Time do in truth cleave to the things themselves wherewith Time is joined ; as for Time it neither causeth things nor opportunities of things, although it comprise and contain both.'

I am not sure how far that is solid criticism of popular usage ; it is true against such a crude view as that the mere ticking of a clock causes of itself growth and decay. But, if Time be taken in a wider sense as the order of successiveness, the very condition of life and death in all sublunary things, the two are so closely 'conjoined' that it seems a false antithesis to separate completely what happens in Time from Time itself.[1]

However that may be, we can find new passages more genially characteristic of English theology at its best than this one of Hooker's, in which a supposed poetical fancy is dismissed in language itself both poetical and shrewd.

[1] M. Bergson once defined Time as 'what prevents things from happening together' ; so, we might say, 'Space makes communication difficult,' meaning not merely mountains or oceans, but the fact of their spatial relation.

FOURTH LECTURE

TIME AND ETERNITY IN MODERN THOUGHT

The things which are seen are temporal; but the things which are not seen are eternal.—2 COR. iv. 18.

IN the last three lectures we have been building up (as it were) the traditional background or setting of the problem of Time and Eternity; in the present lecture we pass to the more critical treatment of the problem in Modern Philosophy.

The obvious division is into three parts: (*a*) the philosophers before Kant; (*b*) the influence of German philosophy; (*c*) modern reactions against German idealism.

(*a*) *The philosophers before Kant.*—The Cartesian school started from the principle that nothing deserved the name of truth which could not at once be seen as *necessarily* true [1]; hence came the 'new method' of clear and distinct ideas, sometimes called the geometrical method, because it aimed at imitating the spirit in which the propositions of Euclid were stated and proved [2];

[1] *Cp.* Descartes' first rule 'to comprise nothing more in my judgment than what was presented to my mind so clearly and distinctly as to exclude all ground of doubt' (*Second Discourse*—Everyman Ed., p. 15).

[2] In the case of Spinoza's *Ethics*, this is true of the form as well as the spirit; it is written just like a book of Euclid with definitions, propositions and corollaries.

the order of geometrical propositions, each related to the other and each following from the other, seemed to Descartes the ideal pattern of all reasoning ; such truths or propositions were eternal in the sense that they did not change, were never truer at one moment than another and were therefore timeless, that is, out of all relation to Time. In contrast to them, the Time series seemed singularly lacking in coherence and clearness ; one proposition in geometry inevitably follows another, but there is no reason why half-past four should follow four o'clock ; that Time goes on at all seemed due to a special though constant intervention of God, a completely arbitrary, though predictable, miracle of the Divine Will.[1] One moment of Time, therefore, has no necessary connection with another ; it is God Who adds the next instant ; from such a point of view the course of Time (as Bergson says) is 'continué,' not 'continue' (continued, not continuous).

[1] From this follows Descartes' doctrine that Creation is Conservation : 'Tout le temps de ma vie peut être divisé en une infinité de parties, chacune desquelles ne dépend en aucune façon des autres ; et ainsi, de ce qu'un peu auparavant j'ai été, il ne s'ensuit pas que je doive maintenant être, si ce n'est qu'en ce moment quelque cause me produise et me crée pour ainsi dire derechef (anew), c'est-à-dire me conserve. En effet, c'est une chose bien claire et évidente à tous ceux qui considéreront avec attention la nature du temps, qu'une substance, pour être conservée dans tous les moments qu'elle dure, a besoin du même pouvoir et de la même action qui serait nécessaire pour la produire et la créer tout de nouveau, si elle n'était point encore' (*Méditation* iii, p. 93, *Œuvres de Descartes*) ; cp. *Principles of Philosophy* (Everyman, p. 173) : 'The nature of Time . . . is of such a kind that its parts are not mutually dependent, and never co-existent ; and, accordingly, from the fact that we now are, it does not necessarily follow that we shall be a moment afterwards, unless some cause, viz., that which first produced us, shall, as it were, continually reproduce us, that is, conserve us.'

Spinoza with his passion for a logically tidy universe would clearly not be content with a system which distinguished God's arbitrary Will from His Reason, and so recognised logical orders on the one side and on the other illogical orders like the Time series ; for Spinoza, God's Will and Understanding are one ; all that He does (and there is nothing He does not do) is the result of an inflexible necessity.

Like Descartes, while he accepts eternity as the attribute of God, he defines, as Durée, the real persistence or endurance of created things and, as Time, our own subjective measurement of motion. It is not easy to arrive at the meaning of Durée ; sometimes it is spoken of as persistence through Time ; in this sense, it is denied of God. 'To attribute it to God is to distinguish His essence from His existence' ; Durée cannot touch essence ; no one will ever say that the essence of the circle or the triangle, as far as it is an eternal truth, has lasted longer now than in the time of Adam. The existence which God would have in the future, belongs to Him now actually in the present, or (to speak more correctly) an actually infinite existence belongs to God in the same way as an actually infinite understanding.'[1] On this view Durée is simply objective Time, and Spinoza will not apply the word to the eternity of God or to the immortality of the soul,[2] because he is afraid

[1] *Pensées Métaphysiques,* Pt. 2, c. 1 ; existence means historical place in the order of time ; essence means the nature of timeless, necessary truths.

[2] *Ethics,* Bk. 5, prop. 23, *n.* : 'The existence (of the mind) cannot be defined by Time or explained by duration.'

that it will be interpreted in the popular sense of going on 'for ever.'[1]

But there are other passages in which Durée seems to be sharply distinguished from Time, notably *Ethics*, 5. 20, where immortality is defined as the 'duration of the mind without relation to the body.' Professor Joachim[2] says: 'Time is, for Spinoza, the result of a limitation of duration: the conception of Time is an imaginative aid to enable us to picture persistence or permanent existence. Time cuts "duration" into lengths, thus destroying its continuity and giving it a beginning, an end, and stages. When this is the case, "duration" is the general term, of which eternal existence and temporal existence are forms,' one apprehending it intelligently, the other imaginatively.[3] On the other hand, some interpreters[4] regard Durée as different

[1] Descartes distinguishes Durée, which is objective and a real attribute of things, from Time, which is a subjective mode of thinking; duration applies to things whether at rest or in movement, but Time is only the measure of movement (taking as our standard 'the greatest and most regular motions that give rise to years and days'); (*Principles*, i. 57); *cp.* Spinoza's (Cartesian) *Pensées Métaphysiques*, Pt. 1, c. 4: 'La durée est l'attribut sous lequel nous concevons l'existence des choses créées en tant qu'elles persevèrent dans leur existence actuelle. . . . Pour déterminer la durée maintenant nous la comparons à la durée des choses qui ont un mouvement invariable et déterminé et cette comparaison s'appelle le temps. Ainsi le temps n'est pas une affection des choses mais seulement un simple mode de pensée . . . un être de Raison.'

[2] *Study of the Ethics of Spinoza*, 295.

[3] Imagination (for Spinoza) is the power of seeing absent things as though they were present; this is possible because of the traces (vestigia) which things leave on the brain; by piecing these together we get the idea of temporal succession, but this only tells us about the order of our sensations and not about the reality of external things.

[4] *Cp.* Hallett, *Aeternitas* (quoted by Inge, *God and the Astronomers*, c. 3).

from Time and Eternity, as an existence, changeless but admitting Before and After, specially used of the human soul after death and, in fact, very much like Aquinas' Aevum of the Angels ; one sees why Bergson chose such a vague word as Durée for his new conception of Time.

In any case Timc itself is merely our subjective attitude and has no effect on things ; Professor Alexander complains : ' It seems to Spinoza that matter is motion because extension expresses God's essence. . . . Substance . . . is not lifeless, but alive, but . . . Life implies change and change implies Time. Yet Time is excluded from the eternal nature of God, Who comprehends Time indeed, but only, to use a paradoxical phrase, in its timelessness. . . . Nothing seems so obvious to us as the proposition that motion takes Time and is unintelligible without it. But Descartes certainly, and it would seem Spinoza as well, conceives motion as change of place.' [1]

On the whole, Spinoza must be set down among the greatest enemies of Time and change ; he longs for ' the eternal order and the fixed laws of nature ' [2] ; this may be partly the love of a scientific mind for law and order, but it certainly expresses itself in the words of a mystic, desiring the Supreme Good that cannot be taken away. ' Amor erga rem aeternam et infinitam sola laetitia pascit animum, ipsaque omnis tristitiae est expers ; quod valde est desiderandum totisque viribus

[1] *Spinoza and Time*, pp. 33, 34.

[2] ' Secundum aeternum ordinem et secundum certas naturae leges ' (*Tractatus*, 12).

quaerendum '[1]; the wise man sees all things 'sub specie aeternitatis '[2]; this does not merely mean that he has arrived at correct scientific method, but that he is happy and blessed, because he lives in a world where chance and accident are impossible; 'he is scarcely moved in spirit (by external causes); he is conscious of himself and of God and of things by a certain eternal necessity; he always enjoys satisfaction of mind.'[3]

While the Cartesian school were always condemning Time by the application of some transcendental standard of their own, the British empirical school failed to 'take Time seriously,' because they pushed their analysis too far; they were continually embarrassed by their favourite doctrine—Particularism, as it has been called, the view that experience can be analysed into separate parts, each of which is a distinct object of perception; this makes them unable to grasp any idea of continuity and Time becomes a mere succession of perishing instants.[4] Hume argues that Time is made up of solid indivisible moments, just as space consists of indivisible points. A Time composed of such atomic instants cannot really be continuous, for Time cannot be passing *through*

[1] *Tractatus*, 10. 'Love towards an eternal and infinite object alone feeds the mind with joy, and itself is utterly free from all sadness; such a state is to be greatly desired and sought after with all our strength.'

[2] *Ethics*, 5. 29; difficult to translate; 'under their aspect of timelessness' is fairly near.

[3] *Ethics*, 5. 42 *n.*

[4] Locke, *Essay*, II, c. 15, § 12: 'Duration . . . is the idea we have of perishing distance, of which no two parts exist together, but follow each other in succession.' He finds it difficult to reconcile this with an identical Self (Green, *Works*, I. 115).

them ; Hume bases his view entirely on *our* experience ; our minds 'can never attain a full and adequate conception of infinity ; . . . the *idea*, which we form of any finite quality, is not infinitely divisible '[1] ; he assumes that we have impressions of different moments given in perception. 'Five notes played on a flute give us the impression and idea of Time ; though Time be not a sixth impression. . . . The mind only takes notice of the *manner*, in which the different sounds make their appearance.'[2]

On the question of eternity, the British thinkers, partly influenced by the Reformation, are contemptuous of the scholastics ; Hobbes pours scorn on the 'Nunc stans' of Boethius (the stationary moment) ; Locke seems to regard the idea of infinity and eternity as mere repetitions of finite ideas. 'The complex idea we have of God is made up of the simple ideas we receive from reflection. . . . If I find that I know some few things . . . I can frame an idea of knowing twice as many ; . . . the same may also be done of the duration of existence without beginning or end, and so I frame the idea of an eternal Being.'[3]

If eternity only means the never-ending succession of perishing moments, it can hardly be predicated of the Divine Life, and Locke himself recognises at times that we must regard the Divine Mind as surpassing the human mind in quality

[1] *Treatise*, I. 35 (Everyman Edition). As usual, he weakens his case by his Subjectivism. 'If we carry our enquiry beyond the appearances of objects to the senses, I am afraid that most of our conclusions will be full of scepticism and uncertainty' (*ibid.*, I. 68).

[2] *Ibid.*, p. 43.

[3] *Essay*, II, c. 23, §§ 33–5.

and not as a larger-sized copy of our successive experiences ; 'What is once past, he (man) can never recall ; and what is yet to come, he cannot make present. . . . God's infinite duration being accompanied with infinite knowledge and infinite power, He sees all things past and to come.' [1]

Leibniz, whose philosophy is best regarded as a first attempt to reconcile empiricism and rationalism, regarded Time and space as imperfect representations of logical relations. Things which appeared to follow one another were really related as ground and consequence ; just as the propositions on two different pages of Euclid are perceived by the reader one *after* the other, but their real relation is logical, not temporal. The human spirit, not being very high in the scale of monads, still represents truth to itself under these pictures of Before and After ; if we could ' clear up ' our ideas, we should see that all truth comes from within ourselves and not from an apparently external world of space and Time.

We may perhaps here add a word on Swedenborg's *Heaven and Hell*, not as representing any particular school of thought, but as interesting in itself.

He says 'Although all things take place in regular order in Heaven, just as in this world, the angels do not know what Time is, because in Heaven there are not years and days but changes of state.[2] . . . Thus the natural ideas of Man

[1] *Essay*, II, c. 15, § 12.

[2] These are real changes. Sometimes angels are in a state of intense love (morning) or of intense wisdom (noon) ; when

are turned into spiritual ideas with the angels. . . . Spring and morning are converted into the idea of a state of love and wisdom, such as angels enjoy in their first state ; summer and noon into an idea of love and wisdom such as they enjoy in their second state ; autumn and evening such love and wisdom as they enjoy in their third state, and night and winter into an idea of such a state as exists in hell . . . by Eternity angels perceive infinite state, not infinite time. . . . It is known (by some men on earth) that Time originates from state, for they know that Time passes according to the states of their feelings. It passes quickly with those who are in an agreeable and joyous state of mind, slowly with those who are in a disagreeable and sorrowful state of mind, and in various ways with those who are in states of hope and expectation.'[1]

Kant somewhat contemptuously described Swedenborg's work as 'Dreams of a Ghost Seer' ; on this particular matter of Time and Eternity we may perhaps judge that the dreams came through the veracious gate of horn.

their wisdom is less intense, it is evening ; night only belongs to Hell ; the reasons for these changes are (*a*) that delight in the heavenly life would gradually lose its value, if they were always in full enjoyment ; (*b*) their less intense states are due not to God but to their love of Self, which leads them astray ; this makes them sad, but their sense of what is good is rendered more exquisite by such alternations of delight and sadness (Everyman Ed., pp. 69–71). The two reasons seem hardly consistent, for the desire of change is first treated as a condition of enjoyment and then as a selfish failing ; it is hard to say whether we should call such a life one of growth or progress. It does not seem to be a perfect life ; they are being perfected (p. 70). It should perhaps be remembered that (according to Swedenborg) angels and devils have been men : All both in Heaven and Hell are from the human race (p. 146).

[1] *Heaven and Hell*, pp. 72–4.

(*b*) *Influence of the German school.*—We may say (if the metaphor be not rather a mixed one) that Kant began the process of 'taking Time seriously' by putting it on its own feet. Hume had tried to treat it as perceived by the senses; Kant shows that this is impossible; a succession of moments in consciousness, in which one perishes before the next is born, can never be the consciousness of succession as an order.[1]

On the other hand, the Cartesians had attacked Time because it could not be 'thought' as a rational order; Kant admits that there is nothing logical about the qualities of Time[2]; the temporal order, therefore, belongs neither to the realm of thought nor to that of perception. It is 'intuited' as an order necessary for our interpretation of experience—separate from what we perceive, and yet of no use or meaning except as applied to what we perceive.

Time is of the utmost importance to Kant for his explanation of experience; the fact that we do perceive change in Time is the foundation of experience and of the categories which make our experience possible.[3]

But the 'forms' of Time and Space (Kant

[1] 'Neither co-existence nor succession would be perceived by us, if the representation of time did not exist as a foundation *a priori*' (*Critique of Pure Reason—Transcendental Aesthetic,* sect. 2. 1).

[2] 'The proposition that different times cannot be co-existent could not be derived from a general conception (of Time)' (*ibid.*, 2. 4).

[3] 'Consciousness of time is a fact whose actuality . . . cannot . . . be challenged. . . . Among the conditions indispensably necessary to all consciousness of Time . . . (is) recognition . . . (which) is conditioned by self-consciousness . . . (which) pre-supposes consciousness of objects' (Kemp-Smith, *Commentary on the Critique*, pp. 241–4).

always treats them together) are only valid within the world of experience ; treat them as absolute things and they come to pieces in your hands ; they perish, riddled with the contradictions which Kant calls the Antinomies. Ask 'Is the World, as a Whole, in Time ?' and you get no answer ; if it had a beginning, then 'there must have been a time in which the world did not exist,' and in such a void time, there can be no beginning ; if the world had no beginning, then 'an infinite series has already elapsed,' which is impossible, for an infinite series can never be completed.[1]

This shows that we have passed beyond the sphere within which the understanding can function ; the cause of this impotence is that all experience through the senses comes in fragments—parts of space and moments of time ; as we never have or could have a sensation of the world as a whole, we try to get as near as we can to it by putting together our piecemeal perceptions into an infinitely prolonged series ; as they are bits to start with, we can never imagine them ending and we can never get far enough to know whether they end or not.[2]

Now since all that is subject to Time and succession is (in Kant's view) rigidly determined, God, Free-

[1] *Antinomy of Pure Reason* (Meiklejohn), p. 260.

[2] So in his solution of the First Antinomy (*ibid.*, p. 325), Kant rejects the view that Time is either finite or infinite ; all we can say is 'We can find no end'—what he calls a Regress in indefinitum ; 'because neither the world nor the cosmical series of conditions to a given conditioned can be completely given, our conception of the cosmical quantity is given only in and through the Regress and is not prior to it.'

dom and Immortality have to be relegated to a world beyond experience, not known by the understanding but implied by the existence of morality ; these ultimate things are placed beyond experience and beyond time, for the same reason, that they may be free ; their timelessness is a moral quality involved in their freedom and recognised by the good will. 'Only on moral grounds . . . can it be proved that the self is an abiding personality, and that as conscious, personal form it belongs to the order of noumenal reality'[1] ; of God, Kant himself says, 'There is a Being in me, distinguished from myself as the cause of an effect wrought upon me, which freely—that is without being dependent on laws of nature in space and time—judges me within.'[2] This Kantian opposition of Time to Freedom is worth keeping in mind.

When we pass from Kant to Hegel, we come (almost for the first time) to a new conception, which henceforth dominates speculation on our problem—namely, the Philosophy of History. Hitherto Modern Philosophy had been mostly associated with science and mathematics ; Kant himself was inclined to contrast History, as the study of what *is*, with Ethics, the study of the unattainable ideal, that *ought* to be ; for Hegel the Ideal was in the real ; he had no patience with the tendency to place perfection in some distant world ; for him 'The Real is the rational' ; here and now

[1] Kemp-Smith, *Commentary*, p. lii.
[2] *Opus postumum*, p. 824 (quoted Webb, *Kant's Philosophy of Religion*, p. 198).

is the work of God, 'Who is not a Spirit behind the stars but a Spirit of spirits.' [1]

It was not, of course, for Christianity a new idea that God was revealed in history, but hitherto what had been meant was, generally, the intervention of God from without, as He interposed at arbitrary intervals to reward or punish. What was new in the Romantic movement of the nineteenth century was that God was to be found within the natural evolution of things, in growth and movement as well as in catastrophe and earthquake. Wordsworth expressed it in the famous lines—

> Not in Utopia,—subterranean fields,—
> Or some secreted island, Heaven knows where!
> But in the very world, which is the world
> Of all of us,—the place where, in the end,
> We find our happiness, or not at all! [2]

Carlyle in an equally well-known passage in *Sartor Resartus* (penetrated with German thought) says:

'O thou that pinest in the imprisonment of the Actual, and criest bitterly to the gods for a kingdom wherein to rule and create, know this of a truth: the thing thou seekest is already with thee, "here or nowhere," couldst thou only see!' [3]

[1] 'Il est le grand ennemi de mécontents de la vie, des âmes sensibles, des perpetuels déclamateurs et agitateurs au nom de la raison et de la vertu. . . . Il haït le Sollen, le devoir être . . . qui doit toujours être et qui n'est pas et qui ne trouve jamais de réalité à lui adéquate, alors qu'au contraire, toute réalité est adéquate à l'idéal' (Croce, *Ce qui est vivant*, pp. 50–1).

[2] *Prelude*, Bk. XI, 140–44; it is not always remembered that the words describe the poet's (hardly justified) expectations as to the power of the French Revolution to recreate human nature.

[3] P. 202 (Temple Classics).

This new idea of normal historical development as a revelation of God had important reactions on the problem of Time and eternity. The historian is accustomed to see change and development everywhere ; he is always on the lookout, in his studies, for the first signs of something new, or the last signs of something old ; the idea of a static period is as repulsive to him as that of a people too happy to have a history. To the old-fashioned mind, Time was imperfect, because it destroyed, and was almost the equivalent of death [1] ; to the more modern taste 'our works and our affections . . . are beautiful only because they are in motion and fugitive' [2] ; to the scientific mind, change seemed almost the same as progress, the very sign of what was alive ; to the aesthetic mind, change gave to the things that grow a new richness and variety,[3] and to the things that pass away a new graciousness and tenderness.[4]

But we are allowing ourselves to be swept along too far. For Hegel himself the very heart of Reality is Becoming ; the poor abstraction 'Being in general' has to unite itself by contrast with the negative pole,[5] 'Not Being,' before there springs,

[1] *Cp.* Milton, 'Triumphing over Death and Chance and thee, O Time.'

[2] Croce, *Logic,* 498 (*vide infra,* p. 124).

[3] *Cp.* Browning's

> 'Grow old along with me ;
> The best is yet to be.'

[4] *Cp.* Corey's

> 'But oh the very reason why
> I clasp them is because they die.'
>
> (Mimnermus).

[5] Hegel regarded electricity as a providentially provided illustration of the Dialectical Method.

from the contact of two abstractions, the concrete Becoming.

In more theological language, the Kingdom of the Father, God by Himself, becomes the Kingdom of the Son, God 'going out of Himself' in creation and history (dying to live) so that He may return to Himself in the Kingdom of the Spirit, His life having become more rich and real through the sacrifice.

This process cannot itself take place in Time; God is perpetually and eternally all three Persons at once; He is for ever overcoming the opposition of the evil and the false, and reconciling them in the synthesis which overcomes by inclusion. 'This determination of itself is not a process of becoming or a transition. Rather the Idea freely lets itself go, absolutely sure of itself, and at rest within itself.' The pure Idea resolves 'to determine itself as external Idea.' [1]

Yet there are tendencies in Hegel to treat the course of human history as in some sense part of the experience of the Absolute by which it comes to self-consciousness; he says 'The Life and knowledge of God may doubtless be expressed as Love's playing with itself; but this idea sinks to triviality, if the seriousness, the pain, the patience, the labour of the Negative are absent therefrom. In Itself that life may well be the untroubled equality and union with Itself, Which has no serious concern with being other and overcoming such otherness. But such "In Itself" is but the abstract

[1] *Logik*, v. 352–3 (quoted by von Hügel, *Eternal Life*, p. 210).

generality, in which we have ignored that Life's nature—of being for Itself. . . . All existent Reality is movement and developed becoming ; precisely this unrest constitutes the Self.' [1]

Is History, then, part of the experience of God? In the *History of Philosophy* Hegel says, 'The World Spirit has no need to hurry ; "it has time enough," precisely because it is out of time ' [2] ; on the one hand he says, 'Comprehended History forms both the memorial and the Calvary of the Absolute Spirit,—that without which It would be lifeless solitude ' [3] ; on the other hand, Philosophy is only 'the recognition, within the appearances of the temporal and transitory, of the Substance and the Eternal, there immanent and present,' [4] and again, combining both ideas, 'This Spirit consists in its becoming what it is from the first in Itself.' [5]

Dr. Inge perhaps sums up justly when he says, 'Hegel certainly did not mean that the logical development of his dialectic corresponded accurately with any concrete historical process. Whether he was careful to preclude this interpretation of his meaning is not so certain.' [6] Full of this new inter-

[1] *Phaenomenologie*, pp. 14, 15 (von Hügel, *l.c.*, p. 213).
[2] *Ibid.*, p. 214.
[3] *Ibid.*, p. 216.
[4] *Ibid.*, p. 215.
[5] *Ibid.*, p. 216.
[6] *God and the Astronomers*, p. 96. Hegel himself says, 'One might believe that Philosophy in the degrees of the Idea should have a different order from that of the concepts produced in time, but on the whole the order is the same ' (Croce, *Ce qui est vivant*, p. 116). It is true that Hegel does tend to identify History with the development of ideas, and thus becomes both determinist and pedantic ; he dismisses ' non-important facts ' to the sphere of Waverley novels : Croce maliciously quotes the example of the Italian Hegelian who ' arrived at the point of maintaining that documents are necessary to decide in what prisons Tommaso Campanella was shut up or

pretation of History and enthusiasm for History, Hegel is ready to make the attempt to place Time and eternity in a real relation ; hitherto, too often Time had been looked upon as a meaningless caricature of the eternal, or else eternity itself had been dismissed as an absurdity. Now it is seen that in some sense the eternal is revealed under the form of Time. But the difficulty remains ; is temporal change merely the gradual unveiling of God's real nature ?[1] Or is it in some sense a change in God's consciousness of Himself ? If the first, then God's eternity seems to have no actual contact with human suffering and struggle and Calvary only reveals the mockery of an absent God ; if the second is true, that God Himself grows and learns and enriches His experience through the historical process, this seems to contradict all the traditional Christian definitions of His perfection.

The uncertainties of Hegel's language led to the schism between the Hegelian Right and the Hegelian Left. The Left laid stress on the immanentist side of his teaching—the Spirit in History—and pushed the doctrine to Positivism and Materialism ; the categories were the laws of Nature or the economic laws of History. The Right stressed the transcendental side—God as the

how many days and hours he suffered torture, but not to determine the historical significance of his thought and action ; that could be deduced *a priori* from the ideas of the Renaissance, the Catholic Church, the Reformation and the Council of Trent' (*ibid.*, p. 119).

[1] This seems Carlyle's view ; 'Nature, which is the Time-vesture of God, and reveals Him to the wise, hides Him from the foolish' (*Sartor*, p. 271). The wise seem to be those who see He is the same, the foolish those who think He changes.

Creator of the world with His own Life apart from and above human history.

In England we had mostly representatives of the Hegelian Right; some of them were Christians, like the Cairds, T. H. Green and Nettleship; others were (in varying degrees) unsympathetic towards Christianity, like Dr. McTaggart[1] and (if we can call them Hegelians) Bosanquet and Bradley.

T. H. Green constantly reminds us of the fact that change demands not only Time but also 'its opposite . . . a law or subject equally operative in all states . . . there is no such thing as mere time.'[2] So, consciousness of Time demands a timeless 'spiritual principle' in knowledge; 'neither can any process of change yield a consciousness of itself, which, in order to be a consciousness of the change, must be equally present to all stages of the change.'[3] This eternal principle must have been present in the world before we existed; it gradually emerges in our consciousness and makes us its vehicles[4]; it must be admitted, however, that he is a little too prone to use language which seems to identify the eternal God with our timeless selves.[5]

Bosanquet regards History as the perpetual renewal of the old in new forms, 'an eternal

[1] Though he professed Atheism, his denial of the reality of Time and his acceptance of the immortality of the soul made him a Hegelian of the Right.

[2] *Lecture on Kant* (Philosophical Works, II. p. 73).

[3] *Prolegomena to Ethics* (4th ed.), p. 25.

[4] *Ibid.*, p. 72.

[5] *Lecture on Kant* (*ibid.*, p. 74): 'What is Nature for an eternal thinking subject? Just what it is for our Reason, which is this eternal thinking subject.'

novelty' ; Bradley looks on Time as an appearance, and a very low one at that. It is riddled with the same contradictions as change ; it pretends that something is and is not at the same time ; the Absolute, the only true reality, 'knows no summer or winter' ; it is the supreme Truth, because it alone contains no self-contradiction and is always fully and wholly itself.[1]

(*c*) *Modern Reactions.*—It is against this denial of change and History that the revolt of the second part of the century begins ; it is represented in Germany by Nietzsche's pronouncement:

'Evil I declare it, and hostile to mankind—this doctrine of the One, the Perfect, the Unmoved, the Sufficient, the Intransitory.

'The Intransitory! it is but a simile—and the poets lie exceedingly.

'But the best similes shall speak of Time and Becoming ; they shall be for praise and justification of all transitoriness.'[2]

In less dithyrambic terms the Oxford writers of *Contentio Veritatis* protested against the Hegelian 'condemnation of all finite values.'

In religious thought, we see the same tendency acting in various ways ; the exaltation of change as in itself good led some people to introduce evolution into the life of God[3] ; it also encouraged the idea of a finite God, in the struggle side by side with us, uncertain of victory over evil, unless we help Him ; this theory is suggested by the

[1] See Supplementary Note on the Neo-Hegelians.
[2] *Thus spake Zarathustra* (Everyman Ed., p. 77).
[3] Compare, for instance, Professor Alexander's emerging Deity.

words of William James: 'I confess that I do not see why the very existence of an invisible world may not, in part, depend on the personal response which any one of us may make to the religious appeal; God Himself, in short, may draw vital strength and increase of very being from our fidelity.'[1] So Mr. Wells speaks of 'this Finite God, Who is the King of man's adventure in space and time. . . . Who fights through men against Blind Forces and Night and Non-existence.'[2]

In more strictly theological spheres of thought, we see a new treatment of Our Lord's Incarnate Life as real human history with a real growth of His mind as well as of His body; He appears (sometimes startlingly) as a Jew of the first century[3]; some thinkers even ascribe to Him real temptations in the sense that He was 'free' to listen to the promptings of the devil.[4]

We can trace the same tendency in the new conception of Church History, profoundly affecting old Apologetic, as in Newman's theory of Development or in the Modernist impatience with 'outworn' formulae; we can see it in the discontent with representations of Heaven as a place where 'we do nothing,' and in the demand for activity, learning, growth as part of our idea of eternal bliss; this view is especially credited to Browning in

[1] From *The Will to Believe*; the extract was selected by Henry James for *The Spirit of Man* (No. 425).

[2] *Mr. Britling*, pp. 429, 432.

[3] Contrast with the conventional figure of a Universal Redeemer the almost roughly Jewish and apocalyptic figure of Schweitzer's Christ.

[4] See Appendix II, p. 274.

virtue of two famous utterances,—his description of old age in *Rabbi Ben Ezra* :

> And I shall thereupon
> Take rest, ere I be gone
> Once more on my adventure brave and new :
> Fearless and unperplexed,
> *When I wage battle next*,
> What weapons to select, what armour to indue ;

and the last words he wrote :

> 'Strive and thrive!' cry 'Speed,—fight on, fare ever
> There as here!'[1]

[1] Epilogue to *Asolando* ; but in the *Prospice* he says of Death : 'One fight more, the best and *the last*!'

The fact is we have become so used to the caricature of Browning which represents him as a blustering optimist, always challenging every doubt and denial, that we forget the tender mysticism which is quite as true a side to his character ; so, in Browning, there are less strenuous pictures of the life to come, as in *The Last Ride Together* :

> 'The instant made eternity,—
> And heaven just prove that I and she
> Ride, ride together, for ever ride.'

In *Old Pictures in Florence* (stanzas 21, 22) he almost seems to withdraw his preference for a 'hectic heaven' :

> 'There's a fancy some lean to and others hate—
> That, when this life is ended, begins
> New work for the soul in another state,
> Where it strives and gets weary, loses and wins :
> Where the strong and the weak, this world's congeries,
> Repeat in large what they practised in small,
> Through life after life in unlimited series ;
> Only the scale's to be changed, that's all.
>
> 'Yet I hardly know. When a soul has seen
> By the means of Evil that Good is best,
> And, through earth and its noise, what is heaven's serene,—
> When our faith in the same has stood the test—
> Why, the child grown man, you burn the rod,
> The uses of labour are surely done ;
> There remaineth a rest for the people of God :
> And I have had troubles enough, for one.'

Bergson

If we turn back to the more technical philosophies, we find this tendency to regard change as a good thing in itself (which Dr. Bosanquet nicknamed 'Progressism') most fully and vividly represented by the teaching of M. Bergson.

We recall that, for Kant, Time and freedom were opposed to each other; for Bergson, Time *is* freedom; how is this transformation achieved?

Kant pictured Time as a chain in which the second link depends entirely upon the nature of the first. Bergson by a *vrai coup de théâtre* turns all this upside down; the whole picture of the chain with its separate links is utterly unsuitable for a living process, like the passage of Time; it is, in fact, a picture suggested by our intelligence ('le fabricant'), which, interested only in how things may be used, loves to treat them as dead and motionless in order to dissect and measure them. But real Time has no links; it does not move jerkily from one moment to another; Life, Movement, Time, as we experience them and feel them, are continuous, or they are nothing.

To picture the passage of Time as a straight line made up of points is much the same as trying to measure the 'flight of thought,' or to ask how much an act of self-sacrifice weighs; Time, as a feeling, is pure quality.[1]

[1] 'Si je veux me préparer un verre d'eau sucrée, je dois attendre que le sucre fonde. . . . Le temps que j'ai à attendre . . . coïncide avec mon impatience . . . c'est de l'absolu' (*i.e.* the feeling) (*Evolution Créatrice*, p. 10).

In a chain the links are side by side in space ; but in true Time (Durée, as Bergson calls it) there are no separate parts, any more than a feeling of affection can be cut up into smaller pieces ; it is all one, in the experience itself, the past not disappearing but flowing into the future.[1]

If we must have an image, let us leave on one side the sense of sight and choose the sense of hearing, in which space plays a much smaller part ; a melody is the nearest approach we can make to a representation of pure Durée. 'A melody to which we listen with the eyes closed, fixing our minds wholly upon it, very nearly coincides with that Time which is the actual flowing of our inner life, but it has still . . . too much definiteness ; first, we must remove the difference between the sounds ; then we must abolish the distinctive marks of sound itself and only retain the continuation of what precedes into what follows—the uninterrupted transition which is multiplicity without divisibility and succession without separation.' [2]

In Bergson's famous phrases, 'There are no things that move, there is only movement' ; 'there are no things that change, there is only change.'

[1] 'La durée est le progrès continu du passé qui ronge l'avenir et qui gonfle en avançant. . . . Le passé se conserve de lui-même' (*Evolution Cr.*, p. 5).

[2] Bergson is very fond of such musical illustrations as the above, which comes in *Durée et Simultanéité*, p. 55 ; *cp.* the brilliant metaphor in *Evolution Cr.*, p. 3 : 'Il est vrai que notre vie psychologique est pleine d'imprévu. . . . Mais . . . ce sont les coups de timbale qui éclatent de loin en loin dans la symphonie.' We shall see later that musical experience plays an important part in discussions about Time and Eternity.

Once we have rid our minds of the idea of parts of Time, stages of movement, links of the chain, notes of the tune, then the conception of Life or Time as mechanically determined is seen to be a pictorial illusion ; there are no parts that cause one another ; there are no links that follow one another ; a melody is not determined in the sense that the first notes cause those that follow ; all the notes are held together by the uninterrupted succession which in this case is the tune. As Durée is continuous movement, at the very moment a thing is, it is becoming different ; there is no static piece of the past called A, which like a dignified old gentleman determines the course of B, the younger present ; present and past are unreal distinctions ; at every moment something old is changing into something new ; life is a perpetual re-creation ; 'chacun de nos moments est une espèce de création. . . . Nous nous créons continuellement nous-mêmes.' [1]

This independence of the past, by which pure Durée is rescued from Determinism and Mechanism, has been the most popular part of the Bergsonian philosophy.[2] But this is only half

[1] *Evolution Cr.*, p. 7.

[2] For completeness' sake, we should add a few words on his theory of Clock Time ; he fully admits that the Durée, which is like the uninterrupted transmission of a melody, is of no use for practical purposes ; we need a time for social life, in which moments can be measured and compared. For this purpose we use spatial measurement as symbols of real Durée ; 'Si je promène mon doigt sur une feuille de papier sans la regarder, le mouvement que j'accomplis, perçu dedans, est une continuité de mon propre flux . . . si maintenant j'ouvre les yeux, je vois que mon doigt trace sur la feuille de papier une ligne qui se conserve . . . elle est mesurable' (*Durée et Simultanéité*, p. 64).

But the line is not the same as the movement ; 'in the case of

the freedom for which Bergson fights ; he wishes to make Durée also independent of the future, that is of rational direction or intelligent purpose ; this part of his system, directed against Finalism and Teleology, is perhaps less attractive, but it concerns the theologian more nearly. We shall have to deal with it in the more constructive part of these lectures ; we can only spare a few words for it now.

At first sight it is hard to understand why Bergson's Vitalism, which calls itself creative, should be so hostile to purpose. This is because Life for him is an absolute value, while the intelligence which plots and purposes is only a subordinate division of life ; even in the animal world, instinct works miracles of swiftness and efficiency, of which intelligence would be incapable. As Baron von Hügel puts it, ' In Bergson's predominant view we struggle, suffer, live, and

a falling star, we distinguish very clearly between the line of fire that we can divide at will, and the indivisible movement it implies ' (*ibid.*, p. 63) ; the difference between felt time and the time of science is well illustrated on p. 76 : ' If, on a sudden, all the movements of the universe were to increase in the same proportion, including the movement which is used to measure time, there would be something changed for a consciousness which is not bound up with the movements of molecules within the brain ; between sunrise and sunset it would not receive the same enrichment . . . but for science nothing would have changed.' This contrasts interestingly with a passage in Professor Taylor's *Faith of a Moralist*, ii. 352 : ' There is an intrinsic connection between the scale on which a thing is built and its qualitative behaviour. . . . A being who got through two of his periods to our one would not be a man living twice as fast as the rest of us, but a creature with a new type and quality of life.' Bergson supposes that the external shapes of things in space would continue the same although the tempo increased ; Professor Taylor supposes that, if the tempo increased, external shape would alter with it.

die, in order to exist, and only to exist'[1]; to ask what life is, where it began, where it will end, towards what it is moving, is to put questions that cannot be answered, because they should never have been put; life does not progress or grow into anything; it moves always 'from the full to the full.'

For this reason 'the gates of the future are fully open.' No divine plan or supernatural design encroaches upon its virgin whiteness; the future has not even an embryonic shape; every moment we are on the edge of the gulf and are only carried over it by the impersonal *élan de vie*. I suppose that in no other philosophy has Time been so crowned and enthroned, for even Professor Alexander, another loyal adherent, would put space by its side as Queen Regnant. We shall consider in our next lecture the truth and usefulness of Bergson's teaching, so inspiring in its freedom and spontaneity, so startling in its repudiation of intelligence; here we may simply note the important historical fact that it is just the isolated sovereignty of Durée, with nothing to support it from below and nothing to guide it from above, which has given rise to criticism.

ALEXANDER

First of all, it seems cut off from what is below, Space and Matter, which play the part of the devil in his dualistic world and are opposed to Time as

[1] *Eternal Life*, p. 297.

death to life.[1] Professor Alexander protests against this antithesis. For him Space and Time are so closely united that only a hyphen can express their intimacy ; true, Space seems at first rather an inert partner : 'Time is the mind of Space and Space the body of Time'[2] ; 'Time is a kind of cosmic gendarme that makes stagnation impossible. . . . "Circulez, messieurs."'[3] 'Space has no distinction of parts ; Time is discovered to supply the element in Space, without which Space would be a blank.'[4]

But Space has also its part to play ; the past instant . . . is dead and gone ; Time would be a perpetually renewed Now ; it is Space that saves it[5] ; the continuity of Time rests on Space ; we could not recognise change as change except against a permanent background.[6]

For Professor Alexander, therefore, the highest spiritual functions, so far from being in opposition to what is material, are built upon and 'emerge' from it ; but as regards guidance of Space-Time from above, he is one with Bergson in denying it ;

[1] Durée and consciousness are inseparable. 'On ne peut pas parler d'une réalité qui dure sans y introduire de la conscience' (*Durée et Simultanéité*, p. 60) ; on the other hand '(un objet matériel) n'a pas d'histoire. . . . Rien ne s'y crée' (*Evolution Cr.*, p. 9).

[2] *Space, Time and Deity*, ii. 38. (Macmillan.)

[3] *Ibid.*, ii. 48. [4] *Ibid.*, i. 47. [5] *Ibid.*, i. 45.

[6] This is illustrated by his criticism of Bergson's view of Memory. In his Durée the past survives in the present, but this is not enough ; the ground subsides and the tower leans . . . a tower, if it had true memory, would remember the earthquake 'as belonging to its past, and not be conscious of it merely in the present effects left behind by the past. . . . If the remembered past is past . . . then the penetration by the past can have no significance which Space does not also share with Time' (*Space, Time and Deity*, i. 141–2). For his Realist theory of knowledge, the past when truly remembered is still there in its old space and time.

all qualities come from below, and Deity is merely a name for our faith that they will emerge in the evolutionary process.

Whitehead

It is here that Dr. Whitehead intervenes with *his* criticism—that Durée is cut off from what is *above*; in his view the temporal process needs a world of 'eternal concepts' to account for it.

Dr. Whitehead divides the universe into 'events' and 'objects'; 'events' represent the changing, Bergsonian aspect of things [1]; 'objects' represent the permanent and eternal world of possibilities,[2] which he compares to the Platonic Forms; they are 'universals,' 'whose conceptual recognition does not involve a necessary reference to any definite actual entities of the temporal world.' [3]

Yet this 'inexhaustible realm of abstract forms' must be brought into contact with events if Becoming, as we know it, is to exist; for Dr. Whitehead Becoming is the determination of the actual by the potential; 'there is a schoolboy now, and there will be a grown man ten years hence; we have not stated the whole truth, unless we add that the schoolboy is now becoming the man he will be. Beyond the actual there is always a range of real possibilities.' [4]

[1] 'Events cannot recur, for they are unique' (Thornton's *Incarnate Lord*, p. 457, an important, if difficult, application of Dr. Whitehead's teaching to Christian Theology).

[2] 'Eternal objects' are 'pure potentials for the specific determination of fact, or forms of definiteness' (*Process and Reality*, p. 29).

[3] *Ibid.*, p. 60.

[4] A. E. Taylor, 'Some Thoughts on Process and Reality' (*Theology*, xxi. 66–79); I must gratefully acknowledge the help gained from this article as an interpretation of Dr. Whitehead's difficult exposition.

To explain process we have to admit two realities, an actual event that is changing and a real possibility that is being realised ; now real possibilities are distinguished from what is impossible by the fact that they form an 'organised and articulated system' ; it is not true that anything may happen ; the future will conform (as it always has) to a certain pattern.

That means that certain things may happen and some cannot, the reason for the distinction being 'the eternal decision of God' which 'lies behind every fact.'[1] Objects themselves have no natural connection with events ; it is God Who so organises them that they are relevant to events and enter history in a certain order.[2]

Bergson had said 'The gates of the future are wide open ; there is no more probability of this happening than of that.' Dr. Whitehead, I think, would reply 'No, they are not as wide open as all that ; there are certain things we are sure will not happen and there are others that are infinitely probable or improbable ; the future may not now

[1] A. E. Taylor (*v.s.*), p. 76.

[2] 'The process of Becoming is constituted by the influx of eternal objects into a novel determinateness of feeling, which absorbs the actual world into a novel actuality. . . . Givenness and potentiality are both meaningless apart from a multiplicity of potential entities. These potentialities are the eternal objects. It is a contradiction in terms to assume that some explanatory fact can flow into the actual world out of a non-entity' (*Process and Reality*, pp. 62–3). God's rôle . . . lies in the patient operation by which He unites the multiplicity of actual fact with the primordial conceptual fact ; 'He is the poet of the world with tender patience leading it by His Vision of Truth, Beauty and Goodness' (*ibid.*, p. 49). The inexhaustible realm of eternal objects has internal connections and modes of ingression into Space-Time. The system is completed in its conception of God (Thornton, pp. 462–3).

be planned out to its last detail, but it will conform to a certain pattern ; to believe less than that is to reduce the universe to a phantasmagoria.'

This may seem only a restatement of the old theological belief that the world is ordered by God. Dr. Whitehead's system is not entirely what a Christian would call orthodox or traditional, as can be seen from such phrases as 'God's primordial nature is free, complete, . . . eternal, actually deficient and unconscious ; His derivative nature (consequent upon the creative advance of the world) is determined, incomplete, . . . fully actual and conscious. . . . God and the World stand over against each other, expressing the final metaphysical truth. . . . In God's nature, permanence is primordial and flux is derivative from the World ; in the World's nature, flux is primordial and permanence is derivative from God.' [1]

When (next term) we come to the second and much harder half of our task—the attempt to face the philosophical issues involved in all this—we shall (I hope) find help in this conception of Dr. Whitehead, especially when we are considering how far the course of Time and change implies a directive and controlling power.

Supplementary Note on The Neo-Hegelians

I must spare a word here for Croce and Gentile. It is well known that Dr. Bosanquet in one of his latest works, *The Meeting of Extremes in Contemporary Philosophy*, made a violent attack upon the Neo-Hegelians

---

[1] *Process and Reality*, pp. 489, 493 ; in other words, God and the World are related, one to the other, very much as the Ideal is related to the Real ; neither is to be regarded as independent of the other.

for surrendering the eternity of the Absolute and dissolving it into change and becoming ; it was generally agreed that the attack was somewhat unfair, but it is not easy to say where they do stand on this question.

Everything individual (including my 'empirical self') perishes ; only the universal concept endures. Spirit, which is expressed in every fact and exhausted in none, is therefore eternal and abides, while they pass away. So much is clear, but is the eternal itself affected by change? Gentile says (*Logica*, ii. 330) : 'Nel tempo astrattamente considerato tutti moriamo e dobbiamo morire ; perche nel tempo c'e la molteplicita, che sparpaglia la vita e la sopprime, ma nell' eternita del pensiero ne moriamo ne possiamo morire perche la molteplicita del tempo vi e risoluta in quell' unita che e immortale . . . Pensiero . . . stringe nel suo istante senza tempo tutti i tempi e ci da il gusto in ogni nostro pensare della vita immortale.'

So Croce : 'In seriously thinking of our immortality as empirical individuals, immobilised in our works and in our affections (which are beautiful only because they are in motion and fugitive), we are assailed by the terror, not of death, but of this immortality, which is unthinkable because desolating and desolating because unthinkable' (*Logic*, p. 498).

But this eternal Spirit (1) seems to have an 'ideal history . . . an eternal going and returning, in which *a*, *b*, *c*, *d* arise from *d*, without possibility of pause or stay, and in which each one, whether *a* or *b* or *c* or *d*, being unable to change its place, is to be designated, in turn, as first or as last' (*Logic*, pp. 85–6) ; (2) seems to be closely connected with the history of the world in time. 'Thought passes, but generates other thoughts, which in their turn will excite other thoughts. . . . No other meaning but this can be found in the vaunted eternity of philosophy in regard to Time and Space' (*Logic*, p. 319), and again : 'All that is born is worthy to perish, but in perishing it is also preserved as an ideal moment of what is born from it.' Here the changes of history seem to leave some trace on the eternity of philosophy, and indeed the famous dictum 'Philosophy is History' seems to put some kind of change at the heart of reality.

What Croce means probably is that we have :

(1) The four distinct concepts (the Four in one and one in Four), Art, Philosophy, Ethics, Economics ; these in their relation to one another do not change ; their 'movement' is represented by an eternal circle.

(2) Inside each are the opposite concepts (the Ugly, the False, the Bad and the Harmful) ; here there is that kind of change which consists in the continual overcoming of the opposite in the process of history.

'L'esprit est développement, est histoire et par cela même être et non-être à la fois, devenir, mais l'esprit sub specie aeternitatis, que considère la philosophie, est histoire idéale, éternelle en dehors du temps ; il est la série des formes éternelles de ce naître et mourir, qui comme le disait Hegel, ne naît et ne meurt jamais' (Croce, *Hegel*, p. 76).

It seems to me very hard to say whether the nature of the Eternal is here regarded as only revealed, or as really modified, by change, but that is perhaps the result of my own obtuseness.

FIFTH LECTURE

ON THE NATURE OF TIME

As for man, his days are as grass: as a flower of the field, so he flourisheth.

For the wind passeth over it, and it is gone; and the place thereof shall know it no more.—Psalm ciii. 15, 16.

In our four previous lectures we have been hugging the shore, following the creeks and indentations of history, calling at harbours graced by famous names, admiring inland prospects through the eyes of great thinkers; now we must launch out into the deep seas of speculation.

As far as it is at all possible to disentangle questions that must be closely interconnected, I shall try to divide the subject-matter of these two lectures into three parts—(*a*) Time considered in its own nature; (*b*) Eternity considered in its own nature; (*c*) the relation between Time and Eternity.

(*a*) *Time considered in its own nature.*—On this ladder of ascending difficulty, we start from the lowest and nearest rung—time in our own experience. At first sight we seem to have a variety of sentiments on the subject.

There are people who 'live in the past'—the old man whose interest is almost entirely in what he remembers, or the conservative who idealises the good old days. Again, there are people who seem to live wholly in the present, the Epicurean with his motto 'To-morrow we die,' the aesthete with his 'cult of the passing moment,' and (as a rule) the child, whether in years or disposition. Then there is the active type, busy with the future and regarding the present only as a jumping-off board for what is to come; Lucan stamps the likeness in his famous description of Caesar—'Nil actum credens cum quid superesset agendum.' [1]

Over against all these we have the mystical temperament which regrets Time in all its three dimensions, perfectly expressed by Shelley in the lines from *Adonais* :

> Life, like a dome of many-coloured glass,
> Stains the white radiance of eternity,
> Until Death tramples it to fragments.[2]

But on further reflection, we can eliminate certain moods; the type of mind which desires change simply for the sake of change is not in itself desirable. It is restless, imprudent, wanting in reverence for the past and generally concerned with the future in a very petty and limited sense.[3] Dante compares the political instability of Florence to the tossings of a feverish patient on his

[1] *Bell. Civ.*, ii. 657; *cp.* the Corinthian description of the Athenians in *Thuc.*, i. 70: *ἃ δ' ἂν ἐπελθόντες κτήσωνται, ὀλίγα πρὸς τὰ μέλλοντα τυχεῖν πράξαντες.*

[2] The idea of Time breaking up as in a prism what in eternity remains whole and entire is not only poetically beautiful but also philosophically accurate.

[3] *Cp.* Burke (*Reflections*, p. 36): 'A spirit of innovation is generally the result of a selfish temper, and confined views. People will not look forward to posterity, who never look backward to their ancestors.'

couch,[1] and, in the case of the individual, we all recognise and condemn the inability to settle down.[2]

Again, there are people who dislike all change, either because they live in the past like the old or because, like cautious conservatives, they fear the future. In itself such an attitude is clearly a refusal to live and learn ; we cannot accept as fully human the child who never grows up or the old man who is unable to die—Peter Pan or Tithonus.

We seem left, therefore, with two views—the Progressist view that change which is continuous and purposeful[3] is an ultimate thing, and the Mystical view that regards all Time and change as signs of imperfection.

Christianity inherited from Judaism a sense of the Divine purpose in History, but at first it was mostly of the apocalyptic kind ; there was no gradual unfolding of the Divine plan ; rather there was a succession of degenerating eras, like the silver, brass, iron and clay of the idol in Nebuchadnezzar's

[1] *Purg.*, vi. 145–51 :

> 'Quante volte del tempo che rimembre,
> Legge, moneta, offizio, e costume
> Hai tu mutato, e rinnovato membre !
> E se ben ti ricordi, e vedi lume,
> Vedrai te simigliante a quella inferma,
> Che non può trovar posa in sulle piume,
> Ma con dar volta suo dolore scherma.'

[2] Of course political and moral conditions might be such that a complete change was necessary, but that is not the same thing as a desire for change, always and for its own sake.

[3] Some evolutionists have justified the caricature of their school as holding that *all* change is progress, but its serious exponents only urge that in the long run the course of human history is directed towards some good end.

dream, till, when things were at their worst, they were destroyed by the stone 'cut without hands.'[1] However, Christianity had the advantage of the doctrine that in the time before the end (the 'While it is called to-day' of the Epistle to the Hebrews) the great work of human salvation was to be proclaimed. Christians did not sit still with folded hands, while the world reeled to its ruin; they had a message of hope and salvation to preach in the interval, however short it might be, before the Parousia; 'the signs of the times' had to be studied as heralds of the New Age when 'time should be no more'; the time was 'short' and had to be 'redeemed.'[2]

The Opponents of Time and Change

I shall begin with a few words about those who dislike change and question its reality; they fall into two schools, which at first sight seem strange allies—the Mystics and the Logicians. The strangeness is due to the popular idea that the mystic is concerned with the vaguest thing in the world, and the logician with the most definite; that the first is ardent and emotional, and the second cool and detached; the one seems to be embracing a

[1] Dan. ii. 36–45.

[2] This view is still prevalent, whenever the Coming of the Kingdom is thought of as catastrophic—not as the peaceful climax of some ever-widening process of conversion, but as a Divine intervention cutting right *into* History rather than springing *from* it; for such people the Time process has less value than for those who, from the direction of the process, try to plan out an almost illimitable future; the difference between the two points of view is brought out by their reaction to the question 'Might the Last Day come to-morrow?'

cloud with passion, the other coldly contemplating a triangle. This may or may not be true[1]; in any case both regard the possession of something unchanging as the very assurance that they are in touch with reality. Thus for Mr. Bradley the idea of a thing changing is a wholly irrational conception; I see A and the next moment I see B; by what right can I say that B is a new state of A? B cannot still be A for the exceedingly simple reason that A has ceased to exist. So for Dr. McTaggart the Time process cannot be rational, because every term of the series becomes present in turn—present to what? If to an unchanging X, then how does the process from past to future begin? If the generating principle of the process is itself changeable (as for example *my* experience), then logic is violated, for 'the relation of a term of the series itself to other terms of it must be unchanging'[2]; in other words (to use the example Professor Taylor gives) the death of Queen Anne must be (absolutely) before or after; the trouble is that in 1600 it is after and in 1800 it is before.

If the Time series is fixed, then there can be no real process and Time is not a mode of being; with it, of course, disappears all that in my own personal experience is historical and changing.

Now it is here that we must tread with caution; most Christians would admit that God, the Highest Reality, is unchangeable and that therefore changing existence, such as human history, is less real than

[1] It is not altogether true. Plato and Spinoza both seem to have felt an emotion about logical processes, which is akin to *religious* feeling.

[2] Professor Taylor, *Faith of a Moralist*, vol. i. (suppl. to c. 3).

He is ; but it is fatal to Christian Theism to suppose that because anything is not completely real (in the sense of being like God), therefore it is unreal ; it may be fully real in its own inferior rank ; so much is implied by any Christian doctrine of creation. Therefore, while we can say with the mystic that human experience is neither ultimate nor wholly satisfying, while we can say with the logician that Time is not the most perfect form of reality, we can never say that it is a delusion [1] or that it is without significance.[2]

Such objections to Time as are purely logical are never likely to impress anyone except the professional reasoner ; the popular mind always grasps change and happening and feels uneasy about the unchanging and eternal ; Christianity itself is so intimately concerned with the Time process as the stage for the salvation of souls and the scene of God's revelation that it is not perhaps necessary to prove that Time is not a phantom.[3] Ordinary people who are neither mystics nor logicians do not feel any doubt about Time and

[1] Any view that says ' If we saw things as they really are, there would only be an unchanging reality ' may be called ' Panlogism ' ; so Professor Taylor says, ' If the rejection of Panlogism is what is meant by "irrationalism," I suppose I must be content to accept the name of irrationalist ' (*Faith of a Moralist*, i. 117).

[2] As, for example, the idea of Cycles, in which the events of past time are exactly repeated in all their details.

[3] I shall not add anything about the mystics, about whom I do not really know enough to say anything profitable. In general we may say that, by laying great stress on the saving experience *here and now* (the eternal life of the Fourth Gospel), the mystic tends to direct the mind away from the Time process to another order, where Time counts for nothing. I know they have been practical and founded hospitals and organised convents ; the question is not whether they worked ' in the world ' but whether they found satisfaction in it.

change ; what they wonder is whether there is anything behind them. We shall try to show, in the rest of this lecture, that the element of Time and change, taken by itself, neither explains reality as we know it, nor satisfies the deepest demands of the human soul.

Objections to regarding Time as ultimate

(1) *The status of past and future.*—One of the prettiest paradoxes about Time is the proof of the non-existence of the present ; if there is nothing but the continuous flight of Time, then what we call existence never really exists. Time cannot stop ; its smallest instant is passing—that is, it is partly future and partly past ; there is no razor edge, when the past has disappeared and the future is not yet ; if therefore the past and the future are literally nothings, the present is made up of two nothings ; even if by some desperate device we could discover a real present in the flow of things, we could not know it ; our experience is always of the past ; owing to the fact that light takes a certain time (however infinitesimal) to reach our eyes, the vision it brings is that of a world past and perished. Did ever any speculation of Bishop Berkeley reduce the 'choir of heaven and furniture of earth' to so precarious a condition ?

Lotze comments on this : 'We readily utter the words : "Past is past." But are we fully aware of their gravity ? The rich past—is it indeed nothing ? And is the history of the world merely the infinitely thin, continually changing, strip of light which constitutes the present?'[1] So Carlyle: 'Is the past annihilated, then, or only past; is the future non-extant, or only future? Those mystic faculties of thine, Memory and Hope, already answer: already through those mystic avenues, thou the Earth-blinded, summonest both Past and Future, and communest with them.'[2]

As long as we think merely of the objective flow of things, it seems impossible to make any sense of the word 'present'; to take Mr. Bradley's simile of the water flowing under the bridge, you cannot suddenly draw a line and say, 'All above this comes down from the hills; all below this goes down to the sea; but here on this sacred line it does neither'; all you can do is to turn your lamp on the waters, take a section that is illuminated by its rays and say, 'All that flows through this lighted part is my present'; so Bergson himself admits that Time without consciousness is meaningless. 'One cannot speak of a reality which lasts without introducing consciousness; . . . it is impossible to imagine a link between Before and After without an element of memory and consequently of consciousness.'[3] In other words, past, present and future are terms of my consciousness and would be meaningless in a mindless world; the present therefore is not 'the moving line that divides past and future'[4] but 'a series grasped as having unity.'[5] The present moment of con-

[1] Quoted by von Hügel (*Essays* (Second Series), p. 140).
[2] *Sartor Resartus* (Temple Classics), p. 267.
[3] *Durée et Simultanéité*, pp. 60, 61.
[4] Inge, *God and the Astronomers*, p. 87.
[5] *Ibid.*, p. 85.

sciousness is always packed with memories of the past ; my perception of the blue sky here and now blends without a break with my immediately past sensations of blue sky ; by means of memory I grasp a certain unity of experience which I call the present state of the world—the present day, more vaguely the present year, more vaguely yet the present generation ; beyond the limits of personal memory the historian groups a whole period or civilisation as one interrelated era ; for him the past becomes part of his present not merely by the imaginative power that can visualise its conditions but by the intellectual process which explains it and relates it to our own world.[1] All this would be generally agreed ; we come to a more difficult question when we ask in what sense the past or the future is '*real*' ; if the past has no reality except in our memory, then the view of Time as a flux is possible ; if the past is real in any other sense, then Time cannot be merely the replacement of a dead past by a living present.

What I wish to say can be said by taking two common phrases, 'the living past' and 'living in the past.' The phrase 'the living past' is often used to suggest that the past lives on in the present—a view something like that of Immortality as a survival in our descendants or in the mind of

[1] An interesting case of our combining or grasping the *future* into a unity is found in the psychology of Expectation ; if I look forward to some welcome event to come, I (roughly) measure the span of time that separates me from that event, and I adjust my mind to it ; if the event arrives sooner or later than I expected, there is a mental shock ; I always sympathise with the prisoner who waited for a year to be freed, and when an extra day was added to his captivity committed suicide.

posterity.[1] It is true, of course, that the present is vitally connected with the past; we cannot understand what a man or a nation *is*, unless we know what they have been, but to say that the past or the best in the past is simply carried on into the present is a vast exaggeration; the cry of the human heart is against it:

> Sorrow's crown of sorrow is remembering happier things.

The mourner by the death-bed will never believe that the old days have passed on into his present without remainder; it is a sad law of human life that, even when the old is reformed, something is always lost.[2]

We can see the point more clearly if we contrast two meanings of the word 'remembering' as used by Bergson; the first is 'learning by heart'; we say to a child, 'Do you remember the Lord's Prayer?' and he recites it correctly. But as far as the act of recitation is concerned, the past may have been completely absorbed in the present; he may have no recollection of the hours spent in learning or the look of the print; the only sign of past effort is the successful act in the present.

Very different is 'remembering' in the sense of dwelling upon pictures of what is gone—'living in the past,' as we call it; here the past, so vividly recalled, has no relation with present action and may indeed be antagonistic to it by making a man a day-dreamer absorbed in his memories.

[1] 'Volito vivu' per ora virum.'

[2] So Froude, passionately as he defended the Reformation, could feel the charm of the Middle Ages.

Now in cases of this kind, memory and observation are not so easy to distinguish ; the present, which we observe, is actually coloured by what we remember having observed just now ; otherwise experience would be a mere splutter of unrelated sparks ; when after the torch has been whirled quickly round we still see the fiery circle, when we perceive a star which has long ago perished, we do actually observe the past. Now suppose that, by some vivid heightening of memory, all our past became as vivid as what we call our present, we should be able to time-travel at least within our own experience.

It will be said, ' This would only be an imaginary, not a real past,' but surely it would be as ' real ' as the vanished star or the after-glow ; all our sensations are packed with the past ; a very distant star might now be ' seeing ' the defeat of the Armada. Would not such a sight be ' real ' for it ? If we take such a case as that described in *An Adventure*, whether we suppose the two ladies actually strayed into the past or that they ' remembered ' vividly through the memory of Marie Antoinette, in either case (for a limited time and space) the past was as real to them as it could have been to the French Queen. It may be said, ' However vivid my act may be which recalls the past, the act of recall is from the present and in the present.' That may be true, but it merely brings out the difference between the conditions of Divine and human knowledge. A past which is still capable of being perceived by possible observers in some far corner of the universe cannot be called dead, and must make part of a universal Consciousness. If God fills space, He includes the different 'presents' of different observers, and if (as Relativity suggests) Time and space are so intimately connected that position affects chronology, and the Where governs the When, then a God who is every*where* present must be also present at every *when*.

It is obvious that in our own lives such a complete recall of the past as we have imagined would interfere with practical life ; life bids us forget and leave the past behind us ; we are changeful creatures and change is the law of our lives. But even we, in our tiny span of consciousness, include the past and even anticipate a little of what is to come (for the prudent man looks 'before and after') ; how much more does God include in His eternal and unchanging present what we call past and future ! I have taken my illustrations mostly from the past ; there is some striking evidence of our ability to see glimpses of the future, but the Divine Foreknowledge has so many problems of its own that I think we had better postpone consideration of it till we discuss the question of Creation and Predestination ; for the moment, all I have tried to suggest is that a view of Time which regards it as pure flux empties reality of much of its significance and value by completely destroying the past.

(2) *The nature of Time . . . infinite or finite ?*—Another question concerning the inner nature of Time is whether it has a beginning or an end. It is obvious that those who believe in Time as the

ultimate reality, must regard it as infinite, for, if Time were to end, reality itself would come to an end and no one can contemplate the complete disappearance of everything. A Christian may, I suppose, believe that Time is infinite and that God has always been a Creator; we have seen that Aquinas, though he accepted the 'In principio' of Genesis as *de fide*, did not see anything inconceivable in there having been no beginning; there is no reason (he says) why Creation 'ex nihilo' should imply 'post nihilum.'

But if it can be shown that infinite Time is difficult to reconcile with rational purpose, then there is an additional reason for believing that Time is not ultimate. I wish to suggest such a view, though I do it with the utmost respect to those who differ from me, and without any idea that I am defending more than my private opinion. I am perfectly incompetent to discuss the mathematical and physical problems involved in the infinity of Time; the question whether Time has a beginning and an end only concerns the Christian consciousness in so far as it affects the presence of rationality and purpose in the universe.

'Time had no beginning and will have no end'—the words are soon said, but their meaning is not always realised. We think of the beginning of Time as so far off that *we* cannot perceive it, but, taken in their full sense, the words mean that we can never get any nearer the beginning. Millions of aeons do not bring us a hair's breadth nearer. We can get some faint image of this nightmare of thought by considering its sister problem—the infinity of space. Even the stellar distances, which we can measure, stupefy our minds ; they leave us with a sense of emptiness and waste ; if we are to consider them as going on for ever, the brain reels. We are told that it makes us feel the greatness of God ; this is to confuse quantity with quality ; a million years do not necessarily reveal God better than a minute ; it depends what happens in each of them. Measureless oceans of interstellar space do not proclaim God's greatness more than the shape of the smallest flower ; it is not how long a thing lasts that matters, but what it is while it lasts.

Now it is just here that infinity seems weakest ; it empties the universe of significance and purpose. I am not a mathematician, but I understand that infinite space cannot be filled without repetitions ; in infinite Time, can a series of significant events be achieved without monotony?[1] It is for this reason that some champions of infinite Time so often fall back on senseless cycles of repetition.

Something which starts from nowhere and leads nowhere can never have a purpose and can never reach achievement. It is replied, 'The world-process as a whole has, it is true, no purpose, but it includes purposes within it. It includes histories that are wholes—the rise and decline of empires, the destinies of individuals—all these stand out separate and entire ; what matter that the succession

[1] I say 'significant' ; it is said that musical combinations are endless ; obviously one could go on repeating two or three notes for ever, but I should imagine that the combinations which give pleasure are finite ; clearly the series of numbers is inexhaustible, but it is largely repetitive.

of pictures is infinite, if each picture is finite? The universe has no history, but the Roman Empire and the Catholic Church each has a history.'

This rather recalls Tyrrell's view that there is no universal Day of Judgment, but that each soul has its own Day of Judgment as it passes into the unseen world.

The traditional Christian teaching asserts that there will be a Day of Judgment for 'the world,' not only for those who are alive at the time but for the risen dead; all the physical universe—the sun, the moon and the stars—is represented as in sympathy with the ending of earthly life and sharing in its destruction.

Such pictures are, no doubt, taken from prophetic descriptions of the Day of the Lord as a trial, to which all nations are summoned and in which the heathen are punished and Israel vindicated; it is hardly a verdict on individuals at all, but on nations. In Christian eschatology, this idea has been somewhat superseded by that of the solitary soul trembling before the angels and the Great White Throne, but, with our revived sense of solidarity and social responsibilities, we can perhaps better grasp the idea of God's judgment on empires and nations; the Last Day is His verdict on history.

You may say 'Surely such a Last Judgment is superfluous; God has already pronounced His verdict on imperial greed and national unrighteousness and the souls of those responsible have already passed to their account.' Not wholly so; God has not yet been publicly vindicated [1] ; nations and epochs as well as individuals must answer to Him.

If souls must answer, then nations ; if nations, then all humanity, for, if the actions of persons affect the destiny of nations, the actions of nations affect the world and those of a generation affect posterity ; all this interlinked responsibility will be made clear at the end.

Dr. Inge, in his work *God and the Astronomers*, supports the view that this world will end by the Law of Carnot and suggests that the universe is running down like a clock, but he goes on to imply that, when this world-order has ended, it may be succeeded by other world-orders—an endless series, each with its beginning and end, just as, before Humanity, there were other world-orders in endless regression ; thus God is always creating and never without a world.

That there may have been and may now be other worlds with value and significance, besides our own, is possible and in many ways an exhilarating thought [2] ;

[1] ' Oh the joy to see Thee reigning,
Thee, my own belovèd Lord !

. . . . . .

Thee, my Master and my Friend,
Vindicated and enthroned,
Unto earth's remotest end
Glorified, adored, and own'd.'

(*Hymns A. and M.*, 203.)

[2] *Cp.* Alice Meynell's *Christ in the Universe* :

' Nor, in our little day,
May His devices with the heavens be guessed,
His pilgrimage to thread the Milky Way,
Or His bestowals there be manifest,
But in the eternities
Doubtless we shall compare together, hear
A million alien Gospels, in what guise
He trod the Pleiades, the Lyre, the Bear.'

but I see nothing gained by saying they are infinite ; we have the old difficulties of repetition, while to create a number of worlds as inexhaustible as the numerical series is not a greater sign of God's power than to create a number defined according to purpose ; completion and not mere number is the sign of God's creative activity.

Finally, we must not multiply these worlds *ad infinitum* from fear that without them God might be 'left alone'; as we shall try to show later, His eternity is self-sufficing. If we can return no answer to the question 'What happened *before* God created?' or 'What will happen *after* Time has ended?' it is because we are trying to use temporal terms with reference to an order which is not temporal.

(3) *The conservation of values.*—We have seen how Plato opposed the Heracleitan flux on the ground that it left no room for the unchanging Eidê of Truth, Beauty and Goodness. In Modern Philosophy these Eidê are generally called values, and so Dr. Bosanquet is really repeating the old Platonic argument when he says, 'If anyone asserts that he knows the universe to be ultimately in change and in time, he must face the question of the kind and degree of its unity, or conservation of values.'[1]

If I say 'This *is* true' or 'This *is* beautiful,' am I not asserting something which cannot change and therefore is beyond the flux? Bergson would

[1] *The Meeting of Extremes in Contemporary Philosophy*, p. 217. The unity of the universe consists in its having the same law or principle. Therefore its oneness is revealed by the Value being present all through it ; Dr. Bosanquet adds, 'This problem is the central crux of philosophy.'

meet this by saying something of this sort : ' Logic and the terms of logic deal with their material as if it were static. To measure Time, we divide it up into moments, which we compare to points on a line. So when we try to measure or value life, we select one aspect of it, put it under a microscope and say " This *is* true or good " ; but this aspect was never really separate from the whirl of life around it ; we only name it and make it stationary because we want to talk about it ; it is already stuffed before it enters our dialectical museums. But the real act of virtue, palpitating with life and actuality, the real undefinable vision of truth or beauty as lived, these can only be appreciated by feeling, by an intuition of life, grown more intense and more worth living. We cannot ask what the life-force is ; we can only feel it as it becomes.'

Now, when I say ' This act *is* just,' I am not using ' is ' in a temporal sense, as when I say ' It is raining ' ; I do not mean that whereas ' it *is* fine ' for ten minutes, this *is* true for a considerably longer time. If it is true that ' Generosity is better than meanness,' this is true always and everywhere, but the ' always ' is not one of duration ; it is not dependent on anything in the nature of the time-process. It is prevalent at every date, because it is true ; it is not true, because it is prevalent at every date.

This is true of the eternal values ; the case of ' becoming ' is more complicated. If the process has a purpose, it is a becoming to be (a *γίγνεσθαι εἰς οὐσίαν* in Aristotle's phrase). If I say, ' He is a generous man,' I do not mean that he has attained the complete ideal of generosity, but neither do I mean that he is not yet generous at all ; it is a paradox that we only become good by doing good actions, and yet the actions are only good, if we are in some sense good already. He is at once 'becoming' and 'being' good. This is an important truth and we shall return to it ; for the moment we remark that precisely because Bergson has only one sense for the word 'is,' that is 'becomes,' he is obliged to banish purpose from his universe.

I wish to add a few words about truth as an eternal value. Those who lay great stress on the practical value of truth (Humanists and Pragmatists) are inclined to regard truth as something variable ; if the pre-Copernican system suited the needs of mediaeval astronomers, then it was true for them.

I have no desire to make a frontal attack on such a view. All Christians would admit that the truth is what satisfies our whole nature—emotional and volitional, as well as intellectual, only the intellectual must not be left out ; it is unworthy of a humanist to deny that a man may long with all his soul to believe something and yet be unable to quiet his intellectual doubts ; or, again, a historian may devote himself to the study of some obscure period, where he can acquire neither profit nor reputation, not because he has any hidden 'interest' in doing so, but because he is 'interested'—a very different matter.

Again, it is true that truth changes in the sense that our apprehension of it changes ; a few drops of water fall and I say (truly from my standpoint), 'It is raining,' but if the rest of England is dry, it would be truer to say from the standpoint of England, 'It is not raining.' That God created the world is true, but the content of the belief would be very different in the case of St. Paul and of Professor Eddington. We must always distinguish the truth from partial truths; in one sense nothing is true but the whole, as it appears to the mind of God, and from His viewpoint our little systems may well seem folly. Yet the very fact that we can advance, that we can say, 'This is truer than that,' shows that the change is not in the goal but in our nearness to, or distance from, it; for Christians the Incarnation carries the assurance that human speech, the speech of a particular time and country, can convey a scintilla of the Divine Wisdom.

But when we say that truth is eternal, we do not mean that every little fact which really happens is in its own nature eternal; the fact is temporal and has no meaning apart from its relation to other facts from which it cannot be separated. Even as present to God's mind, the history of the world is not eternal, for change runs through it from end to end. The unchanging truth is not in the facts but in the principle which makes them a system, namely, God's Eternal Purpose; to be true means to belong to that system of facts, which is what we mean by God's creative act.

(4) *Cause and purpose in Nature.*—Many people, no doubt, would consider that the most formidable argument against the flux is the appeal to cause.

'Who or what started it?' they will ask. 'What caused it to flow?'

Now I think such an argument needs to be stated very carefully. It is somewhat like the way of refuting Atomism by asking, 'What gave the atoms the first push?' People who use it find, apparently, no difficulty in imagining a stationary collocation of atoms as primordial, but, if they are to move, there must be a push from outside. All that is picture thinking; we no longer suppose that movement comes from outside and we can picture reality as always in motion; a flowing stream is no more (and no less) difficult to account for than a stagnant one. In fact, we shall be wise not to discuss the cause of the Time process at its beginning (to us a particularly inconceivable part of it), but rather to look at the process as we see it, and to ask how far it accounts for itself.

Bergson is quite clear that *it does*; life is its own explanation; the *élan de vie* supplies all that is required; the Dean of St. Paul's has compared this life force to a blind mole, shoved from behind and never knowing whither it is going; we have already considered Dr. Whitehead's criticism of the view that the future is completely 'open' and anything may happen. The future is *not* a complete breakaway from the past; there are only a certain number of real possibilities ahead, real because selected by God. This means that if the universe is to be saved from sheer anarchy, its direction must be in the hands of One Who decides and chooses. It is important to notice here the difference between Bergson and Dr. Whitehead; the *élan de vie* is pushed on from behind; the momentum of its past is the only cause of its movement; for Dr. Whitehead the action of God is partly decided by the future, as all rational action is—only we deliberate in the dark and God in the sunlight. A Christian will hardly hesitate as to which theory best explains the universe.

But God's purpose is not wholly postponed till the Last Day; it is already in process of fulfilment or rejection in the world of Becoming, certain things are beginning to 'be'; in the welter of waters, solid foundations begin to emerge. Things, animals, spirits represent at different levels entities which 'are'; on the river of change we see currents going at different rates; in the orchestra of Time we hear differences of tempo and rhythm.

We sometimes use the πάντα ῥεῖ rather too rhetorically; to the ordinary man the stability of things is the most striking feature of Nature; generations of men come and go, but the 'everlasting hills' seem to preserve their shape, the general aspect of the world is the same, and of the ocean it can be truly said:

> Time writes no wrinkle on thine azure brow,
> Such as Creation's dawn beheld, thou rollest now.

All this, of course, is partly due to two different senses of the word 'change'; it may mean mere change of position; it may mean real difference (ἀλλοίωσις, as the Greeks called it); all Nature is changing in the first sense; it is a perpetual dance of electrons, but the movement makes so little 'difference' as to be almost imperceptible; we do not notice that our bodies are changing; the earth spins round so smoothly that it seems the very type of what cannot be shaken.[1] Yet if we look far enough and wide enough, we trace in history change of the other kind—a new kind of thing as in the beginning of life or of consciousness, not sudden, not unled up to, but new ; a man who had seen the first day on this planct and then came to see its present state would say, 'It has changed—there are new things on it.' Therefore the picture of Time as a stream flowing equably along is not really correct ; if we must retain the ancient simile, it is a river which sometimes stands stagnant, and at other times hurls itself down unexpected precipices. Things may move at the same rate ; they change at different rates.

Now this mixture, where sometimes the old predominates and sometimes the new emerges—how is it to be explained ? The persistence of the old, which makes so much of Nature a uniform 'pattern' and renders it rational and predictable, is itself a sign of purpose ; things simply do not happen anyhow, and that means that the future is under direction ; no less does the new call for explanation. If it is the same as the past, it is not new ; if it is really a novelty, it cannot come 'from the blue' ; miracles do not happen in the sense that something comes from nothing. When anything really happens, then a possible is in the course of becoming actual, but the possible is not a mere dream or a non-existence. To some extent it guides and directs the actual, for instance, in the form of end or goal

[1] So the Psalmist : 'He hath made the round world so sure that it cannot be moved' (xciii. 2 P.B.V.).

in evolution. All this means that if the world is in movement, it is not like a ship at the mercy of the waves of chance ; it has a plan, pattern or purpose—whichever word we like to use—and this modifies the flux in two ways : first, the future is not completely open—only certain roads traverse it [1] ; secondly, even in the flux itself, certain parts begin to separate themselves from ' becoming ' in order to ' be.' Of these, human personality is the most conspicuous example.

(5) *Personality.*—I do not intend to go into any of the complicated questions that surround the nature of personality. A Christian is bound to concede to the self unity and reality of a kind superior to that enjoyed by a tree or even by a dog, but I think we are forced to admit that our selves are in the making ; it may seem a paradox to assert that the self both becomes and is, but I think it has to be said. If we say of the soul that it is stable and unchanging, we rule out all real development and growth. The Cartesian school argued that the human soul is immortal and eternal from the first moment of its creation ; in this life it is linked in some inexplicable way to the body, but it is always independent of it, and death merely reveals the soul in what has always been its true and separate nature ; few people now would support such a complete divorce between soul and body.

On the other hand, to say that the soul simply ' becomes ' and never ' is ' would mean that there

[1] See the example given by Shebbeare of the rationality of the universe in the last page of *Problems of Providence* ; no sane person (and it is a good test of sanity) really believes that Reality may at any moment burst into fantastic nonsense.

was no enduring self at all, that I am in no other sense the same person that I was twelve years ago, except that in which my body is the same ; T. H. Green is right in saying that a mere succession of feelings could not feel the succession or know that it was separate from it. But I should not like to say that there was an eternal principle in self-consciousness or that in this life we are in any true sense eternal. We are always changing, but we have momentary experiences of what is eternal and by habit and discipline we create a solid character which is more and more independent of the Time flux.

The paradox as to how the self can change and yet endure is not really met by trying to divide it into two distinct departments—one moving and the other motionless ; Plato's simile of the top is too materialistic ; we find no difficulty in believing that behind a thousand changing examples of courage, one stable principle persists ; we can trace through the most tumultuous shifts of tune and tempo the style of Handel or Beethoven. So through the most erratic actions of an eccentric we can say 'no one else would have done it' (that is, provided he *is* an eccentric and not a maniac) ; yet we cannot separate them ; the musical changes *are* Handel, at least Handel the musician ; the queer acts *are* the character.

But though they are not separate, they are not the same ; there is more in Handel than in all he wrote ; the most microscopic analysis of a man's inward thoughts does not exhaust his personality.

To apply the problem more closely to our purpose,

we can say, 'This man *is* good' in at least three different senses :

(1) He is born with the capacity for goodness [1] ; a Christian believes that at least in this life every human being has a spark of goodness deep down in him, waiting to be kindled. But of course it must be expressed and grow, before he can be called really good.

(2) A man does good actions, but here we have the old difficulty that acts are only good if done by the good man ; they must express a state of soul ; yet, on the other hand, a man cannot achieve this state of soul unless he does good acts. For example, suppose a man is naturally bad-tempered ; he forces himself to actions of courtesy and graciousness ; they do not at the moment express his real self ; they are 'acting' if you like (and so the bad-tempered man always excuses himself on the ground that he is sincere), but by habit and discipline such acts help to release the good in him. Can we say of a man in this life 'He *is* good'? Yes and No ; Yes, because he has the intense desire to be good and is forming habits of good action ; No, because in this life temptations persist to the end, because he is still growing and learning new ways of expressing goodness, because, even if he has obtained perfect stability in one virtue, there are always other directions which he has not completely explored. Therefore the inmost self is always an inextricable blend of change and changelessness ; in some aspects it 'is' ; in others, it is

[1] This is the only tolerable sense of Rousseau's phrase 'L'homme est né libre et partout il est en fers.'

'becoming to be'; the Baron von Hügel quotes Professor Holtzmann as saying, 'We become more sure of the super-temporal unity of our being in proportion to the deepening of our personality. As this our personality becomes established, we cease to know whether the years are flying or are crawling past us.' [1]

(3) To say 'He is good' in the final and unchanging sense of the words is not possible in this life, but it seems to be the ideal of the moral quest; this is why our earthly life never fully satisfies us. Professor Taylor uses this as one of his most impressive arguments for immortality; I have not the courage to paraphrase what he has said so finely about eternal life as the end and purpose of the whole moral struggle [2]; I just quote the main points.

(i) Some people say that progress is the end, that humanity ought to get better and better, yet never comes to the end; this is the ideal of some of the noblest spirits of our age. Professor Taylor answers that the various goods and honours of secular or temporal enjoyment 'cannot be had all together by anyone. They must be had one after another, on the condition that some are always not yet, and others no longer. . . . Just in so far as man takes life seriously, his whole aim is to find and enjoy a good which is never left behind and never to be superseded.' [3] And so he argues that the ideal of

[1] *Essays* (Second Series), p. 49 f.

[2] *Faith of a Moralist*, vol. i. c. 9, 'The Goal of the Moral Life,' and c. 3, 'Eternity and Temporality.'

[3] *Op. cit.*, pp. 94, 98.

the moral life must be other-worldly ; we might put the point in a more concrete way by envisaging the future offered to us by believers in pure progress. Let us contrast the idea of perfection as removed to some future stage of evolution with the belief in a future life which will explain and justify this.

Both one and the other are accepted by an act of faith ; a scientist has, of course, as much right to his faith as a believer in immortality, but he must not pretend it is pure science. As far as the observed facts go, the course of evolution might end in a war that would ruin civilisation or a cosmic catastrophe that would end life on this planet ; to believe in a terrestrial Paradise inhabited by a perfect race is as much a creed as the doctrine of the resurrection of the dead.

We notice at once the neglect of the individual involved in the doctrine of evolutionary progress ; in this it may be true to Nature, which seems to waste a thousand beginnings in the search for type ; the victims have no part in the final triumph ; there is indeed something fine in the cheerful surrender of oneself for the good of the race—the prayer of the soldier, ' Not in our time but in their time, O Lord '—but is it really a fine conception of God or reality or the life-force, that it should care so little for persons and throw them aside so easily and be a God rather of the dead than of the living ?

Again, what are we to say of the goal which evolutionary progress sets before the race ? What, for instance, are we to say of pain and suffering ?

Three alternatives seem possible. They may completely disappear; but might not human life, robbed of such a stimulus, stagnate and degenerate into a lotus-eaters' Paradise? Or they might continue as they are, and man might learn to face them with a new patience and courage. But is such a conception a satisfying goal? A man may face a painful and lifelong illness bravely, but to suppose that the ideal of life, as far as we can conceive it, consists in continually facing long illnesses bravely is a piece of morbidity of which St. Simeon Stylites himself was never guilty. Or (a third alternative) pain and suffering might disappear and man might acquire new and enlarged faculties for appreciating Nature; death might disappear and a perfectly healthy race arise, all artists, thinkers, musicians. Would human life then be complete? Would life never be boring in such hygienic surroundings and amid such a blaze of sweetness and light? The answer must be, I think, that the world, as we know it at present, does not contain material for any such endless enjoyment; the day would come when man would ask either for new faculties to enjoy with, or else a new field of enjoyment, and does not that mean that he wants to go on to a higher and fuller existence, that he craves for another life?

(ii) Other moralists urge that even in another world moral progress would go on. Kant argued that immortality is necessary because self-improvement is an endless task and needs an endless life to achieve (or rather not to achieve). The answer is that such an endless progress is irrational and unsatisfying. To quote Professor Taylor again: 'If life is not a failure, then it cannot be an adequate account of the moral life to say that it is one of advance towards a future fruition which never becomes present. . . . Our experience must be something more than a progress in which the best we can say of every stage is only "not yet good, but rather better." . . . In proportion to its moral worth, the ethical life is . . . undergoing a steady elevation and transmutation from the mere successiveness of a simply animal existence to the whole and simultaneous fruition of all good which would be the eternity of the Divine.' [1]

(iii) He goes on to urge that this eternal life need not be thought of as static. 'The termination of the battle (against evil) in a decisive victory need not put an end to the activity to which the victory has been due. . . . In Heaven itself, though there would be no longer progress *towards* fruition, there might well be progress *in* fruition. Life "there" would be, as life "here" is not, living by vision, as contrasted with living by faith and hope; but might not the vision itself be capable of ever-increasing enrichment?' [2] We shall return to this subject in our last lecture.

Some Musical Analogies

We have been considering the view that the Time flux is ultimate and we have formulated five objections to it: it seems to leave no reality to the past; by declaring that Time is unbounded it makes

[1] *Op. cit.*, p. 100. [2] *Op. cit.*, p. 408.

it hard to suppose a rational purpose in things ; it shakes our belief in ultimate values, like the True and the Good ; it seems to exclude any real cause from the universe ; it is not justified by the achievements, nor by the ideal of the moral life.

We shall now attempt to illustrate the nature of Time by some analogies from musical experience.[1]

Bergson is perfectly right when he distinguishes clock-Time from Durée ; clock-Time is homogeneous, a monotonous repetition like the ticking of a clock, whereas in Durée each note interpenetrates the others and so gives harmony and variety ; if the clock begins to play a tune, the notes form a pattern in which what comes later is modified by what has gone before.

Only, the succession of monotonous ticks is not separated from the tune ; one is based on the other. This is strikingly shown by the fact that when we listen to a series of uniform sounds which have no difference of intensity, pitch, quality or time-interval we tend to group them rhythmically ; that is, we give values of quality to bare quantitative repetition.[2]

Rhythm is the basis of tune, and the whole point

[1] I have been much helped here by the chapter on Rhythm in Mr. How's *Borderland between Music and Psychology*.

[2] See Thornton's *Incarnate Lord*, p. 26 : 'Bergson was right in holding that there is more in Time than a bare succession. But he spoilt his own thesis by splitting Time into two antithetical parts. Duration and succession are barren concepts when thus artificially separated. The true Time of our universe is duration perpetually incarnate in a succession.' In the experiment referred to (How, p. 90), all (except two quite unmusical subjects) 'accented every second, third or fourth tick,' though in reality the sounds were not accented.

of a tune is the mixture of repetition and variety. Now a musical effect is obtained sometimes by the recurrence of the same phrase, like that which gives a sense of torment in the last part of Bach's *Crucifixus*, and prepares the way (by contrast) for the silence and liberation of the *Sepultus est*; sometimes the effect is obtained by a *coup de théâtre* like the sudden change of time in Bach's *Expecto resurrectionem mortuorum*. It is the same with the rhythm of life; it is a tune played upon succession, in which duration, change, variety, uniformity have their parts.

This musical illustration perhaps helps us a little to understand the nature of Time in our consciousness, and that in three ways.

(1) When we are happy and living in an atmosphere of intense activity, Time races along; when we are miserable, Time drags; when we are dull, Time hangs heavy on our hands [1]; when we are in a state of alarm or of great mental stress,[2] Time seems intensely 'packed'; when we are completely absorbed we lose consciousness of Time, and so, when we regain it, Time seems to have flown. We can guess something of what the poet means when he says:

> Stretch Time into eternity
> Or crowd eternity into an hour.

This is because the rhythm of Time depends upon our feelings; the tempo may be slow and sleepy

[1] *Cp.* Meredith's description of the prisoner who had no clock: 'We belong to time so utterly that when we get no note of time, it wears the shrouded head of death for us already' (*Vittoria*, p. 311).

[2] Hence the novelist's *cliché*: 'All these thoughts passed through his mind in a much shorter time than it takes to put them down.'

or it may race along, full of excitement ; each note may be separately stressed or each may lose itself in the whole movement ; all depends upon the feeling of the conductor. Our life is made up of moments of achievement, moments of expectation, moments of intense enjoyment and moments of almost unperceived routine. This is true of Nature also, which has its rhythm of tides, of night and day. 'We have more abundant life, if we make human life pulse with a rhythm in tune with the universal rhythm.' [1]

(2) Secondly, we understand why modern philosophers speak of a higher form of life as having 'freer rhythm.' In pure succession the past note is over before the present begins ; as the rhythm becomes free, the past notes are felt in the present ; they can all recur or have value ; we are free from the tyranny of the moment before. So history is not a mere chronicle of succeeding events ; we are not compelled to explain what happens now by what happened just before ; we can go far back for causes and range widely for effects. The words 'pattern' and 'rhythm' are, of course, metaphors ; what they express is a real, enduring and intelligible relation between parts. The 'pattern' of the jig-saw differs from the unarranged parts because it has a unity of its own ; the tune differs

[1] How, p. 142 ; *cp.* the well-known words of Carlyle in *Heroes and Hero-Worship* (p. 101) : 'All inmost things, we may say, are melodious ; naturally utter themselves in Song. The meaning of Song goes deep. . . . It seems somehow the very central essence of us, Song ; as if all the rest were but wrappages and hulls ! The primal element of us ; of us, and of all things. The Greeks fabled of Sphere-Harmonies ; it was the feeling they had of the inner structure of Nature ; that the soul of all her voices and utterances was perfect music.'

from the unrelated notes because it remains in the ear as a whole. Thus the reason for expecting the sun to rise to-morrow is not that it has done so before very often (that may account for our expecting it ; it does not justify it), but that our 'pattern' of the universe includes it ; the whole frame of things would have to alter if the sun did *not* rise ; pattern is the larger term and includes purpose, which is often too conative ; it treats things too much as means, whereas a beautiful or intelligible system may well be an end in itself.[1]

(3) We must not ride a musical analogy to death, but it is worth while remarking that we find three kinds of Time in our consciousness : Time enjoyed in music, Time used by the will in moral progress, and Time understood in history ; these three experiences throw light on one another by their differences.

The Will is always pressing on ; it has a vision of the future and it sets its face towards that. On the other hand, music does not seem to be a progress towards anything. It has a design ; the past and future control one another ; the 'Unfinished Symphony' could not be finished anyhow—for example, by adding 'Rule, Britannia' to it. The completion must have the style of Schubert and the tone of the piece. But we cannot say in music that any one part of a musical movement advances

[1] Thornton says (*op. cit.*, p. 40) : 'The natural world around us is in a perpetual state of flux. Its procession of events is so swift and their details so minute as to elude for ever the net of human perception. Yet we perceive objects which endure and so transcend the flow of events. We perceive them as enduring within a duration of time.'

beyond another ; when we hear the last note, we cannot say that something has been achieved at the moment of completion, except the whole piece itself. In a moral struggle the last moments are of the utmost importance ; in music the last notes are no more important than the first. When the house is built, we take down the scaffolding, but in music the scaffolding is as important as the house.

In that understanding of the Time process which we call history, we seem to have both the two ideas—that of a movement culminating in an end and that of a movement complete and valuable as a whole.

When we grasp or survey a period of history we *do* see purposes achieved, progress made, development carried out ; historians are sometimes inclined to judge events by their very remote consequences, *e.g.* to regard the work of the mediaeval Papacy as unsuccessful because it led to the Reformation ; on this view there would never be any achievement ; if the event is good, it is good in itself whatever the far-removed effects. It is the fallacy of those who worship progress to measure goodness by some unknown standard in the future.

There *is* achievement, then, for history is full of the efforts and successes of the human will. Yet the historian, unlike the statesman or reformer, is not solely interested in the result ; he has also to study with quite as much interest the process that led to it ; every fact is of importance to him, just as every note is of interest to the musician ; failure is as significant a subject for study as success.

And all this is the more true because the general course of history, while it contains much progress and advance, can with difficulty be described as itself in progress or advance; the positions that have been won cannot be regarded as secured and just left behind, and such advance as there is is not often along the whole line. Our economic conditions may be better than those of Italy in the thirteenth century, but they have not so far produced a Francis of Assisi; the general history of humanity seems rather a continued adjustment than a continued advance.

History, then, grasps in its comprehension real achieved ends and also the processes of achievement. Its aim is to secure a 'togetherness,' as when, for instance, it elicits the 'style' or temper of a period; in times of moral action we may be so 'absorbed' as to feel the same 'togetherness' of the situation, but the phenomenon is most vivid and striking in the case of music, because here it is the succession of notes itself which abolishes our sense of succession; our very enjoyment of Time does away with our sense of it. As Professor Taylor says: 'The music is, for the time, our "universe." The "movement" is movement, and we apprehend it as such, but . . . the apprehension of a musical unit is sensibly simultaneous. It is not an attending first to one note or chord, then to the next, but an attentive awareness of the *form* of a whole phrase which is taken in as a whole. . . . A real musician, I suppose, would have the same apprehension of a whole "movement" as all present at once.' [1]

Such experiences suggest the Totum Simul which

[1] *Faith of a Moralist*, i. 90. This recalls the famous passage in Mozart's letter to the Baron V—— : 'The whole (symphony),

is part of eternity [1]; I would not say that in such experiences we are eternal, for in eternity such an experience would last and would cover all spheres of conscious life, but we can say that they show us an image of eternity in Time, thereby revealing that there is no impassable gulf between the two.[2]

though it be long, stands almost complete and finished in my mind, so that I can survey it, like a fine picture or a beautiful statue, at a glance. Nor do I hear in my imagination the parts successively, but I hear them, as it were, all at once (gleich alles zusammen). What a delight this is I cannot tell! All this inventing, this producing, takes place in a pleasing lively dream. Still the actual hearing of the *tout ensemble* is after all the best' (Holmes, *Life of Mozart*, p. 256 (Everyman)). But the genuineness of the letter is doubtful (*Faith of a Moralist*, i. 427); *cp.* the demand of the mystic for *complete* absorption: 'If any thought rise and will press all ways above thee . . . tread him fast down again . . . although he seem to thee right holy, and seem to thee as if he would help thee to seek Him' (*Cloud of Unknowing*, p. 24).

[1] 'One has a sense that one always has been, and always will be, floating on the tide of harmony' (*Faith of a Moralist*, i. 92).

[2] *Cp.* Bk. 9 of St. Augustine's *Confessions*, c. 10: 'Si continuetur hoc et subtrahantur aliae visiones longe inparis generis et haec una rapiat et absorbeat et recondat in interiora gaudia spectatorem suum, ut talis sit sempiterna vita, quale fuit hoc momentum intellegentiae, cui suspiravimus, nonne hoc est: Intra in gaudium Domini tui?' *Cp.* also Browning's *Last Ride Together*:

'And yet—she has not spoke so long!
What if heaven be that, fair and strong
At life's best, with our eyes upturned
Whither life's flower is first discerned,
  We, fixed so, ever should so abide?
What if we still ride on, we two
With life for ever old yet new,
Changed not in kind but in degree,
The instant made eternity,—
And heaven just prove that I and she
  Ride, ride together, for ever ride?'

Cp. also Longfellow's *Golden Legend* (the Story of Monk Felix); the monk had been reading

'A volume of St. Augustine,
Wherein he read of the unseen

Splendours of God's great town (*a*)
In the unknown land,
And with his eyes cast down
In humility, he said :
" I believe, O God,
What herein I have read,
But, alas ! I do not understand ! "
And lo ! he heard
The sudden singing of a bird,
A snow-white bird, that from a cloud
Dropped down.'

After he returns to consciousness, he finds that

' Such had been the power
Of that celestial and immortal song,
A hundred years had passed,
And had not seemed so long
As a single hour ! '

(*a*) The vision in St. Augustine's *Confessions* (see p. 162) would have perhaps served the purpose better than that in the *De Civitate Dei*.

SIXTH LECTURE

ON THE NATURE OF ETERNITY AND ITS RELATION TO TIME

Thou, Lord, in the beginning hast laid the foundation of the earth:
And the heavens are the work of Thy hands.
They shall perish, but Thou shalt endure:
They all shall wax old as doth a garment;
And as a vesture shalt Thou change them, and they shall be changed:
But Thou art the same, and Thy years shall not fail.

PSALM cii. 25–7 (Prayer Book version).

(*b*) *The Nature of the Eternal.*—In the last lecture we were considering the nature of Time considered in itself, and I was trying to show that it could not subsist without the support of a non-temporal principle; we now pass to consider the nature of that eternal principle in itself.

I shall only say a few words on so difficult and mysterious a subject; we know something of God's relation to the world He has made, but of His own inner life it is written: 'Canst thou by searching find out God?' and 'God is in heaven, and thou upon earth: therefore let thy words be few.'

Nevertheless the word 'eternal,' as applied to God, does mean something. It does not merely assert that He is incomprehensible, nor should I be prepared to assert that it is merely negative, just a 'not' placed in front of our own experience in

Time. We actually have experiences in which, while it would be too much to assert that we are 'out of Time,' yet Time may be said to have ceased to count, and such experiences are by no means negative but startlingly positive.

All philosophers admit an Absolute of some kind, for no philosophy can contemplate the collapse of the pillars of Being and the reign of sheer nothing. Something goes on always, but different schools of thought describe it differently; for Materialism or Naturalism what goes on is everlasting, though neither unchanging nor perfect; systems of Dualism regard the universe as everlasting, but as the scene of a changing battle between the principles of Good and Evil, and therefore not perfect; for Theism and Pantheism (though in different senses) ultimate Reality is everlasting, unchanging and perfect.

For the Christian thinker the conviction that the world is imperfect, finite and changing is in itself a ground for believing in the Perfect and Infinite. Descartes in the 'Third Meditation' [1] has the following passage: 'I am not to imagine that I conceive the Infinite, not by a real idea but only by negating whatever is finite, just as I understand rest and darkness by negating motion and light, since . . . in a certain sense,[2] I have the notion of the Infinite in me before that of the finite, the notion of God before that of myself; for how is it possible

[1] *Œuvres*, p. 90.

[2] Descartes' hesitating language is due, I suppose, to an uneasy feeling that he is abandoning the 'Cogito; ergo sum' as the sole starting-point for thought; he is now suggesting that we know God 'before' we know ourselves.

that I should know that I doubt, that I desire—that is, that I lack something and am not altogether perfect, unless I had some idea of a being more perfect than my own, by comparison with which I can know the defects of my own nature ? '

Descartes' argument is perhaps rather naively put, but, in essentials, it is the argument of all Theists. I have in me ideals of goodness and perfection by means of which I criticise and condemn much in myself and in human life ; they cannot come from me, who am admittedly imperfect, and therefore they come from some higher Being. I am far from being good, yet, unless I knew what goodness was, how could I condemn what is evil ? I cannot grasp all the truth, and yet, unless I had some ideal of absolute truth, how could I doubt ? Unless I had some idea of the Perfect, how could I condemn myself as imperfect ? Unless I knew the Divine, how could I raise myself above what is human ? Can we apply this method to the problem before us and ask, Unless I knew the eternal, how could I recognise a process as temporal ?

We might defend such a position on purely intellectual grounds and say that we cannot conceive of endless Time because it is an attempt to treat as a whole what is always partial, and that we can only recognise that Time *is* partial because we have the idea of a form of existence which is more complete.

But the really religious question concerns not so much the timelessness of the eternal as its perfection ; we have therefore to consider our idea of perfection and ask whether or not it admits of change.

Let us take an example from literature ; if we were asked whether Shakespeare or Dante was the 'perfect poet,' we should probably mutter that comparisons are odious and that each is perfect 'in his own way.' I do not say that is a bad answer ; I only wish to reflect on the idea of perfection involved in it. For, first of all, no one but an idolater would maintain that either Dante or Shakespeare was faultless ; there are lines which, with Ben Jonson, we wish Shakespeare had blotted, and there are metaphysical discussions and historical allusions out of which we may doubt whether Dante himself has quite made poetry. Now a work of art is judged as a whole ; therefore, when we come across scenes or cantos which wholly satisfy us, we say, 'This seems to be perfect,' and yet we know it would have been still more perfect if the whole work had been like that.[1] It is the same (as we have seen) with the moral life ; an action may seem perfectly good, and yet we may say it would be better if it expressed a life wholly lived up to that level ; our very recognition of perfection, therefore, is a recognition that it is not full perfection.[2] Secondly, by saying each is perfect in his way, we show that we have the ideal of a perfection that shall not be perfect 'in its way,' *i.e.* with relation to its time and conditions, but shall

[1] Matthew Arnold, in the famous preface to his poems, justly reproaches the taste of his day, which judged a poem by the 'good things in it' rather than by appreciating the whole. We should remember that a good line makes us feel 'That is just right there' ; a quotation from a really good poem is always better in its context.

[2] I am not now to speak of the perfect life of Our Lord, but we may remember that St. Paul speaks of it as being in some sense 'completed' and perfected in the life of His Church.

be whole and complete, in no sense depending on the time-process but absolute, unchangeable, eternal.

Such is the perfection of God, which cannot change, not because it is fixed in any frozen rigidity but because it already contains all that is good and cannot therefore admit of change or improvement. If we must have a picture, it is like a golden goblet, full to the brim ; movement would only spill it ; it is in the half-empty cup that the liquor foams and is agitated.

We must remember that God is not just a good Person, but Goodness itself—not an abstract idea of the good, from which all individual goods are excluded, but the perfection from which all goods proceed, the inexhaustible treasure-house from which the concrete examples ever issue as from their source and principle. All that is scattered in the world of particulars is there complete and entire ; as Dante says [1] :

> Nel Suo profondo vidi che s'interna,
> Legato con amore in un volume,
> Ciò che per l'universo si squaderna.

(' Within its depths I saw ingathered, bound by love in one volume, the scattered leaves of all the universe.'—Temple Classics, p. 405.)

I do not very much like Baron von Hügel's expression ' simultaneity ' as a synonym for eternity ; it sounds too temporal ; we do not want to stress the fact that God has His experience all at once ;

[1] *Par.*, xxxiii. 85–7.

Time is far transcended in it [1] ; I should prefer to speak of it simply as perfection or fullness.

Dr. Farnell, in his Gifford lectures on *The Attributes of God*, writes : 'In our judgment of values we should place a temporary Shakespeare above an eternal triangle.' [2] This is true, but is based on an interpretation of 'eternal' as equivalent to 'static.' Elsewhere he says, 'If by the constraining essence of His Nature God is eternally creative, an activity that demands a time-determination is part of His essence, and this clashes with the concept of His timelessness.' [3] Whether an activity which creates things in Time need itself be in Time is a question we must raise in our next lecture ; at present we are considering God's inner life. Dr. Farnell says, 'If we could imagine an unending series of changes from one perfect state to another, we should not view it with regret.' [4] Something of the kind is perhaps involved in Aquinas' account of the life of the saints and angels in Heaven, but it is hardly adequate to the Christian idea of God. It has always been held that God is completely and wholly Himself (*Actus purus*). All that it is possible for Him to be He always is. To suppose that He passes from one experience to another is to suppose that He has some subconscious self from which experiences come and to which they retire, and that these perfect experiences themselves perish,

[1] It is important to distinguish God's grasp of history as a whole (which, however extended, is still temporal) from His eternal being ; for the sake of clearness, though I fear without much authority, I use the phrase 'Totum Simul' for the former.

[2] P. 261. [3] P. 257. [4] *Op. cit.*, p. 260.

or at least replace one another and leave reality poorer by their absence.[1]

This fullness of God's inner life is expressed by the Christian doctrine of the Trinity and constitutes its real metaphysical importance. If God's Being be fully alive, there must be room in it for the social relations which make all true love and joy.[2] Christianity refused to find the ground of these relations in the world or in any created thing[3]; God gives life to the world; He does not receive life from it.[4]

It is usual in theology to distinguish what is called the Essential from the Economic Trinity; the Essential means the principle of tri-personality as existing in the inner Life of God; the Economic[5] means the three Persons revealed in human

[1] Underlying all this is attributing to God man's fear of boredom and love of variety; I am not clear, either, about the succession of 'perfect' states; can each of them be, in the full and Divine sense of the word, 'perfect'?

[2] Milton caricatures this idea in *Paradise Lost* (viii. 403–8); Adam asks for a helpmeet because he is lonely; the Almighty answers half-playfully:

> 'What think'st thou, then, of me, and this my state?
> Seem I to thee sufficiently possessed
> Of happiness, or not, who am alone
> From all eternity? for none I know
> Second to me, or like, equal much less.
> How have I, then, with whom to hold converse?'

But then Milton was an Arian.

[3] To say, for instance, that the Begetting of the Son is the same as the creation of the world.

[4] The religious attitude of adoration cannot tolerate any dependence of the worshipped on the worshipper; perfection, as we have defined it, cannot depend on process. To suppose it is to fall into the error opposite to Anthropomorphism, to make God not too concrete but too abstract, a bare principle which waits for the clothing of the concrete; but He is the fullness of all goodness.

[5] From the Greek *οἰκονομία*, a splendid New Testament word (now so pinched and degraded) for the plan by which God governs the world.

history—the Father in the Old Testament, the Son in the Gospels, and the Holy Ghost in the outpouring of Pentecost.

As all theologians know, it is a very delicate matter to discriminate between the two. One cannot help being struck at the outset by what seems the singular coincidence that in both the Essential and the Economic Trinities we have the same three Persons arranged in the same order; one cannot be surprised that many people have suspected that the Trinity really represents the three aspects under which God has been known in human history and that the attempt to find the same three Persons in God's inner life is really a projection back of our human knowledge of Him.

I do not agree with that interpretation, because I regard it as part of the doctrine of the Trinity that the Life of God is full and complete, apart from Creation, and therefore has in itself the relations of love and society which we express by the idea of the three Hypostases.[1]

But it is obvious, at the same time, that the Economic Trinity (which is the only one we can be said, in any sense, to know) presents us with

[1] It may be said, 'Why *three* persons? why not three hundred? Is not the number "three" derived *either* a priori from the idea of a perfect number *or else* a posteriori from the fact that the early Church learned to call God by three names?' I am always reluctant to seem to bring arithmetic into theology, but for us at any rate the number 'three' does convey a certain idea of completeness, *e.g.* of a society (father, mother and child, or lover, beloved and the love that binds them together), or of a process (as in knowledge—subject, object and relation), or of evolution (as in Hegel's thesis, antithesis and synthesis). It seems inevitable that, to human minds, 'one' suggests bare simplicity, 'two' division and conflict, and 'three' the overcoming and reconciliation of differences in a richer unity.

shadows and analogies of something real in the heart of the Divine Being.

Take, for example, the doctrine of the Subordination of the Son ; at first sight it might seem easier to explain such texts as 'The Father is greater than I' as referring only to the Economic Trinity, *i.e.* to Christ revealed as man. But the Church as a whole [1] has generally declared that it goes deeper than that, and that the Son eternally receives life from the Father. If this seems to threaten the equality of the Trinity, in which 'none is afore or after other,' that is because we come with human ideas that it is higher to command than to obey. If the Son receives, serves, obeys, it does not make Him 'lower' than the Father. Because, therefore, in the Essential Trinity, the Son expresses the principle of service, therefore in the Economic Trinity He is the fitting agent, 'through Whom' the world is created and 'in Whom' it is redeemed.[2]

In the deepest and truest uses of the word 'Eternity' we find that the emphasis is much less upon lastingness or duration than upon completeness or perfection ; so Browning in *Abt Vogler*—

When Eternity affirms the conception of an hour.[3]

[1] Especially, of course, the more metaphysically minded Eastern Church ; its real objection to the Filioque clause (and I should say a perfectly valid one) is that it obscures the subordination of the Son to the Father as to the *sole* Source and Fount of all Being.

[2] Redemption is constantly spoken of in the New Testament as a new creation (*cp.* 1 Pet. i. 3, ἀναγεννήσας ἡμᾶς) ; in the case of the Holy Spirit we could say, in the same way, that, being the bond of Love in the Trinity, He is fittingly revealed as the source of fellowship and unity in the Church.

[3] The 'conception of an hour' is thought of as fragmentary—'the broken arcs'—'all we have hoped or dreamed of good'—'the high that proved too high, the heroic for earth too hard.'

So Henry Vaughan—

> I saw Eternity the other night,
> Like a great ring of pure and endless light,
> All calm, as it was bright;
> And round beneath it, Time in hours, days, years,
> Driv'n by the spheres
> Like a vast shadow mov'd ; in which the world
> And all her train were hurl'd.[1]

To sum up, we may say that the Christian concept of Eternity is the Greek idea of faultless perfection, moralised and deepened by the Christian sense of personality.

(*c*) *The relation of Time and Eternity.*—We have now considered the nature of Time in itself and the nature of Eternity in itself, but it is evident that if we left the matter there, we should have shirked the more difficult part of our problem.

For they must be related. It is not possible for a Christian to hold with Aristotle that the world depends upon God and yet that God is completely unaware of, and unaffected by it, like some great cathedral which knows nothing of the birds that perch upon its pinnacles ; on the other hand, it is equally difficult for a Christian to say that the world is part of God or that He needs it in any sense for the fullness of His Being. Somewhere between these two peaks, each of them clear-cut and impossible, lies the shadowy and mysterious valley of the unfathomable truth. The rest of

[1] He adopts the old Egyptian symbol of eternity, the ring or circle representing at once the idea of completion and of having neither beginning nor end ; the 'bright and calm' eternity is contrasted with Time, its shadow ; the 'spheres,' I suppose, are the heavenly circles which create Time by their movement.

these lectures will be concerned with this problem, and therefore it will be well to make clear at once the divisions of the subject.

We shall, first of all, consider the relation of the Eternal to the temporal in general, as far as it can be at all discerned in the world of experience, taking five heads—Beauty, Purpose, Truth, Goodness, Holiness. We shall then, in the last two lectures, proceed to consider two special theological problems which are closely connected with the general problem—(1) The relation of Eternity to Time at the beginning of this World Order—the problem of Creation (and, as flowing from it, the baffling problem of Predestination) ; (2) the relation of Eternity to Time at the end of this World Order—the problem of Eternal Life.[1]

Before we begin to approach the first part of our discussion—the relation of the Eternal to Time in general—I should wish to say something which applies to every part of it.

It is usual to repeat such phrases as 'The eternal as seen *in* the temporal,' 'God as known *in* the world.' I think such words must be used very cautiously ; as we have seen, a great deal of this immanentist language comes from the Romantic movement and is excellent poetry, if not always very good philosophy. Hilton, in his *Scale of Perfection*,[2] has an interesting passage, worth quoting here :

[1] There is also the important problem of the Incarnation, what we may call the relation of the Eternal to the *course* of this World Order ; not having had time to include it in these lectures, I have added some words about it in Appendix II.

[2] Bk. II, pt. 3, c. 3.

'It is commonly said that a soul shall see Our Lord *within* all thing and *within* itself. Sooth it is that Our Lord is within all creatures, but not on that manner that a kernel is hid within the shell of a nut. . . . But He is within all creatures as holding and keeping them in their being through the subtlety and might of His own blessed kind (nature) and cleanness unseeable. For right as a thing which is most precious and most clean is laid *innermost*, right so by that likeness (comparison) it is said that the kind (nature) of God, that is most precious, most clean and most ghostly (spiritual), *furthest* from bodihead (materiality), is hid within all things.'

This is an ingenious attempt to make the metaphor of inness suggest a hidden treasure, or spotless linen folded away and removed from all that is material. But there is no doubt that the preposition does sometimes imply that the greater being is enclosed in the lesser; it is often helpful to reverse the phrase violently, to speak of the temporal as *in* the Eternal, of the world as *in* God.

But even if we set such phrases and paraphrases on one side, there remains the serious question how far the temporal can yield any real apprehension of the Eternal—how far by observation of the world we can be said to know God. We cannot mean that the temporal contains or exhausts the Eternal; the whole glory of the perfect cannot be perceived in any one example taken from the imperfect world of Time; even Our Lord's incarnate life, though perfect of its kind, only revealed to us so much of God as could be revealed under those forms.

We speak of seeing God *in* the world ; Wordsworth has hymned :

> The Being, that is in the clouds and air,
> That is in the green leaves among the groves . . .

and—

> Whose dwelling is the light of setting suns.

So Browning in *Paracelsus* says of God :

> Whom existence in its lowest form
> Includes ; where dwells enjoyment there is He . . .
> Thus He dwells in all,
> From life's minute beginnings, up at last
> To Man—the consummation.[1]

It is always slightly ridiculous to weigh great poetry in the exact scales of logical accuracy, but, from the point of view of the problem now before us, one thing is worth our notice. If we mean that God works through created things, and that therefore by studying them we can understand something of His character, that is a note sounded in the Old Testament as fully as in Romanticism [2] ; but if we mean that God *is* the colour of the sunset or the green of the leaves, or that He *is* the Life of Nature behind them, then we are confusing the Creator with His creation and forgetting that the

[1] Browning (Everyman Edition, i. 140–1).

[2] The Old Testament dwells upon the majesty and sublimity of Nature ; Romanticism more upon its beauty and goodness ; neither aspect is very prominent in the New Testament, as we see by the strangeness that is felt at the apocryphal saying of Our Lord, ' Lift up the stone and there thou shalt find Me ; cleave the wood and I am there ' ; St. Paul says in Romans i. 20, ' The invisible things of (God) . . . are clearly seen, being understood by the things that are made, even His eternal power and Godhead.' Keble with characteristic restraint has :

> ' Give me a heart to find out Thee,
> And read (not ' see ') Thee everywhere.'

Eternal cannot share in the vicissitudes of temporal life.

We shall perhaps make our meaning clearer if we take the analogous problem of God's Omnipresence. I quote some words from Professor Otto[1]: 'This doctrine of the Omnipresence of God—as though by a necessity of His Being He must be bound to every time and to every place, like a natural force pervading space—is a frigid invention of metaphysical speculation, entirely without religious import. Scripture knows nothing of it. . . . It knows only the God Who is where He wills to be, and is not where He wills not to be, the 'deus mobilis,' Who is no mere universally extended Being, but an august mystery, that comes and goes, approaches and withdraws, has its time and hour, and may be far or near in infinite degrees, " closer than breathing " to us or miles remote from us.'

This is perhaps put in a rather controversial manner, but the main point is right—namely, that, though all created things are present to God, He is not equally revealed in all ; He is most revealed in what is most like Him—' more in an angel than in a mouse ' (as Spinoza said) ; He is most clearly known in what has the seal of Divine likeness on its brow ; strictly speaking, we do not find God in Nature, but the signs of His handiwork.

Even when we turn to the revelation of God through human nature, we still do not find the Eternal taking part in the time-process as though He were one with it ; we speak rightly of ' hearing ' the voice of God in our consciences and ' feeling '

[1] *Idea of the Holy*, pp. 219, 220.

His presence in our hearts. But the language of religious intimacy must be balanced by the reserve of religious reverence ; we must not confuse the holy lives of the saints with the very life of God ; we must not say that our holiest inspirations are the very thoughts of God. Our highest moments of communion with Him are mediated through thoughts and feelings that are human. We see Him under a veil and not yet face to face.[1] God, the infinitely perfect, cannot, in our present state, reveal the whole of Himself to us ; we should be 'blinded with excess of light' ; we say that our experience of Him is 'adapted' to our human capacity. We do not mean that the Eternal shrinks to our dimensions, but that there is always in our deepest experiences an element which is human and still of a temporal nature. The Eternal is never in the temporal as part of it, but our apprehension of it is mediated through temporal things, by Nature, by the prophets, by the thoughts of our hearts, by the Son, Who, though He shares the eternal changelessness of God, yet in His incarnate life is 'Immensi Patris mensura Filius.'

(*a*) *Beauty*.—We now pass to that relation between the Eternal and temporal which we call Beauty ; for Plato τὸ καλόν was (of all the Eidê) that which

[1] Even in the deepest religious experiences it seems impossible to get 'out of ourselves.' *Cp*. Dr. Lake's words in *Earlier Epistles of St. Paul* : 'If I do not mistake the signs of the times, the really serious controversy of the future will be concerned with this point . . . and the opposing propositions will be : (1) that religion is the communion of man, in the sphere of the subliminal consciousness, with some other being higher than himself ; (2) that it is communion of man with his own subliminal consciousness, which he does not recognize as his own, but hypostasizes as some one exterior to himself' (p. 251).

was most vividly represented in the world of sense and the examples of which most vigorously 're-minded' us of the perfect Vision we had once enjoyed in Heaven.

It would be difficult, I suppose, to exaggerate the quiet, unpretentious and almost unconscious influence which natural beauty has in making the world an acceptable place and a home for the spirit of man ; how difficult it would be to live in a wholly ugly world! The sunshine, the birds, the green of the grass produce a feeling of health and harmony in thousands who have no theory of aesthetics whatever ; music, too, is a great reconciler. 'If that is so, the world must be all right,' said a listener after hearing Bach ; Browning puts it more poetically in *Abt Vogler* :

Sorrow is hard to bear, and doubt is slow to clear,
Each sufferer says his say, his scheme of the weal and woe :
But God has a few of us whom He whispers in the ear ;
The rest may reason and welcome : 'tis we musicians know. .

If Beauty is in itself so satisfying to the human heart, and if it is so vital and permanent a part of the universe, it seems as though it should be an aspect of God's Eternity. But a difficulty may be felt here, which is not felt in the case of the other eternal values ; it may be said, 'In the case of Truth and Goodness the values are purely spiritual ; we can understand that a "pure spirit" should have true thoughts and a good will ; but Beauty depends so much upon the eye and ear, that we cannot imagine it apart from the created world, as we know it. The phrase "spiritual Beauty" is a mere coupling of dissonant ideas ; Beauty can only be physical, or at least can only work through physical instruments. While we allow, therefore, that Beauty is a gift which God has bestowed on the perceived world, we cannot admit that it could exist apart, either in God Himself or in any form of spiritual existence which may await us.'

It is a perplexing question. It is true, of course (to put it bluntly), that God has neither ears nor eyes and it may be hard to say how He knows colour and sound, but it is impossible to deny that, if perceived things have this aspect of Beauty, God Who created them must know it and enjoy it. Spinoza with characteristic audacity regarded Body and Soul as equal and parallel attributes of God and implied that it was no more (and no less) idolatry to represent God as having a bodily form than as being a person ; I would not go so far as that, but we should remember that it is really Manichean to say that God is mind as opposed to matter. He has the perfections of both.

When we come to the other question, whether Beauty will survive in Heaven, it is necessary to remind ourselves how long in this country theology has allowed itself to be dominated by a false spiritualism, which held that the other world could have no real place for the material. Catholic theology has always taught that we are men (not angels) and that body and soul are necessary for our perfection ; the glorified body implies a glorified environment in which Beauty may well play its part. The Christian phrase, 'A new Heaven and a new earth,' hovers between the idea of this universe purified and renewed, and the idea that God can produce far higher and more spiritual forms of Beauty at His creative Will.[1]

(*b*) *Purpose.*—When we pass to Purpose, we pass to something which seems at first sight the reverse of eternal ; something which seems dependent on Time, gradually achieved from stage to stage and adapting itself to accident and contingency. Yet, when the Christian comes across something in history of which he can say, as the Crusaders said of their adventure, 'Dieu le veut,' he surely feels face to face with something that has been 'decreed from eternity.' At this point we shall perhaps find it useful to recur to the Platonic formula.

According to it, there are two kinds of existence : first of all, the eternal, perfect and self-sufficing

[1] Browning, in *Easter Day*, leans to the latter alternative :

> 'Think, now,
> What pomp in Buonarroti's brow,
> With its new palace-brain where dwells
> Superb the soul, *unvexed by cells*
> *That crumbled with the transient clay !*
> What visions will his right hand's sway
> Still turn to forms, as still they burst
> Upon him ? How will he quench thirst,
> Titanically infantine,
> Laid at the breast of the Divine ?
> Does it confound thee,—*this first page*
> Emblazoning man's heritage ?—
> Can this alone absorb thy sight,
> As pages were not infinite ?'

This seems to imply that Beauty of body and through body is only earthly ; on the other hand, it might be pointed out that Beauty here is spiritual, not because it is divorced from matter but because it dominates and organises the material ; Music is spiritual, not when the notes are faintly audible but when they perfectly express the emotion ; it was Pater who said that all arts aspire to be like Music (*i.e.* in the complete penetration of their material).

Being, only possessed in its fullness by God Himself; secondly, there is the World of Growth and Becoming, the relation of which to the eternal may be described either as 'imitation' or 'participation.'

Being and becoming are really distinct, and the same value which exists perfectly in the eternal is imperfectly imitated in the world of becoming. A Christian would add that the purpose of the world of becoming is to acquire by growth some of that stability which exists in the eternal fact, to become good, true, beautiful; history strives to achieve what already *is* (though in a different sense of the word 'is') in the Eternal Being of God. It imitates the eternal.[1]

We must remind ourselves that the temporal process is neither a mere succession of different things nor an inevitable progress to some predestined end. Not a mere succession of different things, for we have seen before that the pattern or rhythm of the process is far more complicated than that; things do not merely whirl by at the same rate; there are repetitions, things that last—all that makes history a happening and not a chaos. Change and succession achieve things that endure.

[1] As we should expect, the idea comes in the Platonic Epistle to the Hebrews. *Cp.* viii. 5: *οἵτινες* (the priests of the Old Covenant) *ὑποδείγματι καὶ σκιᾷ λατρεύουσιν τῶν ἐπουρανίων*; ix. 9: *ἥτις* (the Tabernacle) *παραβολὴ* (figure) *εἰς τὸν καιρὸν τὸν ἐνεστηκότα*; x. 1: *Σκιὰν γὰρ ἔχων ὁ νόμος τῶν μελλόντων ἀγαθῶν, οὐκ αὐτὴν τὴν εἰκόνα τῶν πραγμάτων.*

Westcott notes (p. 304): 'The difference between the "shadow" and the "image" is well illustrated by the difference between a "type" and a "Sacrament." . . . The one witnesses to Grace and Truth beyond and outside itself: the other is the pledge and the means through which Grace and Truth are brought home to us.'

And just because of that, the world of becoming is not merely a progress to an end which alone will justify it. Much of God's Will is already done; in so far as any age or individual realises something great in art or life, it has copied the Divine; something godlike is already achieved.

Plato's formula includes participation as well as imitation; neither man nor Nature could imitate God without His aid, in Nature by power, in man by grace. It is very difficult for us to draw any accurate line between participation and imitation; between Nature created good by God and the presence of God felt in and through Nature; between the good in man, made as he is in God's image, and the grace which is more than man, which goes before and works with and crowns human action. The world was created to be like God and (false as it has been to its vocation) still, at its best, it bears the marks of its Divine Father. But when God creates things like Himself, it is still a kind of participation; they have something of Himself; and when, at our highest, we come across the supremely good or beautiful, the thought that He is the cause is almost lost in the thought that He is there.[1] If a Christian were asked, 'What is the purpose of the universe?' the Scriptural answer would be, 'To be like Christ'; this is the real meaning of the New Testament phrase

[1] We therefore get the paradox that the more a thing is its true self (*i.e.* in the Divine likeness), the more it yields the place to God; Father Waggett has taught us how in the Blessed Sacrament the Bread and Wine do not disappear but come to their full reality; this is the true sense of Myers' famous line on the Incarnation—

'Jesu, divinest when Thou most art Man.'

'Heir of all things'[1]; Christ is the ideal, the universe as it should be according to the Divine plan. We can compare Eph. i. 10: ἀνακεφαλαιώσασθαι τὰ πάντα ἐν τῷ Χριστῷ, τὰ ἐπὶ τοῖς οὐρανοῖς καὶ τὰ ἐπὶ τῆς γῆς (to unite together again the universe disordered by sin); i. 23: τὸ πλήρωμα τοῦ τὰ πάντα ἐν πᾶσιν πληρουμένου (Christ Who all in all is being fulfilled); Col. i. 16: τὰ πάντα δι' αὐτοῦ καὶ εἰς αὐτὸν ἔκτισται.

These texts remind us that it is sin which has prevented the 'imitation of Christ' in the world of becoming.[2] The essence of the finite is that it is fragmentary. We do not enjoy the good as a whole or all at once; we experience it πολυμερῶς καὶ πολυτρόπως[3]; hence that dissatisfaction which lies at the root of human experience; therefore, in default of Supreme Beauty or Goodness, we see different aspects, which by their variety and succession imitate the perfect fullness of the Absolute.

The idea that eternity holds in one what we see here piecemeal is a useful picture. We have seen how Dante speaks of the temporal process as made up of scattered leaves which eternity binds up in one volume; we have seen how Shelley describes it as the prism breaking the white radiance of eternity into many colours.

But like all pictures of the supernatural it has to

[1] Heb. i. 2: ἐν υἱῷ, ὃν ἔθηκεν κληρονόμον πάντων.

[2] Not (as I have so often had occasion to say) development *ad infinitum*; this is the myth of inevitable progress. Each generation is called to imitate God in different ways; St. Francis is not necessarily in advance of St. Augustine, because he was born later; it is the fact of sin and failure that makes us think of the end as endlessly postponed.

[3] Heb. i. 1.

sacrifice much in return for its simplicity, and in particular it sacrifices the idea of growth in the temporal process ; the successive experiences are not just there as in a kaleidoscope, nor are they just unreal refractions, a mere trick of the light. There is a real finite goodness and beauty and truth, not of course independent of the Infinite but in some sense distinguishable from it ; otherwise we have pure Pantheism.[1] The finite reality is an achievement ; we have to struggle for goodness , truth has to be learned ; beauty needs the trained mind.

This is particularly so in the case of Truth.

(*c*) *Truth.*—We have already seen that Truth is itself eternal :

> It gives me strength to know
> That, though I perish, truth is so.

But St. Paul could say (though he was speaking of knowledge given by supernatural revelation),[2] 'We know in part. . . . I spake as a child. . . . Now we see through a glass, darkly.' [3]

Fragmentariness—childishness—obscurity ; so he sums up its character. You say, 'Well, at any rate we know much more about man and the universe than St. Paul did.' True, but precisely because of that, how much more complicated are our problems ! What modern psychologist could

[1] Thus, however convinced a Christian theologian may be that the goodness of a saint is entirely caused by the goodness of God, it would be very risky to say that such goodness 'just *is* God.'

[2] As is shown by the next phrase, ἐκ μέρους προφητεύομεν, and indeed by the whole argument—superiority of charity to the supernatural gifts enjoyed by the Corinthians.

[3] 1 Cor. xiii. 9, 11, 12.

say with St. Paul's simplicity, 'I knew a man . . . caught up to the third heaven'?[1] What historian of the ancient world would not feel some modification was necessary in the judgment 'Professing themselves to be wise, they became fools'?[2] What political philosopher would subscribe unhesitatingly to the aphorism 'The powers that be are ordained of God'?[3] The obvious observation, that the more we know, the more we are puzzled, shows that St. Paul was right at least in his estimate of human ignorance, and it also shows the great gulf between our apprehensions and the Absolute Truth; our finite apprehensions, one succeeding to another, have value and importance of their own, but we can hardly imagine any development of them which would make them one with the Truth itself.

(*d*) *Goodness*.—When we pass to the eternal value of Goodness we find the same double truth—that it is independent of us and that our experience of it is fragmentary.[4] Of the eternal values, Truth is the one that seems most objective; when all the arguments for Pragmatism have been stated, the sound common sense of the ordinary man will always distinguish 'what I want' from 'what is.' Beauty perhaps comes next in objectivity; few lovers of Nature would say that we put the loveliness or the splendour there ourselves[5]; few lovers

[1] 2 Cor. xii. 2. [2] Rom. i. 22. [3] Rom. xiii. 1.

[4] These two truths are not in the least contradictory; on the contrary, if the ideal *were* created by ourselves, we should expect to find more satisfaction in it.

[5] Coleridge's address to Nature, 'Lady, we receive but what we give,' is only true in the trite sense that the beauty of Nature needs us to appreciate it—if we are to appreciate it.

of art would say that there is no right or wrong in the matter of admiration. But Goodness might seem at first sight the creation of human longing for a better and purer world, the child of a romantic aspiration. But religion has always asserted that our highest ideals and deepest desires are pale shadows of the Divine goodness ; as the Baron von Hügel was always asserting, 'In Religion Ought is the same as Is.'

I need not recapitulate what has been said in the last lecture about the moral life, in which being and becoming are so strangely mixed together and the ideal of pure 'being' lies before us in another world.

(*e*) *Holiness.*—As for Holiness, I should regard it not as a separate value but as a sense of mystery which accompanies them all. The Greeks were sometimes apt to speak of *τὸ αἰώνιον* as the reasonable, the rounded-off, and to speak of the finite and limited as being the realm of mystery ; we should agree with them that the universe is reasonable, but we should add that to our limited understandings it must seem mysterious ; also that our human nature is so 'wonderfully made' that while we rejoice to know, we also find a different kind of joy in accepting what we cannot understand ; if we find mysteries in the finite, we find still greater mystery in the infinite.

I add a last word about personality. Much of what I have said in this lecture may have seemed dry and arid to the religious soul, which has listened to a discourse on values while what it prizes is intimacy with a Person. Whether, and in what sense, God is a Person is a question dusty with controversy ; Bradley declared 'To me a person is finite or nothing' ; Lotze maintained that only in God do we find personality that is real because freed from our limitations. For our purposes, it is enough to say this : The values we have spoken of would have no meaning for us unless accompanied by consciousness ; Truth, Beauty, Goodness for us are experiences of persons. But we must always remember that in God subject and object (Goodness and the good person) are united ; therefore (in Dr. Webb's phrase) it seems safer to say that God's Nature includes personality rather than that He is a Person.

In the next lecture we approach more definitely theological problems ; if I have been building rather metaphysical castles in Spain, I shall then have to face the test of more concrete examples.

SEVENTH LECTURE

THE PROBLEM AT THE BEGINNING OF THIS WORLD ORDER — CREATION AND PREDESTINATION

In the beginning God created the heaven and the earth.—GEN. i. 1.

IN the last lecture we were considering the relations (as far as we can grasp them at all) between the eternal World of Being and the World of Becoming. But there remains, of course, the momentous problem of origin ; why, from a Being Which is Perfection itself, should there arise an imperfect process of becoming ? Or (if we answer with Plato that God was not jealous and that He wished to share His goodness with others) the question *How ?* still remains ; how from Perfection could anything new arise ? for if the new thing be bad, then Perfection has produced what is imperfect,[1] and if the new thing be good, it can only be a repetition of what is there in the Perfect, and therefore cannot be new.[2]

We might therefore feel that it is simpler to adopt

[1] *Cp.* Plotinus' view that the Time process was a fall of the good from good.

[2] Perfection by definition already includes all that is good ; anything, therefore, that is new (*i.e.* added to Perfection) must be bad ; that is the problem of Creation seen from its logical side.

what we may call the Hegelian synthesis (though I do not assert that it was what Hegel meant) and say that God is *not* perfect without His creation, which is necessary to the full expression of Himself; God *and* the world make up total reality; as Dr. Whitehead says, 'God and the World stand over against each other, expressing the final metaphysical truth.' [1]

Before I say a few words about this problem, may I ask you to dismiss from your minds a kindred problem which (to the general confusion of the argument) may be entangled with it—I mean whether Time had a beginning or not? We have seen in a previous lecture that this second problem is quite open to discussion; Aquinas regarded the pros and cons as well balanced and thought the matter was only decided by the explicit revelation contained in the first verse of the Bible; I ventured to suggest that the rationality of the universe made it on the whole probable that Time had a beginning and will have an end. But the world may be as infinite and boundless as you like; no effort of rolling back its origin or its end into nothingness necessarily makes it less contingent; the question Why is the world at all? is quite distinct from the question When did the world begin? God might have been always a Creator without creation being a necessary part of His Being.

We are told 'It *is* a necessary part of His Being, because He was morally bound to create; we cannot imagine or conceive a God Who is not

[1] *Vide supra*, p. 123.

creative.' It is true, of course, that what God does, He *must* do, in the sense that He must always choose the best course, but that does not prevent the act being free, unless we identify freedom with indecision. No doubt, in the case of a human being, I can say, 'He felt a moral or aesthetic demand in his nature which made it necessary for him to write a book, and, since he has written it, it has become part of himself; he would not have been the same person if he had not written it,' but one cannot use such language about God; He has no need to express outside His Nature something which is within; goodness flows from Him to satisfy the needs of others, not His own. If we are to say that God 'needs the world,' it destroys our whole idea of perfection. A Being Who is perfect and eternal cannot depend upon the fragmentary and temporal; such a God cannot be Reality itself and cannot be an object of worship, for who can prostrate himself in utter abasement and adoration before what is in the slightest degree dependent upon the worshipper? [1]

What therefore is this one-sided relation in which God is all Reality and yet there is a World of Becoming which is real and (in a sense) other than God? How can God and the world both be real, if God is All Reality without the world? If God is already complete Reality, how can anything new arise?

[1] 'God begs Man: "My son, give Me thy heart." . . . But this same paradox . . . is so great . . . because God has not a sheer necessity to create, or a sheer need of creatures, even once they are created' (Von Hügel, *Essays and Addresses* (Second Series), p. 150 f.).

At this point it may help us (and perhaps rest us a little) to consider what

NEWNESS

means. We should perhaps begin by suggesting it is 'what has never existed before.' But if we heard 700 strokes of a gong, in which the sound quality never varied, we should tend to say, at each note, with pardonable irritation, 'There is another of them'; and if to our relief a different note should intrude, we should say, 'There is something new at last'; newness has something to do with felt difference.[1]

The problems and puzzles that surround the question, When does a thing become new? all really turn on the question, When is difference felt?[2] It would be possible to make a list of the seconds from one second past the hour, which could hardly be called 'late for a lecture,' up to five minutes past and never find any exact point at which we could say 'Here lateness begins,' yet it begins somewhere on the line. Some vigorous contrast with

[1] Compare with this the curious uses of 'again'; πάλιν in Greek implies repetition, *e.g.* Matt. xxvi. 44: πάλιν . . . προσηύξατο ἐκ τρίτου (of the third prayer in the Agony), but ἄνωθεν suggests movement backward, going back to the beginning, starting our course 'all over again'; so in Gal. iv. 9, νῦν δὲ γνόντες Θεόν . . . πῶς ἐπιστρέφετε πάλιν ἐπὶ τὰ ἀσθενῆ καὶ πτωχὰ στοιχεῖα, οἷς πάλιν ἄνωθεν δουλεύειν θέλετε; where πάλιν ἄνωθεν is 'a strong expression to describe the completeness of their relapse' (Lightfoot, *ad loc.*). Also ἄνωθεν, meaning 'from the very first,' can come to carry an idea of qualitative difference, 'going back and starting over again in a better way'; so in John iii. 3, ἐὰν μή τις γεννηθῇ ἄνωθεν; if the word means 'again' and not 'from above,' the sense is not merely that the believer is to be born a second time (δεύτερον as Nicodemus takes it in verse 4), but that something entirely new is to happen—the beginning of a changed life; R.V. well translates it 'anew,' not 'again'; so Shelley's 'The world's great Age begins anew,' where 'again' would spoil the sense.

[2] *Cp.* the pair of socks which had been darned and redarned.

the old is generally necessary to make us feel ' This is new ' ; we do not realise how much Johnny has grown up unless we see him (in a photo or in someone's memory) as he was a year ago. Before we have had much experience we all tend to be impressed with the sharp contrast of old and new and to rejoice in it ; young people are easily bored and like to feel everywhere the variety of life ; the reformer imagines a new heaven and earth ; the journalist is on the lookout for sensational ' news.' On the other hand, the old and experienced veteran shrugs his shoulders and sometimes becomes cynical in his repudiation of any real change in human affairs. ' You can't alter human nature,' he says, or (forgive the inevitable quotation), ' Plus ça change et plus c'est la même chose.' The historian tries (and it is one of his hardest tasks) to discriminate between what is really new and what was there all the time. ' New presbyter is but old priest writ large.'

Milton may have been right from the point of view he was adopting (freedom of the press), but it remains true that England under the régime of the Directory of Public Worship was interestingly different from England under the Book of Common Prayer.

We can hardly conceive absolute newness, a new entirely unrelated to anything old.[1] This point is of

[1] We speak of turning to a wholly new thought, but (*a*) the sense of personal consciousness survives ; (*b*) the thought may have been there subconsciously. Try to imagine a new animal entirely unlike any known specimen. Even a blind man, seeing for the first time, has some idea of the external world from touch. I suppose the first awakening of life in the womb is the nearest we can get to an absolute beginning, which is why we cannot really grasp it ; strong as our memories of childhood may be, we do not ever remember suddenly becoming conscious.

importance in the case of evolution ; we are told the new comes ‘ from the old ’ ; such a statement is a clear contradiction ; out of the bosom of the old only the old can come, for if the new has been lurking there all the time it is an impostor if it calls itself new. What we mean is that the course of Nature is continuous ; it changes every moment in quantity ; the dance of the electrons never ceases ; now and then we perceive changes of quality ; we say, ‘ There is something new,’ though if we had watched the process we should have been much puzzled to say at what moment life supervened on matter or self-consciousness on life.

But the new cannot come from nowhere ; we have seen that it comes from the creative activity of God—from His supply of real possibilities. ‘ Then,’ you will say, ‘ it was not really new ; it was in God’s mind all the time ; at best, it is only new for us.’ That, if I mistake not, is the kernel of the problem we are discussing in this lecture.

Of course, in a sense, if something is new for us, it does not matter where it comes from ; our parents may be making up a game for us as they go along or they may have learned it when they were young ; never mind ; we have never heard it before. So (it might be said) all the course of history is there already in God, but it unrolls itself to us with the thrilling excitement of a real drama. Yet it is just when we begin to adopt the formula ‘ Old for God, but new for ourselves ’ that the difficulties inherent in the problem begin to become formed and formidable ; let us take three points.

In the first place, is there not something actual in the 'happening' of an event? It may lie from all eternity in the inmost shrine of God's counsel, but it has not yet happened. You may say, 'It has already happened in the Divine mind, and it only happens again.' Yes, but even happening again is a new event.

Secondly, if this is true of events, much more is it true of our knowledge and appreciation of them. If newness consists in my saying, 'Here is something I have not experienced before,' then God may have foreseen or determined that event from all eternity; from all eternity He may have looked forward to, and sympathised with, my enjoyment of it, but till I was born and the event occurred to me it could not have been true to say, 'I enjoy it.' For if God's enjoyment of it is the same as mine, then the last distinction between God and man is gone and the dykes that keep out Pantheism are down.

Thirdly, as we have had occasion to remark before, we must not regard eternity as a box, from which the products of Time are brought out one after another, or as a bundle of sticks, which are seen loose and separate in the Time process; God does not throw us bits of eternity. Time is no doubt a fragmentary representation of eternity, but the difference between them is not one of quantity—a mere more or less.[1] The Time

[1] Cp. *Fortunes of Nigel* (last chapter); James I says: 'We propose to grant him an augmented coat-of-arms . . . and we purpose to add Time and Eternity for supporters, as soon as the Garter King-at-Arms shall be able to devise how Eternity is to be represented.' Archie Armstrong, the Court Fool, replies: 'I would make him *twice as muckle as Time.*'

process has a reality and dignity of its own, which would be ruined if we could say of any part of it, not only 'It has been decreed or known beforehand by God,' but 'It *is* God, *i.e.* is already part of His life.'

If we may make use of our Platonic formula, we may say that nothing exists in the World of Becoming which is not already present more perfectly in the Eternal Being of God, but events in the World of Becoming are new in the sense that they take on the inferior form of *γένεσις καὶ φθορά*. The Time process is new in its own right, as not having happened before; it is not new in the sense that it adds anything to the Eternal Being of God.[1]

But this is only half the problem, for God is not only the Transcendent Being Whom the process of becoming imitates; He is also Immanent, at least in the sense that He guides and directs the process by His Providence. Not only does He contain in His own Being the eternal values which human history tries to realise on the lower temporal stage, but He has (it has been taught) the whole course of that history spread before Him like a map; therefore, however new creation may be when compared with the Being of God, yet the Creator finds nothing new in it, for 'all things are naked and opened unto the eyes of Him with Whom we have to do.'[2]

We have to pass on, then, to the problem of

[1] In the problem of the Incarnation, we have a similar paradox; the perfect manhood of Our Lord did not make His Divine Nature 'better'; rather it was a new expression of His perfect Goodness in a lower sphere.

[2] Heb. iv. 13.

Predestination and Foreknowledge

The main interest of the subject for us lies in the question how far God's complete knowledge of history is compatible with freedom, newness and contingency. But before we come to that, I should like to say a few words as to the manner of God's knowledge; we have touched upon it before and it is not very profitable to speculate about the organs of Divine Wisdom, but two reflections may help us to remove certain difficulties from the imagination.

First of all, when we speak of God as thinking, we do not mean abstract and separate thinking; He does not spend His time among abstruse problems of Euclid; He does not study the universal apart from the particular. It is we who break up reality and apprehend it partly by sense-perception, partly by reason, partly by faith, and so on. The Divine intuition sees things as they are in their inner unity and reality.

Secondly, because He sees them as they are, He sees them as related, for it is only our fragmentary apprehension which divides them up. We see in Space 'from here' and in Time 'at this moment,' but the real universe is not made up of our tiny glimpses; God sees it as a whole; He penetrates Time and Space, for the present event is what it is not only because of what is past, but (if we believe in a rational and knowable universe at all) because also of what will be.

Now this Divine intuition, which sees history as an articulated whole, sees it as in some sense outside itself, for however far you press the fore-ordained decrees of God, however rigidly you trace the smallest details of human happening to a code or a plot composed, cast and produced by the Divine Author, the fact remains that in the last resort it happens to them and not to Him—or (at the very least) to them as well as to Him.

Such a concession even Calvin would make [1]; how far does it take us? Does it simply mean that we repeat the parts, the words, the gestures laid down for us, or does the fact that *we* take the parts introduce any element of chance or accident? [2]

Three answers are possible, and only three.[3]

First of all, there is the view that all things are foreknown and predestined by God; the intolerable consequence of this is not so much that good men get no credit for their goodness (that matters very little) but that the acts of bad men are willed and planned by God.

Calvin was logical when he said that Adam was created with free will but lost it by the Fall and that our urge to sin is the punishment of his voluntary

[1] *Cp.* Calvin's ironical account of the 'grosse fouasse de Quintin,' who, on seeing a man dead in the road and on being asked if he had murdered him, answered (in Picard dialect): 'It was me; it was God, because whatever we do it is God does it, and whatever God does, we do it' (Faguet, *Seizième Siècle*, p. 193).

[2] Anatole France caricatures the teaching of the Church in *L'Ile des pingouins*, pp. 43, 44: 'Il convient que ma prescience (God is speaking) n'entreprenne pas sur leur libre arbitre. Afin de ne point porter atteinte à la liberté humaine, j'ignore ce que je sais, j'épaissis sur mes yeux les voiles que j'ai percés et, dans mon aveugle clair-voyance, je me laisse surprendre par ce que j'ai prévu.'

[3] The view that it is a mystery we cannot penetrate (maintained in Dr. Mozley's *Predestination*) is perhaps true, but can hardly be called an answer.

sin; modern Determinists who would hardly accept Genesis regard evil as a necessary foil to good. I cannot myself believe that we can come to terms with any such belief; God may overrule sin for His purposes; He may include it in His plan; it cannot have been part of His original plan.[1]

Secondly, there is the view that the whole course of history is foreknown, but not in every detail predestined by God; His all-knowledge distinguishes the necessary from the contingent. Thus Dr. Inge says, 'God may foreknow the future as that which is going to happen, not as that which could not have been otherwise'[2]; Lotze says, 'Let us conceive that the entire reality, which for us unfolds itself as a succession, is present all at once to the eye of God. Then what is not really future, but only seems future in the object, will be perceived by God not as an uncertainty, but as something real, nor will its character as free be impaired thereby. In brief, a knowledge of what is free is possible, but a foreknowledge of it is inconceivable.'[3] So Dr. Sorley: 'I confess that the ancient arguments about the inconsistency of freedom with foreknowledge do not appeal to me. If we remember that the

[1] Dr. Shebbeare (*Problems of Providence*, p. 87) says: 'For Christian Theology, God, in the person of Christ, weeps because Jerusalem will not seize its God-given opportunity. Does Determinism do away the tragedy? Is there for the Determinist any loss of that pathos to which only the infinite pity can be adequate?' I can see that the Fall of Jerusalem could be regarded as a Drama of Destiny on the lines of Greek Tragedy, but I cannot see any meaning in Our Lord's denunciation of the Pharisees as the blind leaders who brought the people to this pass if there is no freedom and no responsibility.

[2] *God and the Astronomers*, p. 97.

[3] *Outlines of a Philosophy of Religion*, p. 120.

Infinite Mind is not limited to a finite span of the Time-process, we must allow that, notwithstanding the free causation of finite minds, the actions which we call future are yet eternally present to His knowledge. To a mind which transcends Time there cannot be the difference which exists for us between memory and foresight ; the past and the future must be equally open to His view. Universal determination contradicts freedom ; universal knowledge does not.' [1] When we were speaking of Boethius, you may remember how strenuously he attacked the idea of God knowing things before they happen ; the whole point is that for Him they have already happened. He has two parables to illustrate this ; when we see, at the same time, a man walking on the earth and the sun rising in the heavens, we see them simultaneously and yet we know that the first is moving voluntarily and the second from necessity ; so God may know an action and yet that action be voluntary. Again, he says we cannot escape the Divine foreknowledge any more than we can escape the glance of an ' ever-present eye.'

Professor Taylor stresses the same point. ' Nor do I see,' he says, ' that the admission of contingency conflicts with belief in the Divine Omniscience, as is often supposed. It would do so, if we impiously thought of God as inferring our future from our past much as an astronomer calculates the future positions of a planet from a record of positions it has occupied in the past. . . . It will not be imagined that God calculates the course of

[1] *Moral Values and the Idea of God*, p. 472.

events, like a " Laplacean demon," from a multitude of differential equations.' [1] We may sum up this point of view by saying : A Determinist says that God sees [2] the future event B because it is necessarily involved in the past event A, while this kind of traditional theology would say that God knows the future event B *whether or not* it is involved in the past event A. Omniscience becomes a kind of Omnipresence in Time.

A third view is that God neither foreknows nor foreordains all the details of history. So Martensen writes : 'A God literally foreknowing all things, would be merely the spectator of events decided and predestined from eternity, not the all-directing Governor in a drama of freedom. . . . The final goal of this world's development, together with the entire series of its essentially necessary stages, must be regarded as fixed in the eternal counsel of God ; but the (means for the) practical carrying out of this eternal counsel, . . . in so far as these are conditioned by the freedom of the creature, can only be the subject of a conditional foreknowledge, *i.e.* they can only be foreknown as possibilities, as *Futurabilia*, but not as realities, because other possibilities may actually take place. . . . While God neither foreknows, nor will foreknow what He leaves undecided, in order to be decided in time, He is no less *cognizant* of and *privy* to all that occurs. . . . His knowledge penetrates the entanglements of this world's progress at every point ; the unerring

[1] *Faith of a Moralist*, ii. 422.

[2] Or (if he does not believe in God) 'An Omniscient Mind *would* see . . .'

eye of His Wisdom discerns in every moment the relation subsisting between free beings and His eternal plan ; and His almighty power, pregnant of great designs, guides and influences the movements of the world as His counsels require.' [1] William James in a well-known simile compares God to the expert chess-player. ' He cannot foresee exactly what any one actual move of his adversary may be. He knows, however, all the *possible* moves of the latter ; and he knows in advance how to meet each of them. . . . And (his) victory infallibly arrives.' [2] So Dr. Martineau : ' What is needed, in order that the intending causality of God, and His moral government, may secure their ends and shape their means ? Simply, that no one of the open possibilities (of the future) should remain in the dark and pass unreckoned ; and that they should all, in their working out, be compatible with the ruling purpose of God, not defeating the aim, but only varying the track.' [3] So Dr. Clement Rogers : ' If the idea of foreknowledge is still a trouble to us, if we cannot reconcile it with our idea of Free Will, we are at liberty to say that He does *not* know, that His knowledge of the future is limited by the Free Will He has given us. For, after all, we recognise that His power is limited by it. But it is a self-limitation, one He has imposed on Himself.' [4]

[1] *Dogmatics*, pp. 218–19 (quoted Bicknell's *Thirty-Nine Articles*, p. 287).

[2] *Will to Believe*, p. 181.

[3] *A Study of Religion* [2], ii. 263.

[4] *Modes of Faith* (S.P.C.K. pamphlet *Atheism and Theism*, p. 25) ; *cp.* Martineau, *op. cit.*, p. 263 : ' Foreknowledge of the contingent is not a perfection ; and if, rather than have a reign of universal

I feel rather diffident of saying anything on so famous and knotty a problem, about which so many distinguished doctors disagree, but after having come so far along the path I can hardly turn back and be content with a mere catena of authorities. What I should say would be something like this :

Most of the believers in foreknowledge lay great stress on the fact that it is not like any kind of human knowledge ; our knowledge of the future (such as it is) is always from the past ; we argue from what has happened to what will happen, and therefore what we foreknow must always be determined and inevitable. But God's knowledge sees the future not in the past but side by side with the present. If this means that there is in God a miraculous and to us completely incomprehensible knowledge [1] which can be aware of future facts without affecting their contingency, it may perhaps be right to bow before it as before another mystery of faith. But it seems to me that we must admit it *is* a mystery ; knowledge, in any sense *we* understand it, is not compatible with contingency ; indeed they are opposite conceptions ; the contingent is just what (in a human sense) cannot be known.

With the contingent in Nature I am not now

necessity and stereotyped futurity, He willed, in order to prepare scope for a gift of moral freedom, to set up a range of alternative possibilities, He could but render some knowledge conditional for the sake of making any righteousness attainable.'

[1] Boethius' analogy of my seeing a man walking and the sun rising at the same time is more ingenious than satisfying ; the walking may be voluntary, but when I see it, it has already passed into an unalterable action.

concerned ; in the case of human freedom (clearly the heart of the problem) it is of the first importance to get clear, if we can, the relation between what is free and what is contingent.

Let us take first the case of good actions. A saint may live in the perpetual presence of God and under the continual Hand of Divine Grace ; we should call him free, because his actions are perfectly voluntary ; they are *his* actions ; yet we cannot suppose that they could have been otherwise ; the will is now invincibly set towards the Divine Will ; nothing the saint does is contingent. As against this, let us put the case of an ordinary man trying to do well ; he sometimes stumbles and slackens his pace ; now he overcomes his temptations and now his temptations overcome him. We feel uncertain about the result ; his action is free in the sense that the conflict is within himself ; not free, in the sense that he cannot do effectively what his deepest self wants to do. Endless confusion in moral philosophy has been caused by asking which of these two states—saintliness or struggle—is the best and by the suggestion that real freedom means a struggle, in which we could fall at any point ; the truth is they are two different kinds of goodness, and as a matter of fact we can hardly conceive a normal human life [1] without both. The most inevitable progress of serene holiness has generally had at least one earlier stage, when choice has meant a battle against temptation, and the most persistent combatant finds that, as habits are formed, the

[1] I should, myself, make an exception of Our Lord's perfect humanity (see Appendix II, p. 274).

struggle becomes easier and, at least on one point of the line, there is peace.

Take again the case of the bad man. He may be a sinner who is completely in the bondage of bad habits, Aristotle's Akolastos ; whatever the case may have been with him or may be in the future, he cannot at the moment help falling into sin. But the Akrates is still struggling ; we will suppose he is conquered every time, but there is an ever-weakening protest from his better nature. The Akolastos is free only in the paradoxical sense that it is he, and no one else, who has enslaved himself ; the Akrates is not free, in that he loathes what he is continually doing ; his actions get ever less and less contingent, as he is pushed nearer and nearer to the abyss of Akolasia.

There is therefore a large area of human action, lying between the extremes of good and bad, which to us seems contingent, that is, where we cannot tell what the result will be. It has, of course, been suggested that this is merely due to our ignorance ; it is said that if a man torn by moral conflict could really estimate the opposing forces within himself, he would see at once what the result was bound to be, and that, as a matter of fact, his friends in their unclouded judgment can often shrewdly forecast how it will all end.[1]

[1] The case of an external observer may seem simple enough ; the case of a man observing himself during a moral struggle seems excessively complicated. If he knows which side will win, can there be a struggle ? If he knows, and yet the struggle is unaffected, it means that ' he ' has really no concern with the struggle, for either the knowledge makes a difference, in which case the matter was *not* fully settled before the knowledge, or it makes none, which really destroys the unity of the self. I add a word as to the psychological

Now, of course, it is perfectly true that a mind possessed of all the facts would in many cases be able to foretell the result ; by penetrating into the very depths of a man's character (open to the observer in every chink and corner), by taking into account all the man's history, heredity and environment, one could in all cases make a good and in many cases a confident guess as to the future. But if the prophecy is in all cases accompanied by complete certainty, then struggle is an illusion and the moral conflict meaningless.

I may perhaps sum up what I want to say by reverting to the question of newness ; the history of the world, as we have remarked before, is made up of infinite variety against a background of uniformity. As you come nearer to the individual, variety seems to predominate ; as you leave him, uniformity prevails in its turn [1] ; this uniformity is

effect of believing in Predestination. Mr. John Buchan in his *Gap in the Curtain* has discussed very interestingly the results on different characters of the disclosure of one detail in their future. One of the characters—a politician—knows that he will make a brilliant maiden speech in the House ; he says ' Of course, I did my best ; if you knew that you were bound to win a race, you would run as hard as you could.' The popular impression is rather the opposite ; if you are bound to win anyhow, why take any special trouble ? But this is bad psychology because it leaves out the factor of desire ; if I want to win the race, to make a good speech, to serve God with all my heart, then the suggestion that I am predestined to do these things works on the will with a tremendous encouragement. Nor must we omit the motive of gratitude ; I must serve God with all my heart, just because He has given me this glorious certainty of salvation ; for the effect on those who believe themselves predestined to hell, we have the case of Cowper as presented in Lord David Cecil's masterly analysis, *The Stricken Deer*.

[1] Buckle (*Civilization in England*, p. 24), noticing that the yearly average of suicides is fixed, argued that certain people must kill themselves every year to keep up the average ; in other words, he

largely made up of repetition ; things happen again, but they are enough alike to make prediction safe. But in the more complicated forms of life we get what is really different ; the doctor of the soul has a harder task than the doctor of the body, because it is truer of Moral Theology than of Medicine that every case is a *new* case. For us the drama and interest of life come largely from what is new and unforeseeable, but (I say it reverently) there is no reason to suppose that the Deity needs excitement ; He is completely satisfied with the richness of His perfect and all-inclusive Being.

Therefore a vast amount of the detail of history is new and exciting to us because of our ignorance ; the result of the Battle of Waterloo was, I suppose, known to the Divine mind though not to ours. The amount of action which is strictly contingent (new in the sense that it could not have been deduced from the old) we cannot estimate. It seems to us to cover a large area of human action, in which (for instance) we give way to temptation and yet cannot but believe that God did leave open a door of escape for us,[1] if we had only used it.

'But' (we may ask) 'is it really rational to say that God, when He maps out a plan for the world, leaves large areas of unexplored territory where He cannot tell what will happen?[2] Can there be gaps in His eternal counsel? Is it not easier to

supposed that people commit suicide because the average is fixed. Of course the opposite is true ; the average is fixed (as far as it *is* fixed) because people commit suicide.

[1] 1 Cor. x. 13.

[2] Especially if God is 'at' every moment of Time and therefore there is no unknown 'future' for Him.

fall back on a mysterious foreknowledge?' I do not propose to decide such a question; we have not the elements necessary for a Divine Epistemology. I shall merely conclude with three general considerations. (1) The unknown (if we suppose the contingent to be unknown to God) is so small compared to what He knows, and even in the case of incomplete prediction the knowledge of God must be so near to absolute certainty, that we do not lose much by saying, 'God does not know.'[1] If we suppose a carefully trained and sympathetic teacher of children, we see that, though the children are free (the teacher cannot always predict what they will do in detail), yet he knows them so well that he can seem to them like Omniscience; the Infinite Mind of God knows us far better than that, and to Him our perversities must seem as unoriginal and (in a sense) as monotonous as those of children; Dr. Schiller has propounded as a test question for Theists—'Can God be surprised?' At least we may be sure that He cannot be taken by surprise.

(2) God has already limited His Power by the act of creating us. Everyone (except perhaps an extreme Pantheist) will admit that, though our future actions may be clear as crystal to God's eyes, we have not yet *done* them. Therefore against the background of God's eternal purpose and knowledge, something really moves—namely, our doing; there are gaps in God's all-power; it is conceivable there might also be gaps in His all-knowledge. I suppose that the most convincing argument against any relaxation of God's foreknowledge is

[1] God's guesses, we might say, are better than man's certainty.

that it seems to imply change in Him, as though He suddenly adapted His plans to unforeseen contingencies. On the other hand, we must remember that on any theory of the Divine Providence it *appears* to us to change ; the sending of the Son of God into the world may have been completely foreknown and predestined from eternity ; for us it does not happen till a certain date. But actually change is in the created, not in the Creator ; God does not really change His mind, love Israel one day and reject them the next ; the events of history call out what is already there in His Eternal Being. It does not seem to me, on the whole (though the question is very mysterious), that the question of complete or incomplete knowledge makes much difference here ; my plan is equally fixed, whether I say, 'When A does B, I will do C,' or whether I say, 'If A does B, I will do C ; if he does C, I will do D' ; in the latter case the alternatives are fixed. If one may make so crude a comparison, the working of an automatic machine is fixed ; it depends on someone else which handle is pulled.

In any case, I would suggest that it is by insisting on the absolute perfection and self-sufficiency of God that freedom and contingency are retained for creation ; it is by separating (not, of course, by isolating) God and man rather than by muddling them up that freedom can be best ascribed to either.

(3) The most helpful way of conceiving this baffling problem, practically and devotionally, is the idea of God's *overruling Providence* ; the evil which man does God turns to good ; his worst

sin becomes part of the Divine Providence[1]; Calvary is at once the blackest and the brightest moment in human history. The course of the world seems to us accidental and contingent, but to God it seems full of His design and purpose. A fact is what it is partly because of its consequences, and therefore the same fact would be contingent to us and yet to God part of His unfailing plan; *we* see the beginning without the end; God sees the end in the beginning.

On this subject I feel I have too long transgressed St. Augustine's precept, 'Non ut dicatur, sed ne sileatur'—and so, now at last, I will be silent.

[1] *Cp.* Psa. lxxvi. 10. 'The fierceness of man shall turn to Thy praise' (P.B. The A.V. has 'Surely the wrath of man shall praise Thee').

EIGHTH LECTURE

THE PROBLEM AT THE END OF THIS WORLD ORDER—ETERNAL LIFE

Beloved, now are we the sons of God, and it doth not yet appear what we shall be: but we know that, when He shall appear, we shall be like Him; for we shall see Him as He is.—I JOHN iii. 2.

'IT doth not yet appear what we shall be'; that warning has been so often forgotten from the time when Pope Gregory constructed his theory of the state of the departed from visions and revelations to the details described by modern spiritualists [1]; only the highest imaginative geniuses have been able to speak of the world to come without making themselves ridiculous.[2] But we may perhaps be allowed to consider cautiously some principles which apply to any world under God's government; for neither the Divine Nature nor human nature is completely transformed by the mere fact of death.

One term which all Christians would accept

[1] I take it that the general objection entertained by Christians against Spiritualism is not the assertion of close relation between the living and the departed (we also believe in that), nor even the assertion of possible communication with the dead in exceptional cases (the author of Matt. xxvii. 52 clearly believed in that), but the idea of constant and normal contact between our world and theirs; they have gone on; we do not mean that they are out of reach but that they are not still hanging about the world they have left.

[2] Such subjects are best dealt with by art and music, but a great deal of imaginative religious work is of a low order and needs criticism now and then by the cold, dry light of Reason.

as describing eternal life is 'perfection.' Hitherto we have been thinking mostly of the eternal perfection of God and the words 'finite perfection' may seem almost self-contradictory; they imply that each finite creature is meant to imitate, to reproduce certain aspects of the Divine Nature and, when it has achieved this, it is perfected. Our Lord said, 'Be ye perfect, even as your Father which is in heaven is perfect'[1]; but the image of the Father is unequally and diversely reflected among His family of children; the old descriptions of Heaven illustrate the point; the Divine glory reflected in mirrors of different sizes, or the Divine grace poured into vessels of different shapes, though all equally filled; the text from 1 Cor. xv. 41: 'One star differeth from another star in glory' has had a strong influence on such representations, though it seems to have no such meaning in its context.

The word 'perfect,' Teleios, in the New Testament is closely connected with Telos, implying that something or someone has reached an *end* in accordance with purpose.[2] It sometimes has reference to intellectual growth, implying the ripe sense of the grown man as opposed to the ignorance of a child.[3] In Hellenistic usage it can mean a person who has been initiated into the mysteries; so in

[1] Matt. v. 48.

[2] *Cp.* the Word from the Cross, τετέλεσται; the adjective itself is often used of achieved human perfection, but it is also used of God (Matt. v. 48, where achieved human goodness is compared to Divine perfection); it is used in the 'already-complete' sense of God's Will (Rom. xiii. 2), of the Heavenly Tabernacle (Heb. ix. 11), of God's gifts (Jas. i. 17), of the Christian Law (Jas. i. 25), and in 1 Cor. xiii. 10, 'the perfect' is equivalent to Heaven.

[3] Heb. v. 14.

Col. i. 28, St. Paul says, 'that we may present every man *perfect* in Christ Jesus,' and there is probably a contrast intended between the small circle of initiates and the universality of the Gospel.[1] In the mysteries the stress was mostly on advance in knowledge, though moral progress was not completely neglected; in St. Paul the idea is connected with that of Christ's perfect humanity as setting the standard for our lives; we grow up 'into Him' in body, soul and spirit.[2]

The word Teleios has also affinities with the Aristotelian philosophy; a thing is perfect when all that is latent in it (Dynamis), all that it had it in it to be, has burst into the full bloom of Energeia; the perfection of man is the life of contemplation.[3]

The idea of perfection, therefore, has special reference to a final state of attained knowledge and holiness.

If this Teleiosis meant absolute knowledge we should reach omniscience and become as God; rather, it means the fulfilment of our capacities as men and as individuals; man is not meant for omniscience, and I suppose that even in Heaven the seraphic doctor will know more than the charcoal-burner.[4]

[1] See Lightfoot, *ad loc.* [2] Eph. iv. 12–14.

[3] The conclusion of the *Ethics* cannot, I think (in spite of many efforts), be interpreted in any other way than as meaning that true Eudaimonia lies in the Contemplative Life *alone*, but the Practical Life makes some contribution to it, at least in being a preparation for it.

[4] St. Paul in 1 Cor. xiii. says that Knowledge καταργηθήσεται because it is ἐκ μέρους; we shall see πρόσωπον πρὸς πρόσωπον; Knowledge in heaven would be without a veil, but the words 'even as I have been known' *may* suggest that the fullness of knowledge there will have some relation to the capacities of the soul revealed here on earth.

So, again, in the case of holiness ; saintliness does not remove distinctions ; even in Heaven St. Francis would retain his bent towards poverty and St. Thomas his bent towards learning. I suppose all the blessed have a touch of kinship with all that is good, but surely in differing proportions ; otherwise how could personalities still be distinct ?

After these introductory considerations, let us approach two questions which concern more nearly our subject of Time and Eternity.

(1) Can we conceive, after death, a 'progress to perfection,' such as is suggested by the idea of an Intermediate State ?

(2) When perfection has been achieved (when, as we say, we have 'come to Heaven'), is there still room for progress or change or anything in the least degree resembling Time ?

(1) We must remember, what it is easy to forget, that the adjective 'intermediate' as applied to 'state' means not a place between Heaven and Hell but the span between death and the Day of Judgment. In this case, it would be clearly absurd to talk in terms of our chronology. For instance, it would be too great a 'coincidence' if the 'periods' necessary for the perfection of the departed should all have expired together precisely at the Last Day.

But if souls have still to learn and grow, there will be a state of progress, roughly analogous to what we mean by Time ; if our poor limited souls were on the track of the Divine perfections, the process of our purification would indeed be infinite, but if we take the goal as being defined and perhaps different for each soul, we can conceive the process continuing in another world till it ends.

The whole question has, of course, been complicated and obscured by the controversies of the Reformation. The Reformers laid great stress on complete justification, assured and final, through faith in Jesus Christ; they tended to reject the mediaeval theory of gradual growth by means of Grace and Sacrament; the truly converted soul was already 'saved'; his sins were blotted away and with them all fear of punishment after death [1]; they quoted Rom. viii. 1: 'There is therefore now no condemnation to them which are in Christ Jesus.' [2]

The mediaeval doctrine of Purgatory was too much concerned with penal theory, and some descriptions only discriminate Purgatory from Hell by the fact that in the former an end is in prospect. It is true that the idea of punishment after death has nothing in it inherently absurd. Forgiveness of sin does not at once blot out all sin's consequences in this life, and there is no particular reason why it should in another; suffering for sin (gladly and willingly borne) is itself a purification.[3] But some mediaeval teaching was far too legal; so much sin,

[1] 'Luther maintained . . . that the completely contrite Christian has complete remission both of punishment and guilt. . . . The main reason alleged was that the doctrine (of Satisfaction, Penances, etc.) obscured the power of the satisfaction of Our Lord' (Symonds, *The Council of Trent and Anglican Formularies*, p. 85).

[2] The 'condemnation' here means the final sentence against us (*cp.* the οὐδὲ ἐγώ σε κατακρίνω of John viii. 11).

[3] Thus Purgatory is not 'another chance for everybody'; it is only meant for those who die penitent and therefore can accept punishment as reformatory. Whatever may be held about the 'hardened sinner,' the doctrine of Purgatory does not strictly apply to him.

so much suffering. We cannot accept details of that kind. Suffering is not just the payment of a debt ; it is part of an education which enriches as well as purges. The doctrine of an Intermediate State is based on the view that death cannot of itself fit the soul for Heaven.[1] Still, it is true that the shock of death and the introduction of a soul into the spiritual world would probably have of themselves a converting effect, where there is a germ of faith ; the Intermediate State is not a time of second probation ; there is no sin there (that is, no new sin ; only what the soul carries with it), and no fresh temptation to sin ; therefore there would be absent from it that special character which makes progress under earthly conditions so slow and chequered. We may say (if such epithets can be used in such a condition) that the spiritual growth would be far more *rapid* in a world of light and peace than in our surroundings of darkness and conflict.

(2) We now pass to the second question : can we suppose a state in which, the process being ended and perfection complete, all kind of change or process becomes inapplicable ?

[1] It is said that the doctrine is not in the New Testament ; this is true, for in 1 Cor. iii. 15 the 'so as by fire' probably refers to the fire of the Last Judgment, and the payment of the last farthing in Matt. v. 26 refers to the unrepentant sinner. On the other hand, it must be remembered that much of the New Testament, if not all, is dominated by the expectation of the immediate Parousia, which would make questions about the Intermediate State of very little interest. It is this important fact (here as in other matters) which makes one believe that Our Lord must have left provision in His Church and her authority for the enlarging horizon of His followers ; the only alternative seems to be the view that He also expected His immediate return and that, when this hope was disappointed, the Church was thrown on her own resources.

Professor Sorley says[1]: 'Can we assert that the training of the active life has been of such a kind as to fit a man for the contemplative life, so that in the beatific vision he will really find the satisfaction of his nature? . . . The artist may be enchanted with the perfection of beauty; but will he be content to be only a gazer? Will not the artist in him demand *a material not yet beautiful* to which he may convey the new ideas he has received? . . . Would it suffice even for the thinker? . . . The contemplative life which the thinker really prizes is, after all, not a single and eternal beatific vision, but a life in which truth after truth is discovered *as the result of repeated intellectual effort*. . . . Experience does not fit a man for motionless ease, but for new endeavour. . . . One of two things he will be apt to demand of the future: either that the *call of service* come to him anew, and that *fresh enterprises* may be his, or else that his individual life may lapse into the source of all being.' If, in this eloquent passage, we weigh the phrases I have italicised, it is clear that they imply unending progress at least in aesthetic and intellectual activity, to encourage which ignorance and ugliness would in some sense remain.[2]

[1] *Moral Values*, pp. 522–4.

[2] *Cp.* p. 526: 'As long as the time-process continues we can conceive free minds as working towards the goal of moral perfection; we can even think of them as, *themselves made perfect*, still pressing forward into new and untried ways, enhancing the values of the world' (I am not quite clear *what* world). 'It is not only evil—that is, moral evil—that has to be mastered. The artist or the man of science has not been fighting against moral evil . . . yet he has been producing values. In this way it is conceivable that moral evil might be overcome, and yet that adventure would not cease.'

On the other hand, Dr. Inge says:[1] 'I am disposed to think that while Space and Time are the necessary framework of our thought even about Eternity, we cannot accept the view that the life of blessed spirits is essentially "durational".'

Professor Taylor has suggested as a compromise the admirable formula, 'Not progress *to*, but progress *in*.'

'There would be no more progress *towards* goodness of environment or character, but there might be abundant progress *in* good, onward movement in the manifestation of the principle of the good life in ever more varied and richer forms.'[2]

I take it that the main difference between this view and Professor Sorley's is that Professor Sorley retains ugliness and ignorance because he wishes to make room for active achievement, while Professor Taylor makes the environment perfect, because he only admits discovery by contemplation (his artist does not paint nor his scientist calculate). I cannot now, in my last lecture, again enter the lists in favour of the contemplative life: I have been trying to suggest all along that enjoyment, not pursuit, is the goal and that (as Aristotle says) 'restlessness is for the sake of rest'; but I should not wish anyone's judgment on the point to be misled by contrasts of the active and passive; God's Eternity is the fullest activity of enjoyment and it would be very crude to believe that, whenever we are not 'doing things,' we are passive in the sense of asleep.

[1] *God and the Astronomers*, p. 282.

[2] *Faith of a Moralist*, i. 417.

To return to Professor Taylor's statement ; there seems at first some difficulty about the value of the element of ' surprise ' in the experience of the blessed spirits ; he says on p. 428 that ' in men . . . whose enjoyment depends almost wholly on being perpetually taken by surprise, I suppose we might say the appreciation of narrative and dramatic art is at its lowest,' and yet on p. 431 he says that for the blessed spirits ' there are always possible surprises in store, though in a world from which evil had disappeared the surprises would always be joyful,' and on p. 421, ' Heaven . . . must be a land of delightful surprises.'

I may misunderstand him, but I should suppose he means that there will be (so to speak) no surprise of quality but only of transition. To take his own illustration on p. 418, the ' supreme three ' of Shakespeare's tragedies show no progress from one to the other ; each is equally good and perfect, but we pass with joy from one to the other because we find there is still more of the same excellence. As he suggests, this is probably something of what Aquinas meant by the Aevum of the Angels ; as we saw in the third lecture, the angelic time is discontinuous ; it grasps 'simul' all that can be taken in at one glance and then passes on to another act of intelligence ; its state is not progress from darkness to light, but a series of bursts of illumination.

It is clear, I suppose, that if the temporal process, as we know it, exists for the sake of growth, learning and improvement, then it can have no place when Teleiosis has been achieved. At the same time no finite spirit ever becomes omniscient or omnipotent ;

it is always limited by the existence of other and perhaps superior finite spirits—angels or saints [1]—and by the Divine Being, the inexhaustible Source of all knowledge and holiness.

'New' experiences therefore may stream in from the communion of saints and from the Beatific Vision; they will not be new in the sense that they are different in quality, but as being more of the same kind; this is symbolised in Aquinas by the *tempus angelorum*, which is not continuous (*i.e.* not representative of growth, change and decay) but discontinuous—a succession of experiences all equal in perfection and permanence.[2]

Can such a life be called eternal except in the sense of 'everlasting'? Is it not still a Time series 'concentrated into semi-simultaneities,' to use Dr. Inge's rather deprecating phrase?

It would be both tasteless and ridiculous to use technicalities in such a matter; if scope is wanted for parading our philosophical theories, some other field should be found than the life of Heaven. As

[1] Notice the words of Our Lord's prayer in John xvii. 23, 'that they may all be perfected into one'; this cannot mean that all Christians shall become one undistinguishable mass, but that this unity—the dependence of each on the other—is part of the Teleiosis of each member *and* of the whole Body of Christ.

[2] A friend, in a private letter, puts it thus: 'Any ultimate arrest in knowledge of God would be an arrest in imperfection; the bliss of the creature would therefore imply the eternal possibility of going further and further in knowledge and enjoyment of God, which would imply successiveness. Only one must suppose that in Heaven the loss, which is attached to the passage of Time, would be done away and no good possessed would pass away but would be continually added to.' I should agree with that, only I should hesitate about the word 'successiveness,' and I should add that there is a limit not to the mass but to the direction of the experiences—set by the capacity of each.

far as I can see (and it is not very far) two principles are involved. We have defined the 'eternal' as what is perfect and unchanging; the life of the blessed must be perfect in the sense that it is all of one quality—and that the highest and holiest; it is unchanging in the sense that nothing is lost and nothing gained, for all is at the same level. On the other hand, the blessed are not the same as God, nor are they the same as one another; therefore outside (so to speak) the perfection of each there is an ocean of perfection that can be the object of their experience. God is unchanging, because there is nothing outside Himself; the blessed, while firm in the unity of their inner perfection, may have constant enrichment *from outside*—if I may again use what is only a metaphor. But it is time to be done with the dull schemata of our definitions; the thought comes home to us more closely in the music of the famous hymn which combines the thought of praising God and of enjoying our fellowship in praise:

> Illic ex sabbato succedit sabbatum;
> Perpes laetitia sabbatizantium;
> Nec ineffabiles cessabunt jubili,
> Quos decantabimus et nos et angeli.

There are two further questions, each of which deserves a separate treatise: I shall only say a few words about them in relation to our main problem.

The first is the Resurrection of the Body. It was historically connected with the Jewish sense of personality, vigorous but slightly crude and very antimetaphysical; if Abraham was to rise again, then it must be the Abraham of history; the Jews felt a not unjustifiable suspicion that when the Greek philosophers had refined away all that was bodily and therefore destined to perish, what remained was hardly Abraham at all ; they knew of no other personality than that which God had created at the beginning—body as well as spirit.

The doctrine also comes from the prophetic tradition of God's Kingdom, as the glorification of *this* world and the return of the saints with their bodies to enjoy it. We know how this was combated by the Apocalyptic idea that the Kingdom of God would come not here but in another world. The two strains of thought ran on into Christianity ; on the one side, we have the old prophetic idea of the 'restitution of all things' (Acts iii. 21) ; and the 'new heaven and new earth' ('heaven' here means 'sky,' of course) in the Apocalypse.

On the other side, the difference of the two worlds seems to be stressed by such texts as 'They neither marry, nor are given in marriage: . . . they are equal unto the angels' (Luke xx. 35, 36), and 'Flesh and blood cannot inherit the kingdom of God' (1 Cor. xv. 50).

Between these two theories the doctrine of the Resurrection of the Body was apt to hang in the air ; sometimes (as in the very meaning of 'rising *again*') the likeness between our present and our risen bodies is prominent ; at other times, it is the difference, as in 1 Cor. xv., where the new and heavenly environment calls for a πνευματικὸν σῶμα and not for a ψυχικὸν σῶμα such as we have on earth. In too much modern teaching the risen body appears as an anomaly, the ghostly relic of a material world in purely spiritual surroundings. If it were maintained (in any 'millennial' sense) that the present world went on after the Day of Judgment, we should be presented with a paradox that a state of growth survived when the need for growth was over; it would be just the same as if we were to ask, 'What will be the age of the resurrection body?' We could not arrest the growth of our bodies or the course of nature and say 'That moment is perfect; stay like that for all eternity.'

But we are told that our bodies shall be 'changed' and glorified 'in a moment, in the twinkling of an eye'; we may be sure that whatever is beautiful or healthy or good in the physical universe has some place in the world to come: if we need organs for communication and a world of environment in Heaven, why should it not come from the intensification and glorification of all that is best here? Why should we suppose that God's great work of Creation is going to disappear like so much rubbish at the Last Trump, and be forgotten as if it had never been? May we not believe that this universe (the home already of so much serenity and solemnity) will be transformed to become an antechamber to God's Palace? I say 'antechamber' because, however glorified the material may be, it can only be *part*—and a small part—of heavenly experience, just as the risen body is subordinate to the spirit. We may, if we like, picture the blessed as able to enter this transfigured world at will, but the way is always open to Heaven and the inner shrine which is purely spiritual; we may compare the saying, 'Heaven will be like a summer's day, but there will be no more curse and we shall see God.'

The controversies have mostly raged about the one point—what is the connection, what is the continuity between the body which is laid in the grave and the body of resurrection? Here too we shall find it a help to hold closely together in our minds our own bodies and the whole world of matter; the problem is the spiritualisation of the material, the glorification of our present environment; clearly we cannot conceive how it will happen; the Last Trumpet, the rending tombs, the great White Throne are what we may call frontier-pictures—material images used just to cover the moment when the material is being renewed and restored; we rightly desire and expect continuity of some kind both for our resurrection bodies and for the new heaven and earth.

The second question is that of eternal punishment. To me it seems a singularly endless and unprofitable problem; people who believe that one can extract absolute truth by careful analysis of the inspired words and syllables of the Bible—with the help of lexicons, which themselves would have to be inspired—may hope for an answer, but we do not, most of us, any longer regard scriptural language in this way; apart from that, it all seems a question of 'if's.' *If* certain beings cannot by any process be made better—*if* the consequences of sin pass on into the next world unchanged—*if* God can never destroy or bring to an end the soul He has once made, *then* some kind of unending punishment seems inevitable.

Aquinas devotes much of his energy to showing that the sentencing of souls to hell is just ; such considerations of transcendental jurisprudence make little appeal to our minds ; it is easier to say that the unrepentant, by their characters, automatically exclude themselves from Heaven 'exiles' (Aquinas calls them) ' from the celestial society.' [1]

Our difficulty, I suppose, is to conceive how God's Kingdom should have come and ' all manner of things be well,' and God be all in all, while all the time this hopeless tragedy of the lost continues. It seems to us that *either* we must accept Traherne's words : ' Hell . . . is fitly mentioned in the enjoyment of the world. And is itself by the happy enjoyed, as a part of the world,' [2] *or else* (if that seems intolerable) one must suppose some kind of final annihilation, when all hope of conversion is over.

It is said that the soul cannot be destroyed ; such a view is founded on Platonic metaphysics [3] and really implies that the soul had no beginning either.

It is said that God cannot withdraw His gift of life once bestowed ; but surely it is rather terrible to plead God's gift of life as an argument to justify eternal death.

The phrase ' eternal death '—framed as an antithesis to ' eternal life '—is a difficult one to justify.

[1] *Cp.* Dr. Bigg (*Origins of Christianity*, p. 139) on the views of the Gnostics : ' Those who are fit only for earth will remain in the region of sense, immortal, but knowing and seeking nothing better than earth, " that they may not be tortured with impossibilities, like fish desiring to live upon the mountain-top." '

[2] *Meditations*, No. 48 (p. 32).

[3] The Archbishop of York in this pulpit described the mediaeval doctrine of hell as a mixture of the Jewish teaching of destruction by fire and the Greek teaching that the soul is indestructible.

Unless one believes in a Devil, who is the complete fullness and perfection of evil, a Totum Simul of darkness,[1] we must suppose that evil is partial, not perfect ; it is the ruin of good, not a structure in its own right. Hell might be the fixation of bad habits for ever—a petrification of the unholy character—but there is no need to reverse our description of heavenly bliss and apply it to some Satanic revel in wickedness ; the worst punishment of the wicked would be to know what their wickedness meant, when it was too late ; we need no further details, either about people or places, to make us walk soberly.

Conclusion

In bringing these lectures to a close, I ask myself (as I suppose all Bampton Lecturers have asked themselves, but I perhaps with more reason than many) What does it all come to? Have I not been abusing the licence to speculate, which goes with this lectureship, and have I not remembered too infrequently that the Christian pulpit is meant for edification ?

I might answer that, even in theological matters, it is a good thing to know the meaning of the words we use, and that the word 'eternal' comes often enough in our forms of prayer and praise ; or I might say that speaking before a University one has no need to excuse oneself for being academic. But, after all, it is the glory of the Christian

[1] It has never been held that Satan is Badness itself ; that would be Manichean ; he was a fallen angel, not a rival to Deity.

religion (as it was of Stoicism) that its metaphysic is never too far removed from its ethic, and so I conclude with a few words as to the application of what I have been trying to say.

I might perhaps sum up that application by saying that the consideration of Time and Eternity should help to train us in a Christian sense of proportion—' the right judgment in all things ' of the Whitsunday Collect. And that in three ways.

First, in that sense of proportion which we call *Reverence* ; we are being told from many sides that our religion is not God-centred enough ; that it is too often an instrument for the improvement of man and not for the glory of God. Thus in Continental Protestantism the movement associated with the name of Karl Barth is a protest against a perverted Humanism,[1] and has for its own motto ' Only God matters.' Newman bade us remember that Time is short and Eternity is long, and the prayer of Pope Clement XI asks for grace to realise, ' quam tenue quod terrenum, quam grande quod divinum, quam breve quod temporaneum, quam durabile quod aeternum.' To see ' what matters ' is the mark of wisdom in the individual as in the Church at large ; the thought of God's Eternity is the fountain from which reverence flows—not a negative reverence which shrinks nervously from thinking or talking about certain subjects—not an effusive reverence which seeks to please by piling up

[1] In its bad sense, I take it to be a tendency always to adopt (generally very late in the day) the newest popular fad, thus giving the impression that Christianity never has anything independent to say on any problem.

epithets for God and the saints, like the 'Lord, Lord' which Jesus rejected, but a reverence which can speak or be silent—alike with holy fear.

There are times when human interests are so rich and so glittering that the Divine seems crowded out; but such a concentration on this world generally leads to catastrophe, as it did in 1914. The Church preaches no lack of interest in the abundance and variety of worldly affairs, but it preaches (and Death preaches much more eloquently) that all these things 'perish in the using' and that on our use of them depends our own relation to the eternal things which must remain.

The intense realisation of what is eternal may so press upon the mind as to disturb this right sense of proportion. It may create the feeling that the temporal is so fragile and so fleeting that it is hardly worth our serious attention, with the result that we become indifferent and detached; life becomes a vale of tears to be hurried through with eyes averted and fixed upon the distant goal. Or the vivid feeling of eternity may produce not indifference but fanaticism; here there is no lack of care for others, but the interest is feverish, hurried, impatient. The time is so short and the danger so terrible.

In Our Lord's own life there is no trace of these extremes; His ever-present sense of the Father in Heaven and of Judgment to come does not obscure His delight in birds and flowers and children; His parables reveal an interest, always exact and often tender, in human life and character; He preached indeed the urgency of immediate choice, but He did not frighten men into the fold ; He accepted, but He made more gentle, the fierce Revivalism of the Baptist ; whatever He believed about the Parousia, His methods and His outlook are patient, wide-ranging, unhurried. He appeals to men to pause, to reflect, to count the cost, and the Christian Church, wherever she has been faithful to His Spirit, has caught the same blend of fervent passion and infinite patience—' true to the kindred points of Heaven and home '—like St. Paul, who passes from the mystical state, in which he hardly knows if he is in the body or out of it, to the simple realities of daily life, ' Be not high-minded but condescend to lowly things.'

And, *secondly*, *Aspiration*, a sense of proportion as to our own capacities and possibilities. We have been thinking during this sermon about Teleiosis—our chance (if we humbly take it) of final perfection—and perhaps we have been inclined to smile as at the thought of something inconceivably remote ; for the most part, brethren, in moral and spiritual matters, lack of ambition is our principal temptation ; either we are timorous and despondent, or else we are self-satisfied—which equally means that we have set bounds to our aspirations for ourselves. To the Church at Corinth, which might have been thought almost too ambitious in these matters, St. Paul writes, ' Covet earnestly the best gifts.' [1] The consideration of the heavenly Teleiosis should help to deliver us from two dangers

[1] 1 Cor. xii. 31 ; the following words, ' And yet show I unto you a more excellent way,' modify but do not in any sense destroy the force of the first exhortation.

which beset our spiritual ambitions—Impatience and Self-centredness. We are in a hurry and we cannot put up with the long road and the hard training ; true, God's ways are not always gradual ; dull, plodding days are sometimes followed by moments of vision ; we must be ready for either method ; the slow progress must not make us discouraged, nor the sudden crisis find us unprepared.

And yet—I know how easily these well-balanced and polished antitheses translate themselves into stagnation when the time comes to carry them out. The blend of Christian colours (as Chesterton has said somewhere of the Middle Ages) is not a neutral tint, but some riotous contrast of black and gold ; to take one point only, our private devotions—for most of us the message of moderation and restraint, the exhortation to rein in our exuberance or to temper our ardour, all the nice balance between going forward and standing still, is not what is needed ; we need the call to go forward—the trumpet, not the flute. We are mostly the slaves of routine, narrow, unimaginative, without large horizons, saying the dull prayers we have always said, so sure that the heights of meditation and devotion are not for us. The consideration that we are meant for the heavenly life of perfection means that, in some sense and in different degrees, the heights *are* for us ; we too are 'partakers of the heavenly calling' ; we too must be worthy of 'the vocation wherewith we were called.'

But it remains true that the warning against impatience has also a meaning for us, for what else is slackness but a form of impatience, a fear that the task will be too long and too exacting? To advance calls for steadiness as well as for eagerness; the very fact that our perfection seems so distant is a test of all the manliness in us; there are ideals so near that we attain to them too easily; there are ideals so remote that we accept them as beautiful dreams—an escape from Reality rather than a way to it (the source of that degrading consolation by which we seek to atone for what we are by romantic representations of what we would like to have been); a true ideal is far enough off for unresting effort and near enough for unconquerable hope, and such is the ideal of eternal perfection seen from the world of Time. It should also keep us from self-centredness; it is sometimes said that the goal of self-perfection makes a man narrow and unsympathetic; it was an accusation levelled against the Stoics; 'Leave me undisturbed, while I become good' has sometimes seemed to be the paradoxical claim of the ascetic. The thought of the heavenly Teleiosis should cure us of any such mood; our goal is to be living members of the Church, militant here, expectant beyond the grave, triumphant at the last; when we have reached that stature, in which we can best serve God and our fellows, we desire to grow no more.

Lastly (to pass to the third application of these lectures), their subject-matter rightly considered should teach us a sense of proportion as to knowledge, that is, the right attitude to *mystery*. Mystery is the salt of life; a simple God or a simple Christianity would be profoundly dull; God is only simple in the sense of being wholly and completely what He is ; Christianity is only simple in the sense that it is too hard for everybody and so creates no separate categories of initiates.

To suppose Reality exhausted is the mark of a decadent age ; faith is a delighted acquiescence in mystery. This is no bar to intellectual research, for the more we know the more we are filled with wonder. This is a sign that Reality is not poor and starved, but so rich and varied that we shall never penetrate to its empty coffers. Nothing has been further from my intention than to use glib formulae (Platonic or other) in order to make the nature of Time and Eternity and their relation to one another either less difficult or less wonderful. Again and again I have sought relief, when the definitions and distinctions seemed too dusty and abstract, in analogies from art and music and poetry, that spring from fresh and living experience. Only, this awe in presence of the Unknown, without which religion would be a petty thing—this fascination before the unutterable, without which poetry would be only a self-complacent playing with words and syllables—must not be turned into a glorification of ignorance and obscurity. Just as true reverence has a place for this world as well as for the next, just as right aspiration has an eye for the next stage as well as for the distant goal, so a just sense of mystery does not relinquish the known in its thirst for the unknown. We do not want (to use a famous phrase) ‘ a God in the gaps,’ only brought in where human knowledge has broken down. A normal Christian consciousness has always felt the mystery of what is known as well as the assurance of what is not known. It has had moods of strangeness and exile in the midst of what is familiar as well as the sense of being at home in the spiritual world beyond. Phrases and analogics do not help us much ; we can only say that life is full of contradictions, moral and intellectual ; there are different roads to the appreciation of Reality and we do not see how they can ever meet. A narrow logic would say, 'Choose one, follow one ; the rest are blind alleys.' To the Christian they all meet, but somewhere higher up beyond our ardent gaze. This is involved in our initial act of faith, 'I believe in God.' But it is not so different from other acts of faith ; the scientist, too, believes that, beyond contradictory phenomena, Reality is somehow explicable ; the moralist believes that in spite of disappointment and failure the struggle is worth while. So, too, the mystery of the temporal and the eternal is somewhere resolved in an experience which loses nothing that is real in either.

I hope I have not been presumptuous in discussing matters which 'angels desire to look into' ; my desire has been only to take the soundings once again, to see where the great deep lies. Everywhere in us and around us the incomplete yearns towards what is perfect and has glimpses of it. Mysticism in its fully human sense (in the experience of the poet, the saint and the lover) is the sudden sense that beyond the changing appearances of Time there lies a life which does not change and which is our home.

APPENDICES

APPENDIX I

ON THE WORDS FOR 'ETERNAL' IN THE BIBLE

(Except where necessary, I have not repeated the examples given in the Second Lecture, pp. 35–45.)

(*a*) Hebrew Words

OLAM.

The old derivation of *olam* from 'lm (' hidden ') is now generally abandoned ; it has been suggested that it is connected with the Assyrian ullû(m), meaning ' yonder, remote.' [1]

As an adjective, it is used of land which has long lain desolate (Isa. lxi. 4, ' They shall build the old wastes ') and of the good old customs (Jer. vi. 16, ' Ask for the old paths ').

As an adverb, it means 'from of old' ; the giants were ' of old ' (Gen. vi. 4) ; the ancestors of Abraham dwelt ' of old time ' beyond the Euphrates (Jos. xxiv. 2) ; it is used of those who have been long dead (Ps. cxliii. 3) ; of God's lovingkindnesses which ' have been ever of old ' (Ps. xxv. 6) ; and of His judgments (Ps. cxix. 52) [2] ; Wisdom was ' set up from everlasting, or ever the earth was.' [3]

It occurs in the phrases ' the ancient mountains ' (Deut. xxxiii. 15) and ' the ages which were before us '

[1] This information was supplied by Mr. Driver of Magdalen.

[2] *Cp.* Is. lxiii. 16, ' Our Redeemer from everlasting is Thy Name.'

[3] See below, p. 239.

(Eccles. i. 10). It can also mean the indefinite future, and thus it gains the sense 'for ever'; it may refer to the duration of life, as in the hyperbolical address to the Persian King, 'Let the King live for ever' (Neh. ii. 3); there is, as a rule, no need to extend beyond an ordinary life such phrases as 'He that doeth these things shall never be moved' (Ps. xv. 5); 'They (God's saints) are preserved for ever' (Ps. xxxvii. 28); 'I will bless Thy name for ever and ever' (Ps. cxlv. 1); 'The righteous is an everlasting foundation' (Prov. x. 25); 'So shall I observe Thy Law continually for ever and ever' (Ps. cxix. 44).[1]

As there is not (except in the Book of Daniel) any idea in the Old Testament of the end of the universe, 'for ever' refers to the duration of the world; so Tyre shall 'never be found again' (Ezek. xxvi. 21); Jerusalem shall be 'perpetual desolations' (Jer. xxv. 9)[2]; Isaiah has his prophecies inscribed in a book, 'that it may be for the time to come for ever and ever' (Isa. xxx. 8); it is used of nations (Edom shall be 'cut off for ever,' Obad. 10), and of families ('I said that thy house . . . should walk before me for ever,' 1 Sam. ii. 30), and of national relations ('perpetual enmity' between Israel and Edom, Ezek. xxxv. 5).

Two striking uses with reference to God's Nature are (1) Isa. xxvi. 4, 'In the Lord Jehovah is an everlasting Rock' (A.V. mg. 'Rock of Ages'); and (2) Isa. lvii. 15, 'The High and Lofty One that inhabiteth eternity,' where our rendering comes from the LXX, *κατοικῶν τὸν αἰῶνα* (Vulg., 'habitans aeternitatem'); the Hebrew means 'that sittest enthroned for ever.'

When speaking of God's eternal attributes, the Old Testament refers them to His attitude towards Israel, 1 Kings x. 9, 'Because the Lord loved Israel for ever';

[1] Certain phrases in the Psalms, *e.g.* Ps. xli. 12, 'Thou settest me before Thy face for ever,' and Ps. lxxiii. 26, 'God is my portion for ever,' may possibly refer to a future life.

[2] As the prophet speaks of restoration, the epithet may be rhetorical.

Ps. lxxxix. 2, 'Mercy shall be built up for ever'; Ps. cxxxviii. 8, 'Thy Mercy, O Lord, endureth for ever'; Ps. civ. 31, 'Let the glory of the Lord' (as revealed in creation) 'endure for ever; let the Lord rejoice in His works'; Ps. cxvii. 2, 'The truth (*i.e.* trustworthiness) of the Lord endureth for ever'[1]; Exod. xv. 18, 'The Lord shall reign for ever and ever' (over His people); Mic. iv. 7, 'The Lord shall reign over them in Mount Zion from henceforth, even for ever.' His Covenant with Israel is everlasting (Gen. ix. 16), and of His Law it is said, 'For ever, O Lord, Thy word is settled in heaven' (Ps. cxix. 89).

In connection with the details of the Mosaic Law, the Shew-bread is holy to the Lord by a 'perpetual statute' (Lev. xxiv. 9); the words 'perpetual statute' and 'ordinance for ever' are used of the Passover (Exod. xii. 24), the lighting of the lamps (Exod. xxvii. 21), the Levitical priesthood (Exod. xxix. 9), the law against the eating of blood (Lev. iii. 17), the Sabbath (Lev. xvi. 31), the offering of first-fruits (Lev. xxiii. 41), the sounding of the trumpets (Num. x. 8), the 'water of separation' (Num. xix. 21) and the Temple (1 Kings ix. 3). One can see how texts like these would give pause to a scrupulous Jewish Christian; it was to such people that the writer of the Epistle to the Hebrews addressed himself, showing that these outward ordinances were the shadows of what was really eternal.[2]

So the promises of God stand fast 'for ever' (Isa. xl. 8), especially His promises to David: 'The throne of David shall be established before the Lord for ever' (1 Kings ii. 45); Palestine is given to the chosen people as an 'everlasting possession' (Gen. xlviii. 4).

Special phrases—some of them liturgical—are 'Blessed be the Lord, the God of Israel, from everlasting even to

[1] *Cp.* Ps. cxlvi. 6, 'Which keepeth truth for ever.'

[2] He was much helped by his exegesis of Ps. cx. 4; against the promises of perpetuity to the Levitical priesthood he could quote, 'Thou art a priest for ever after the order of Melchizedek.'

everlasting' (1 Chron. xvi. 36); and 'We will bless the Lord from this time forth and for evermore' (Ps. cxv. 18).

Death is spoken of as 'a perpetual sleep' (Jer. li. 39) and our 'long home' (Eccles. xii. 5)—a jewel of translation (LXX has *εἰς οἶκον αἰῶνος αὐτοῦ*; Vulg., 'in domum aeternitatis suae').[1] Only in Daniel do we find the resurrection to 'everlasting life' and 'everlasting contempt' (Dan. xii. 2), but the conception is already apocalyptic. We may sum up by saying that *olam* denotes what lasts through ages—'secular' in the old sense of the word, where the horizon recedes according to the context; it may mean the past lying far back or the future lying far before. In the plural[2] it generally means duration, sometimes including past and future; there is as yet no idea of a division of history into periods or ages; the word still denotes great ranges of time, undefined.

QEDHEM.

This word means originally 'in front' or 'in the east' and so 'aforetime'; a good example of the three

[1] Eccles. iii. 11 has 'He hath set the world in their heart, yet so that man cannot find out the work that God hath done from the beginning even to the end'; R.V. mg. has 'eternity' for 'world' (LXX, *σύμπαντα τὸν αἰῶνα*. Vulg., 'mundum tradidit disputationi eorum'). The word is *olam*, and if it means 'eternity' would imply human longing for a larger and fuller life; but Peake (*Com.*, p. 413) suggests *elem*—something hidden; 'God, jealous lest man should rival Him, has set ignorance in his heart'; the Hebrew dictionary prefers 'the world' in the sense of the duration of the world; the R.V. 'yet' suggests that, though we know 'the world,' the beginning and ending of things are shut out from our view.

[2] The plural is probably intensive, a kind of plural of majesty to heighten the effect. Examples are: Is. xxvi. 4, 'Rock of Ages'; Dan. ix. 24, 'everlasting righteousness' (of the ages); Ps. lxi. 4, 'I will dwell in Thy tabernacle for ever' (for the ages); Ps. lxxvii. 8, 'is His mercy clean gone for ever?'; 1 Kings viii. 13, 'a place for Thee to dwell in for ever'; Ps. cxlv. 13, 'Thy Kingdom is an everlasting kingdom' (of the ages); Is. xlv. 17, 'Israel shall be saved with an everlasting salvation.'

different senses is Job xxiii. 8 ; the R.V. has 'Behold, I go *forward*, but He is not there' ; the LXX has εἰ γὰρ πρῶτος πορεύσομαι ; the Vulgate has 'Si ad orientem iero, non apparet.' [1] It is used in Ps. lxxiv. 12, 'God is my King of old' (LXX, πρὸ αἰῶνος ; Vulg., 'ante saecula'), and it would seem to have little connection with the subject of eternity, if it were not for the important text Prov. viii. 22, 23. The R.V. has 'The Lord possessed me (*i.e.* Wisdom) (mg. 'formed me') in the *beginning* of His way' (mg. 'as the beginning' ; LXX, ἀρχὴν ὁδῶν ; Vulg., 'In initio viarum suarum'),

'Before His works of old (mg. 'the first of').
I was set up from everlasting (*olam*),
From the beginning (Vulg., 'ex antiquis' ; LXX, πρὸ τοῦ αἰῶνος),
Or ever the earth was.'

The words italicised stand for *qedhem* in its sense of 'beginning' ; there has been much controversy as to whether Wisdom is represented as co-eternal with God. Peake says in his *Commentary* (p. 401), 'Wisdom is not conceived as eternally coexistent with God, but as formed before Creation to be the instrument of creation.' On the other hand, the *New Commentary* says (p. 387), 'It is difficult to see how "created me" could be right, for Wisdom must be an eternal attribute of God. . . . Dr. Burney renders "The Lord begat me as the beginning of His way, the antecedent of His works, of old."'

NECAH.

This word means primarily 'eminence' and so everlastingness or perpetuity ; so in 1 Sam. xv. 29, 'The strength of Israel will not lie nor repent' ; the A.V. has in the margin 'Eternity' ; the R.V. margin has 'Victory

[1] *Cp.* also Is. ii. 6, 'they be filled with customs from the east' (LXX has ἐνεπλήσθη ὡς τὸ ἀπ' ἀρχῆς ; Vulg. has 'ut olim'), and Ps. lxviii. 33, 'The heavens of heavens, which are of old' (LXX, κατὰ ἀνατολάς ; Vulg., 'ad orientem').

or Glory'; the Vulgate 'Triumphator.'[1] It is used of life as enduring, *cp*. Lam. iii. 18, 'My strength is perished,' lit. 'my endurance doth vanish'[2]; it can mean endurance in time, *e.g*. Prov. xxi. 28, 'The man that heareth shall speak unchallenged' (mg. 'so as to endure')[3]; so, as *La-necal*, it is used as 'for ever.'

Two curious examples of the ambiguity of the word are Hab. i. 4, 'Judgment doth *never* go forth' (*i.e.* just sentences are not rendered), where the margin has 'goeth not forth unto victory,' and Isa. xxv. 8, 'He hath swallowed up death *for ever*,' where the LXX has κατεπόθη ὁ θάνατος εἰς νῖκος, so familiar to us from its quotation by St. Paul in 1 Cor. xv. 54.

'AD AND WA 'EDH

are defined in the *Oxford Dictionary* as 'Noun masculine. Perpetuity (= advancing time).' It can be used of past time, as in Job xx. 4, 'Knowest thou not this of old?' (LXX, ἀπὸ τοῦ ἔτι; Vulg., 'a principio'), but more often of indefinitely receding time, as in Prov. xxix. 14, '(The King's) throne shall be established for ever.' Job wishes that his words 'were graven in the rock for ever' (xix. 24); it is used of God's righteousness enduring 'for ever' (Ps. cxi. 3), of the King's 'length of days for ever and ever' (Ps. xxi. 4); Ps. xlviii. 14 has 'God will be our guide even unto death' (R.V. mg. 'according to some ancient authorities, "for evermore"').

(*b*) Greek Words

Αἰών, Αἰώνιος in classical and Hellenistic Greek.

The translators of the Septuagint chose the Greek word *αἰών* to render the Hebrew *olam*, and it will be convenient to begin by discussing the use of this word

[1] LXX has a different reading: διαιρεθήσεται εἰς δύο.
[2] LXX has ἀπώλετο νῖκός μου.
[3] Vulg. has 'Vir obediens loquetur *victoriam*.'

(and its adjectival form *αἰώνιος*) in extra Biblical usage.[1]

The word *αἰών* is used in Homer of human life regarded as a span allotted to each man ; so in *Iliad*, iv. 478 f. :

> *μινυνθάδιος δέ οἱ αἰὼν*
> *ἔπλεθ' ὑπ' Αἴαντος μεγαθύμου δουρὶ δαμέντι,*[2]

and in *Iliad*, v. 685 :

> *ἔπειτά με καὶ λίποι αἰὼν*
> *ἐν πόλει ὑμετέρῃ.*[3]

We find the same use in the papyri, *e.g.*

Θεωρήσατε ἕνα ἀπ' αἰῶνος ἀπαγόμενον ('Behold one led off from life, *i.e.* to death ').[4]

Plato uses it for eternity, as in the famous phrase in the *Timaeus*, in which Time is described as *εἰκὼ κινητόν τινα αἰῶνος*[5] ; the idea is still that of indefiniteness ; the duration of human life cannot be measured beforehand, and in the same way the duration of eternity has no end and no beginning.

Αἰών itself is thought of as divisible into *χρόνοι* or *περίοδοι.*[6]

Aristotle is inclined to bring down *Αἰών* from the supra-celestial sphere and connect it with the indefinite duration of the Cosmos : *ὅτι μὲν οὖν οὔτε γέγονεν ὁ πᾶς*

[1] I need hardly say that I do not speak with the authority of a scholar in the case of either Greek or Hebrew ; I have had to rely upon lexicons, especially in the case of Hebrew, which I do not know at all.

[2] 'For short his term of life, By Godlike Ajax' mighty spear subdued ' (Lord Derby's translation).

[3] 'Then in your city let me end my days ' (Sarpedon to Hector).

[4] *Ox. Pap.* 33 iii. 9 (Moulton and Milligan, p. 16).

[5] 37 *d.*

[6] So Timaeus, a fourth-century Pythagorean, says (97 *c*, *d*) : *Χρόνω δὲ τὰ μέρεα τάσδε τὰς περιόδως λέγοντι, ἃς ἐκόσμησεν ὁ θεὸς σὺν κόσμῳ· οὐ γὰρ ἦν πρὸ κόσμω ἄστρα, διόπερ οὐδ' ἐνιαυτὸς οὐδ' ὡρᾶν περίοδοι, αἷς μετρέεται ὁ γεννατὸς χρόνος οὗτος· εἰκὼν δέ ἐστι τῶ ἀγεννάτω χρόνω, ὃν αἰῶνα ποταγορεύομες· ὡς γὰρ ποτ' ἀΐδιον παράδειγμα τὸν ἰδανικὸν κόσμον ὅδε ὁ ὠρανὸς ἐγεννάθη, οὕτως ὡς πρὸς παράδειγμα τὸν αἰῶνα ὅδε ὁ χρόνος σὺν κόσμῳ ἐδαμιουργήθη.*

οὐρανὸς οὔτ' ἐνδέχεται φθαρῆναι . . ἀλλ' ἔστιν εἷς καὶ ἀΐδιος, ἀρχὴν μὲν καὶ τελευτὴν οὐκ ἔχων τοῦ παντὸς αἰωνος, ἔχων δὲ καὶ περιέχων ἐν αὑτῷ τὸν ἄπειρον χρόνον.[1]

In more popular literature *αἰών* could be used (as in Hebrew) of vast and indefinite ranges of time whether in the past or in the future. Menander has *αἰὼν γίγνεται*, ' 'tis an age '[2]; Longinus speaks of *τοὺς ἀπ' αἰῶνος ῥήτορας*,[3] ' the orators of old '; sometimes it is used in the plural: *μόνος τῶν ἀπ' αἰώνων νικήσας*, in an Olympian record of victory; in Diodorus we have *τὴν ἐξ αἰῶνος ἀρχὴν λαβόν* (of the temple of Venus), also *τοὺς ἐξ αἰῶνος βασιλεῖς* and *τὴν ἐξ αἰῶνος παραδεδομένην ἐλευθερίαν*; it is used of the future in Isocrates: *τοὺς δὲ μετ' εὐσεβείας καὶ δικαιοσύνης ζῶντας ὁρῶ ἔν τε τοῖς παροῦσι χρόνοις ἀσφαλῶς διάγοντας καὶ περὶ τοῦ σύμπαντος αἰῶνος ἡδίους τὰς ἐλπίδας ἔχοντας.*[4] At public meetings the cry of loyalty was *Ἄγουστοι κύριοι εἰς τὸν αἰῶνα*[5]; the Greek Anthology has *εἰς αἰῶνας*, and Sextus Empiricus *εἰς αἰῶνα διαμένει.*[6]

Meanwhile in philosophers like Plotinus and in religious rites the word maintains its strict sense of ' eternity.' *Αἰών* was a god, whose mysteries were celebrated at Alexandria from 200 B.C. A Mithraic inscription runs[7]: *Αἰὼν ὁ αὐτὸς ἐν τοῖς αὐτοῖς ἀεὶ φύσει θείᾳ μένων, κόσμος τε εἷς κατὰ τὰ αὐτά, ὁποῖος ἔστι καὶ ἦν καὶ ἔσται, ἀρχὴν μεσότητα τέλος οὐκ ἔχων, μεταβολῆς ἀμέτοχος, θείας φύσεως ἐργάτης αἰωνίου (κατὰ) πάντα.* Epictetus uses the word in the sense of ' divine being ': *οὐ γάρ εἰμι αἰών, ἀλλ' ἄνθρωπος, μέρος τῶν πάντων ὡς ὥρα ἡμέρας,*[8] and Epicurus in the sense of ' eternity ': *τοὺς ὑπὲρ τοῦ αἰῶνος φόβους.*[9]

As an adjective, *αἰώνιος* is probably not to be distinguished too sharply from *ἀΐδιος*. The latter is the more stately word, and perhaps rather the more metaphysical, as *αἰώνιος* is somewhat negative (timeless, un-

[1] *De Caelo*, ii. 283 *b*.
[2] Men., 36 (5).
[3] 34.
[4] 8. 34.
[5] *Ox. Pap.*, 41. 30.
[6] *Adv. Phys.*, 1. 62.
[7] *Syll.*³ 1125.
[8] 2. 5. 13.
[9] *Sent.* 20.

limited). Plato speaks of οἱ ἀΐδιοι θεοί,[1] while the φύσις of the παράδειγμα is called διαιωνία.[2] Aristotle prefers ἀΐδιος; cp. *Ethics*, 1096, *b*. 3 : τῷ ἀΐδιον εἶναι (by the fact of being eternal); 1139, *b*. 23 : τὸ ἐπιστητὸν ἀΐδιον . . . τὰ γὰρ ἐξ ἀνάγκης ὄντα ἁπλῶς πάντα ἀΐδια, τὰ δ᾽ ἀΐδια ἀγένητα καὶ ἄφθαρτα; 1111, *b*. 32 : τὰ ἀΐδια καὶ τὰ ἀδύνατα (what we cannot alter); so 1112, *a*. 21 : περὶ δὴ τῶν ἀϊδίων οὐδεὶς βουλεύεται; *Pol.*, 1299, *a*. 8 : τὰς ἀρχὰς ἀϊδίους (perpetual, for life); στρατηγία (1285, *a*. 8); βασιλεία (1301, *b*. 27); cp. *De Anima*, II. 7. 3: ἐν τῷ ἀϊδίῳ τῷ ἄνω σώματι (the everlasting empyrean essence, the upper heaven); cp. *De Caelo*, 270, *b*. 23, where αἰθήρ is derived ἀπὸ τοῦ θεῖν ἀεὶ τὸν ἀΐδιον χρόνον. In looser language, both the words could be used of more or less prolonged duration; an inscription ascribes τιμὰς ἀϊδίους to Berenice,[3] and Josephus says ἐφυλάχθη ὁ Ἰωάννης δεσμοῖς αἰωνίοις (perpetual imprisonment).[4] Αἰωνιότης finally becomes an official title for the Emperor.[5]

The Mystery Religions helped, of course, to popularise the idea of an 'everlasting' life after death.[6]

The Septuagint.

In translating *olam*, when it occurs in the phrase 'days of old,' the LXX has either αἰώνιος or τοῦ αἰῶνος[7]; αἰώνιος is used for the land long desolate,[8]

[1] *Tim.*, 37 *c*. [2] 38 *b*.

[3] *OGIS.*, 56. 54. [4] *B.J.*, 6. 9. 4.

[5] *Conc. Chalc.* ii. 40 *d*, Letter of Theodosius, ἡ ἡμετέρα ἔγνω αἰωνιότης.

[6] 'One recipient (of the fourth century A.D.) states that he is 'taurobolio criobolioque' (by the Bull-bath and Ram-bath) '*in aeternum* renatus.' The earlier belief limited the efficacy of the rite to 20 years. . . . Does it represent rather the hope of the devotee than any dogma? Is it influenced by Christianity?' (*Essays on the Trinity and Incarnation*, p. 119).

[7] Is. lxiii. 11, 'He remembered the days of old' (ἡμερῶν αἰωνίων); Is. lxiii. 9, 'He . . . carried them all the days of old' (πάσας τὰς ἡμέρας τοῦ αἰῶνος); Deut. xxxii. 7, 'Remember the days of old' (ἡμέρας αἰῶνος).

[8] ἐρήμους αἰωνίας (Is. lxi. 4).

and the ancient landmark[1]; 'which were of old' is ἀπὸ τοῦ αἰῶνος[2]; 'the people of old time' is λαὸν αἰῶνος[3]; in Deut. xxxiii. 15 'the everlasting hills' appear as βουνῶν ἀενάων.[4]

As Greek equivalents for the phrase 'for ever' we find :

εἰς τὸν αἰῶνα (Deut. xv. 17).
ἕως αἰῶνος (1 Sam. i. 22).
διὰ παντός (Lev. xxv. 32).
εἰς αἰῶνα (Ps. xli. 12).
εἰς αἰῶνα αἰῶνος (Ps. xxi. 6).
εἰς τὸν αἰῶνα καὶ εἰς τὸν αἰῶνα τοῦ αἰῶνος (Ps. cxlv. 1).
εἰς τὸν αἰῶνα καὶ ἐπέκεινα (Micah iv. 5).
ἔτι εἰς τὸν αἰῶνα (Ezek. xxvi. 21).
ἕως εἰς τὸν αἰῶνα (Deut. xxiii. 3).
εἰς τὸν αἰῶνα χρόνον (Isa. xiv. 20).
ἕως τοῦ αἰῶνος (Isa. xxxii. 17).
τὸν αἰῶνα καὶ ἐπ' αἰῶνα καὶ ἔτι (Exod. xv. 18).
εἰς γενεὰς αἰωνίους (Gen. ix. 12).
δι' αἰῶνος (Isa. lx. 21).
εἰς τέλος (Job xiv. 20).
τὸν αἰῶνα (Prov. x. 30).
εἰς τὸν αἰῶνα τοῦ αἰῶνος (Ps. lxxxix. 29).
αἰῶνος (1 Kings viii. 13).
εἰς τοὺς αἰῶνας καὶ ἔτι (Dan. xii. 3).

Two points should be noted here.

The curious addition of ἔτι after εἰς τὸν αἰῶνα suggests that the *olam* itself has limits, as do also the phrases πρὸ αἰῶνος[5] and πρὸ τοῦ αἰῶνος.[6]

The Hebrew had strengthened the phrase by saying 'to the Age of the Age' or 'to the Ages,' the plural

[1] μὴ μέταιρε ὅρια αἰώνια (Prov. xxii. 28).
[2] οἱ γίγαντες οἱ ἀπ' αἰῶνος (Gen. vi. 4, the Nephilim).
[3] Ezek. xxvi. 20.
[4] *Cp.* 2 Macc. vii. 36, 'a short pain that bringeth everlasting life, (mg. 'a short pain of ever-flowing life'), from νάω or νέω, to flow, float, swim, πόνον ἀενάου ζωῆς.
[5] Ps. lxxiv. 12, 'God is my King of old' (Vulg., 'ante saecula').
[6] Prov. viii. 22.

being an intensive form, like Elohim for God,[1] but the Greek had no such idiom ; in Greek, therefore, the plural (and the definite article) may have helped the idea that history was divided into ages which we find in apocalyptic speculation.[2]

THE APOCRYPHA, PHILO, JOSEPHUS, ETC.

In the case of the Apocrypha and the Apocalyptists, it is necessary to distinguish the writings of the Second and First Centuries B.C. [3] ; the Second Century writers still believe in a Messianic Age on earth after the Day of Judgment ; the First Century writers, feeling that the earth is unfit for the coming of God's Kingdom, suppose an ever-shortened Messianic Age on earth *followed by* the Day of Judgment and the coming of the Heavenly Kingdom.

SECOND CENTURY B.C.

In Daniel, *ζωὴ αἰώνιος* means the Life of the Age—God's Kingdom on earth ; the Kingdom is itself perpetual, but individuals in it do not necessarily live for ever ; in Enoch i–xxxvi, the righteous eat of the Tree of Life, live as long as the patriarchs of old, and have a thousand children.[4] In x. 10 *εἰς τὸν αἰῶνα* is 500 years, and in x. 5 it stands for 70 generations. The Messianic Kingdom is distinguished as *ὁ αἰὼν ὁ*

[1] The double plural ' to the ages of the ages ' is said not to occur before the New Testament.

[2] *Cp.* Is. ix. 6, ' Everlasting Father ' (mg. ' Father of Eternity ') is, in the LXX, *πατὴρ αἰῶνος* or *πατὴρ τοῦ μέλλοντος αἰῶνος* (Vulg., ' futuri saeculi ').

For liturgical forms of blessing we have *εἰς τὸν αἰῶνα καὶ εἰς τὸν αἰῶνα τοῦ αἰῶνος* (Ps. cvi. 48), and in ordinary contexts *ἐξ αἰῶνος καὶ ἕως αἰῶνος* (Jer. vii. 7), *ἀπὸ τοῦ νῦν καὶ ἕως εἰς τὸν αἰῶνα* (Micah iv. 7), *ἀπὸ τοῦ νῦν καὶ εἰς τὸν αἰῶνα* (Is. lix. 21).

[3] Having no authority for myself to speak in these matters, I use (for the dating of these works) Dr. Charles' *Between the Old and New Testaments.*

[4] Charles, *op. cit.*, p. 54.

μέγας ; *cp*. xvi. 1 : μέχρις ἡμέρας τελειώσεως τῆς κρίσεως τῆς μεγάλης ἐν ᾗ ὁ αἰὼν ὁ μέγας τελεσθήσεται.[1] In xx. 9–13 sinners who have not been punished on earth remain 'in great pain, till the Great Day of Judgment . . . for ever'; on that Day they rise to bodily torments; those who have received punishment on earth shall not be punished on the Day, nor shall they be raised from Sheol.[2]

The Book of Ecclesiasticus has ὁ θεὸς τῶν αἰώνων,[3] and in the first verse we read πᾶσα σοφία παρὰ Κυρίου καὶ μετ' αὐτοῦ ἐστὶν εἰς τὸν αἰῶνα (for ever).[4] In xviii. 10 we have ὡς σταγὼν ὕδατος ἀπὸ θαλάσσης καὶ ψῆφος ἄμμου, οὕτως ὀλίγα ἔτη ἐν ἡμέρᾳ αἰῶνος : 'As a drop of water from the sea, and a pebble from the sand; so are a few years (of our lives) in (that is, compared with) the day of eternity.' The word here must refer to the everlasting duration of God ; we cannot refer it to the Messianic Age.

In Tobit iv. 12 we have 'Noah, Abraham . . . our fathers of old time' (οἱ πατέρες ἡμῶν ἀπὸ τοῦ αἰῶνος) ; in xiii. 6, ὑψώσατε τὸν βασιλέα τῶν αἰώνων, while in iii. 6 Sheol is described as 'the everlasting place' (τὸν αἰώνιον τόπον).

In Susanna, God is addressed as ὁ θεὸς ὁ αἰώνιος ὁ τῶν κρυπτῶν γνώστης, ὁ εἰδὼς τὰ πάντα πρὶν γενέσεως αὐτῶν (verse 42). In Jubilees v. 10 'for ever' seems to refer to the period before the coming of the Kingdom.[5]

First Century B.C.

Here it is sometimes difficult to know whether the writers mean the earthly Messianic Kingdom or the heavenly Kingdom which follows.

[1] Quoted Sanday and Headlam, *Romans*, p. 354. *Cp*. Dan. ix. 7, συντέλεια καιρῶν ; xii. 13, συντέλεια ἡμερῶν.

[2] Charles, *Between the Old and New Testaments*, p. 122.

[3] xxxvi. 19. [4] i. 1.

[5] 'Until the Day of the great condemnation, when judgment is executed.'

1 Esdras (ii. 23) speaks of *οἱ Ἰουδαῖοι ἀποστάται καὶ πολιορκίας συνεσταμένοι ἐν αὐτῇ* (Jerusalem) *ἔτι ἐξ αἰῶνος* (hardly a generation before). In 2 Macc. i. 25 God is spoken of as *παντοκράτωρ καὶ αἰώνιος* ; the seven Jewish martyrs hope for an *αἰώνιον ἀναβίωσιν ζωῆς* (vii. 9) ; as in verse 36 we have *ἀενάου ζωῆς* (everflowing life), the meaning is probably in both cases 'everlasting.'

FIRST CENTURY A.D.

4 Macc. describes the torture of the wicked (x. 15), *μὰ τὸν αἰώνιον τοῦ τυράννου ὄλεθρον*, and (xii. 12) *ταμιεύεταί σε ἡ θεία δίκη πυκνοτέρῳ καὶ αἰωνίῳ πυρὶ καὶ βασάνοις, αἳ εἰς ὅλον τὸν αἰῶνα οὐκ ἀνήσουσίν σε.* This might mean 'for the duration of the Kingdom on earth,' but, as the Day of Judgment seems to have passed, it probably means everlasting punishment in Sheol.

1 Baruch (iv. 8) has *ἐπελάθεσθε τὸν τροφεύσαντα ὑμᾶς θεὸν αἰώνιον* ; in 2 Baruch xl. 3, the 'principate (of the Messiah) will stand *for ever*, until the world of corruption is at an end,' where the phrase refers to the temporary Messianic Kingdom.

In the *Sibylline Oracles* (3. 50) the Messianic Kingdom stands 'for all ages,' *i.e.* till the Universal Judgment; the *Secrets of Enoch* (33. 2) has the interesting statement 'In the beginning of the eighth millennium there is no reckoning of time.' [1]

In 4 Esdras the earthly Kingdom is to last only 400 years and a privileged few are to have a 'first resurrection' to enjoy it (vii. 28–9).

But 'Dabo eis tabernacula aeterna, quae praeparaveram illis' probably refers to the Heavenly Kingdom after the Judgment.[2]

Ἀΐδιος occurs in the Platonic Book of Wisdom in its full

[1] *Cp.* Rev. x. 6, *χρόνος οὐκέτι ἔσται*, which may, however, mean 'There shall be no more interval before the Day' (Scott, *Commentary*, p. 214).

[2] 5 Esdras, ii. 11 (quoted Plummer, *St. Luke*, p. 386).

philosophical sense ; Wisdom is ἀπαύγασμα φωτὸς ἀϊδίου (vii. 26) ; in ii. 23 some read a phrase which recalls the *Timaeus*, ὁ θεὸς ἔκτισε τὸν ἄνθρωπον εἰκόνα τῆς ἰδίας ἀϊδιότητος (' God made man as an image of His own everlastingness '), but others omit the α and read ἰδιότητος, ' His own proper Being.' Αἰών appears as ' the course of the world ' in xiii. 9 : εἰ γὰρ τοσοῦτον ἴσχυσαν εἰδέναι ἵνα δύνωνται στοιχάσασθαι τὸν αἰῶνα ; it refers to the beauty and grandeur of Nature, ' The things that they look upon are beautiful ' ; (v. 7). . . . ' If they had power to know so much, that they should be able to explore the course of things ' (R.V. mg. Or, ' life ' or ' the world ') ' how is it that they did not sooner find the Sovereign Lord of these His works ? '

The word is also used in a rather new sense as ' the coming generations of men,' *e.g.* xiv. 6 : ἀπέλιπεν τῷ αἰῶνι σπέρμα γενέσεως (The Ark ' left to the race of men ' (mg. ' future time ') ' a seed of generations to come '); and xviii. 4 : δι' ὧν ἤμελλε τὸ ἄφθαρτον νόμου φῶς τῷ αἰῶνι δίδοσθαι (' Through whom (the Israelites) the incorruptible light of the Law was to be given to the race of men ' (mg. ' future time ')).

Philo (also Platonic) uses ' eternal ' for the supersensuous world—the κόσμος νοητός ; αἰών is spoken of as πᾶς, μακρός, μήκιστος, ἄπειρος, πολύς ; such phrases as δι' αἰῶνος, πρὸ αἰῶνος, ἐξ αἰῶνος occur more loosely. Eternal life is (some fifty times) ζωὴ ἀΐδιος, but αἰώνιος is used of ζωή, as also of κόλασις and θεός.[1]

Josephus uses ἀπ' αἰῶνος (' from the beginning of the world,' *B.J.*, 1. 1. 4), δι' αἰῶνος (' through all ages,' *B.J.*, 6. 2. 1), εἰς αἰῶνα (' always,' *Ant.*, 4. 8. 18), ἐξ αἰῶνος (' from the beginning of the world,' *B.J.*, 5. 10. 5) ; αἰών is used of eternity (*B.J.*, 1. 21. 10 : Herod desires to transmit the memory of his family and friends to eternity), and, in a curious mixture of Greek thought and Hebrew idiom, of the periods of reincarnation

[1] See references in Grimm-Thayer, *New Testament Lexicon.*

(ἐκ περιτροπῆς αἰώνων, *B.J.*, 3. 8. 5, 'in the revolution of ages these souls are again sent into pure bodies'). *Αἰώνιος* is used of happiness after death (*B.J.*, 1. 33. 2), of the worship of God on earth (*B.J.*, 6. 2. 1), of endless fame (*B.J.*, 3. 8. 5), and of perpetual imprisonment (*B.J.*, 6. 9. 4 ; δεσμοῖς αἰωνίοις of John). His usage is eclectic and characteristic of Josephus' type of mind.

The general conclusions seem to be :

(1) αἰών and αἰῶνες still refer to long and undefined periods of time, especially to that which precedes the Day of Judgment ;

(2) αἰών is not yet technical for the Messianic Age, and εἰς τὸν αἰῶνα seems to have no special reference to it ;

(3) αἰώνιος never seems to mean 'belonging to the Messianic Kingdom,' nor 'lasting for a (defined) aeon.'

NEW TESTAMENT.

A word first as to the two occurrences of ἀΐδιος.

In Rom. i. 20 St. Paul says that the works of creation bear witness to God's ἀΐδιος δύναμις καὶ θειότης ; the contrast is clear between the perishable world and the Divine everlastingness ; it is just possible that St. Paul avoids the use of αἰώνιος because, in the passage he has in mind (Wisd. xiii. 9), the word αἰών is used in the sense of 'the course of the world' (see p. 248).

In the other passage, Jude v. 6, we have : ἀπολιπόντας τὸ ἴδιον οἰκητήριον (ἀγγέλους) εἰς κρίσιν μεγάλης ἡμέρας δεσμοῖς ἀϊδίοις ὑπὸ ζόφον τετήρηκεν ; had the word used been αἰώνιος, we might have translated it 'chains belonging to the Age preceding the Day of Judgment,' but ἀΐδιος never has such a meaning ; we should therefore perhaps render it 'age-long' and compare it with Josephus' δεσμοῖς αἰωνίοις.

We shall now consider the use of αἰών and αἰώνιος in each book of the New Testament. It may be well to remind ourselves of three possible meanings of αἰώνιος : (*a*) lasting for ever ; (*b*) indefinite—without defined end—

age-long ; (*c*) belonging to an age or aeon, especially to the Messianic Age.[1]

In St. Matthew we have *εἰς τοὺς αἰῶνας* in the (? interpolated) doxology to the Lord's Prayer (vi. 13), and we have (negatively) in the curse on the barren fig tree *οὐ μηκέτι ἐκ σοῦ καρπὸς γένηται εἰς τὸν αἰῶνα* (xxi. 19). The Ages have become definitely two, *e.g.* *οὐκ ἀφεθήσεται αὐτῷ οὔτε ἐν τούτῳ τῷ αἰῶνι* (the time before the Judgment) *οὔτε ἐν τῷ μέλλοντι* (xii. 32). This Age means the present world with its cares and attractions (*ἡ μέριμνα τοῦ αἰῶνος*, xiii. 22) ; it will be summed up or completed at the Day of Judgment (xiii. 39, *ὁ θερισμὸς συντέλεια τοῦ αἰῶνός ἐστιν* ; *cp.* xiii. 40, 49, xxviii. 20).

Αἰώνιος occurs twice of the fire reserved for unbelievers (xviii. 8, xxv. 41), once of their punishment (xxv. 46), twice of eternal life (xix. 16, xxv. 46). There is no reason here to desert the ordinary Greek sense of indefinite duration, and in this case (though not in all cases) the context certainly suggests that it means everlasting.

St. Mark (iii. 29) has the remarkable phrase : *οὐκ ἔχει ἄφεσιν εἰς τὸν αἰῶνα, ἀλλὰ ἔνοχός ἐστιν αἰωνίου ἁμαρτήματος* ; some (with an eye on Matt. xii. 32) have translated, ' he is in the grip of a sin which extends beyond this *αἰών*, the consequences of which reach to the future *αἰών*.'

This is possible, but it seems more natural to take the second part of the phrase as a restatement of the first in positive form. Now in the first part *εἰς τὸν αἰῶνα*

[1] Dr. Liddon (*Sermons in St. Paul's*, p. 184, n. 2) says : ' In the LXX *αἰώνιος*, like *αἰών*, when applied to future time, varies with the senses of *olam* . . . but when the Gospel had brought life and immortality to light more distinctly, the word *αἰώνιος* was limited (within the precincts of the New Testament) to the idea (taken at the lowest) of indefinite continuance ' ; he only admits Philemon v. 15 and Jude v. 7 as possibly having a ' limited meaning.' In the text of the sermon he is more severe. ' In the New Testament there is a substantive which varies with the various meanings of the Hebrew word, but there is also an adjective derived from that substantive which, at least as used in the New Testament, does not vary, but means what we English mean by " everlasting." '

would seem to mean 'for ever' (*cp.* xi. 14 of the fig tree, μηκέτι εἰς τὸν αἰῶνα).

In x. 30 we have νῦν ἐν τῷ καιρῷ τούτῳ . . ., καὶ ἐν τῷ αἰῶνι τῷ ἐρχομένῳ.[1] Besides uses which are parallel to St. Matthew, we have τῆς αἰωνίου σωτηρίας in the alternative ending of the Gospel.[2]

St. Luke has εἰς τοὺς αἰῶνας for the prophesied kingdom of the Messiah (i. 33) and εἰς τὸν αἰῶνα for the promise to Abraham and his seed (i. 55); in the Benedictus he has τῶν ἁγίων ἀπ' αἰῶνος προφητῶν (i. 70). In xx. 34 ὁ αἰὼν οὗτος is contrasted with τοῦ αἰῶνος ἐκείνου (the only use of this phrase in the New Testament); in the parable of the Unjust Steward we have οἱ υἱοὶ τοῦ αἰῶνος τούτου, and in contrast the sons of light are to look forward to αἰωνίους σκηνάς (xvi. 8, 9); as σκηναί means emphatically temporary dwellings,[3] the epithet (by contrast) implies that they are eternal.

In St. John's Gospel εἰς τὸν αἰῶνα is the usual phrase; it is used eschatologically seven times.[4] It is used twice of the Christ (viii. 35), ὁ υἱὸς μένει (ἐν τῇ οἰκίᾳ) εἰς τὸν αἰῶνα, where the reference is probably to Isaac remaining when Ishmael was cast out, and xii. 34, where the crowd say they have heard from the Scriptures that ὁ Χριστὸς μένει εἰς τὸν αἰῶνα—a reference to prophecies of an everlasting Messianic Kingdom.[5]

[1] καιρός would not naturally be used of the future age; *cp.* Matt. xvi. 3, σημεῖα τῶν καιρῶν; Eph. i. 10, τοῦ πληρώματος τῶν καιρῶν; Rev. xii. 14, καιρὸν καὶ καιροὺς καὶ ἥμισυ καιροῦ (three and a half years). 'καιρός is a definitely limited portion of time, with the added notion of suitableness'; in modern Greek it means 'weather' (*New Testament Lexicon*). It can be used of the Day of Judgment, πρὸ καιροῦ βασανίσαι (the evil spirits in Matt. viii. 29), ἐν καιρῷ τοῦ θερισμοῦ (Matt. xiii. 30).

[2] τὸ ἱερὸν καὶ ἄφθαρτον κήρυγμα τῆς αἰωνίου σωτηρίας; ἄφθαρτον seems to show that the meaning is 'eternal.'

[3] It has this force in Heb. xi. 9.

[4] οὐ μὴ διψήσει (iv. 14), ζήσει (vi. 51, 58), θάνατον οὐ μὴ θεωρήσῃ (viii. 51), οὐ μὴ γεύσηται θανάτου (viii. 52), οὐ μὴ ἀπόλωνται (x. 28), οὐ μὴ ἀποθάνῃ (xi. 26), all followed by εἰς τὸν αἰῶνα.

[5] *Cp.* 1 John ii. 17, ὁ ποιῶν τὸ θέλημα τοῦ θεοῦ μένει εἰς τὸν αἰῶνα.

In the weakened negative sense St. Peter says that Our Lord shall never wash his feet *εἰς τὸν αἰῶνα* (xiii. 8); the Paraclete is to remain with the Apostles *εἰς τὸν αἰῶνα* (xiv. 16). In ix. 32 we have *ἐκ τοῦ αἰῶνος* for 'from the beginning of the world.'

In St. John's Gospel *ζωὴ αἰώνιος* is of course regarded as spiritual—as the Life of the Age, in which all things are spiritual. Its quality is stressed far more than its quantity; its very definition is 'to know the Father and the Son' (xvii. 3); nevertheless, the thought of lastingness is not absent; it is contrasted with the earthly water which perishes (iv. 14); with the wheat which is consumed (iv. 36); with the bread that gives life in this world-order (vi. 54). How far it is eschatological it is hard to say; in some cases the view that eternal life begins 'here and now' is the consequence rather than the content of the Johannine sayings.[1]

In the Acts we have no use of special interest; *ἀπ' αἰῶνος* occurs twice—once with reference to the holy prophets (iii. 21) and once in a quotation from the LXX (xv. 18; *cp.* Isa. xlv. 21); *ζωὴ αἰώνιος* comes twice—once about the Jews who rejected it (xiii. 46) and once about the converts who were appointed by God for it (xiii. 48).

Turning to St. Paul's Epistles, we have in Romans *εἰς τοὺς αἰῶνας* three times in doxologies (i. 25, ix. 5, xi. 36), and in xvi. 27 the new form *εἰς τοὺς αἰῶνας τῶν αἰώνων*; in xii. 2 *τῷ αἰῶνι τούτῳ* is used of 'this world.' *Αἰώνιος* is used of Life four times (ii. 7, v. 21, vi. 22, vi. 23), once of God Himself (xvi. 26); in this last

[1] *ἔχει ζωὴν αἰώνιον* may mean 'shall have'; *cp.* *ὁ τρώγων μου τὴν σάρκα. . .ἔχει ζ. α., κἀγὼ ἀναστήσω αὐτὸν τῇ ἐσχάτῃ ἡμέρᾳ* (vi. 54), *πηγὴ ὕδατος ἁλλομένου εἰς ζ. α.* (iv. 14), *καρπὸν εἰς ζ. α.* (iv. 36), *βρῶσιν μένουσαν εἰς ζ. α.* (vi. 27), *ὁ μισῶν τὴν ψυχὴν αὐτοῦ ἐν τῷ κόσμῳ εἰς ζ. α. φυλάξει αὐτήν* (xii. 25), *ὑμεῖς* (the Jews) *δοκεῖτε ἐν αὐταῖς* (*ταῖς γραφαῖς*) *ζ. α. ἔχειν* (v. 39), (the Jews would hardly believe they had eternal life here and now). On the other hand, such texts as xii. 50, *ἡ ἐντολὴ αὐτοῦ ζ. α. ἐστιν*, and 1 John iii. 15, *πᾶς ἀνθρωποκτόνος οὐκ ἔχει ζ. α. ἐν αὐτῷ μένουσαν*, suggest it as present.

passage comes κατὰ ἀποκάλυψιν μυστηρίου χρόνοις αἰωνίοις σεσιγημένου; this would seem a very paradoxical phrase to a Platonist, to whom χρόνος and αἰών are contradictory conceptions. In the LXX it would simply mean 'ancient times'; St. Paul probably means the indefinite stretch of the past—going back perhaps beyond Creation.[1]

1 Cor. is rich in the use of αἰών in the sense of 'this present world'; συνζητητὴς τοῦ αἰῶνος τούτου (i. 20), σοφὸς ἐν τῷ αἰῶνι τούτῳ (iii. 18); ii. 6–8 has an interesting reference to οἱ ἄρχοντες τοῦ αἰῶνος τούτου, whose wisdom betrayed them into crucifying the Lord of Glory. It is doubtful whether the reference is to Herod and Caiaphas or to the evil angel-rulers of this Age. In v. 7 we are told they did not know the purpose of God, ordained πρὸ τῶν αἰώνων, which may perhaps mean 'before the course of human history'; the rulers of the aeons could not see beyond the aeons to God's pre-temporal counsel. In x. 11 we have the famous phrase ἡμῶν, εἰς οὓς τὰ τέλη τῶν αἰώνων κατήντηκεν. Peake's *Commentary* (p. 841) has: 'The record is for their benefit who live where this age and the age to come meet; the terminal point of one is immediately followed by the initial point of the other.' On the other hand, the *New Commentary* (p. 501) says: 'Christians . . . were the heirs of former ages.' Τέλος generally means 'end' and κατήντηκεν seems to have a temporal sense; so perhaps 'end of the age' rather than 'fulfilment of prophecies' seems slightly the more probable meaning.

2 Cor. has ὁ θεὸς . . . εὐλογητὸς εἰς τοὺς αἰῶνας (xi. 31), and in iv. 4 the interesting phrase ὁ θεὸς τοῦ αἰῶνος τούτου, the Angel-ruler of this world-order.[2] Αἰώνιος is

[1] No doubt in these verses αἰώνιος and χρόνοις αἰωνίοις 'notice' one another; God was ruler of the Ages during which the secret was kept.

[2] St. John prefers ὁ ἄρχων τοῦ κόσμου τούτου; κόσμος has a special reference to the definite forces arrayed against God.

used of the weight of glory ready for us in heaven (iv. 17), of the οἰκίαν ἀχειροποίητον ἐν τοῖς οὐρανοῖς—the Resurrection body (v. 1), of τὰ μὴ βλεπόμενα as opposed to τὰ βλεπόμενα, which are πρόσκαιρα (iv. 18). In all three cases, the emphasis seems to be on the spiritual nature of what is αἰώνιον, but (especially in the last case) the sense of 'everlasting' seems to be present.

In Galatians we have the phrase ἐκ τοῦ αἰῶνος τοῦ ἐνεστῶτος (now present) πονηροῦ (i. 4) [1]; the doxology has εἰς τοὺς αἰῶνας τῶν αἰώνων (i. 5), and ζωὴ αἰώνιος occurs once (vi. 8). In Eph. i. 21 we have the contrast ἐν τῷ αἰῶνι τούτῳ ἀλλὰ καὶ ἐν τῷ μέλλοντι; in ii. 2 comes the curious combination κατὰ τὸν αἰῶνα τοῦ κόσμου τούτου (R.V., 'according to the course of this world'); the genitive is perhaps adjectival, *i.e.* 'the Age which consists of this Cosmos.' [2] In ii. 7 God is said by the sending of Christ to show the riches of His Grace ἐν τοῖς αἰῶσιν τοῖς ἐπερχομένοις; this would seem to refer to an eternity in a far removed future, for St. Paul's views on the Parousia would hardly have allowed for many future ages on earth.[3] In iii. 9 we have again the Mystery τὸ ἀποκεκρυμμένον ἀπὸ τῶν αἰώνων ἐν τῷ θεῷ; this means, of course, not 'concealed from the ages' but 'from all ages (*i.e.* from the beginning) hid.'[4]

In iii. 11 we have κατὰ πρόθεσιν τῶν αἰώνων, which should probably be taken as 'enduring purpose,' like 'Rock of Ages'; in iii. 21 we find the ἅπαξ λεγόμενον: εἰς πάσας τὰς γενεὰς τοῦ αἰῶνος τῶν αἰώνων, which has

[1] The author of the (Gnostic) *Clementines* seems to have interpreted it 'from the Aeon, the dominion, of the present evil one' (Lightfoot, *ad loc.*). This text and 2 Cor. iv. 4 prepared the way for the Gnostic theory of Aeons.

[2] 'Conformably to the Age to which this (wicked) world belongs' (*New Testament Lexicon*, p. 19).

[3] 'The Age after the return of Christ in majesty' (*loc. cit.*).

[4] Speaking of the parallel in Col. i. 26, ἀπὸ τῶν αἰώνων καὶ ἀπὸ τῶν γενεῶν, Lightfoot says: 'An αἰών is made up of many γενεαί'; I think, however, that αἰών has still the quite indefinite sense of *olam*. In Isa. li. 9, which he quotes, ὡς γενεὰ αἰῶνος means 'as the generations of old.'

been taken to mean 'unto all generations of the Age which consists of shorter ages.' Such a subdivision of *αἰών* into *αἰῶνες* nowhere else occurs, and it seems easier to regard it as a rhetorical variant of *εἰς τοὺς αἰῶνας τῶν αἰώνων*: 'to all generations of the age-long age.'

In 2 Thess. the wicked suffer *ὄλεθρον αἰώνιον* from the face of the Lord (i. 9) and God gives us *παράκλησιν αἰώνιον* (ii. 16); in both cases 'everlasting' seems the natural rendering. In 1 Tim. i. 17 the doxology is addressed *τῷ βασιλεῖ τῶν αἰώνων*[1] . . . *τιμὴ καὶ δόξα εἰς τοὺς αἰῶνας τῶν αἰώνων*; the meaning is 'eternal King.' In vi. 17 we have *τοῖς πλουσίοις ἐν τῷ νῦν αἰῶνι. Ζωὴ αἰώνιος* occurs twice, possibly three times.[2] In vi. 16 *τιμὴ καὶ κράτος αἰώνιον* comes in the doxology.

In 2 Tim. Demas is said to have loved *τὸν νῦν αἰῶνα* (iv. 10) and glory is ascribed to God *εἰς τοὺς αἰῶνας τῶν αἰώνων* (iv. 18). We have also the curious phrase (i. 9) *πρὸ χρόνων αἰωνίων*; it would be a mistake to analyse too closely a semi-liturgical phrase, which is meant to be solemn rather than scientific. In Titus ii. 12 *τῷ νῦν αἰῶνι* means 'this present life'; *ζωὴ αἰώνιος* has been promised *πρὸ χρόνων αἰωνίων* (i. 2), and we are heirs of *ζωὴ αἰώνιος* through hope (iii. 7). In Philem. v. 15 we have the only use of *αἰώνιος* of the individual Christian; St. Paul says *τάχα γὰρ διὰ τοῦτο ἐχωρίσθη πρὸς ὥραν ἵνα αἰώνιον αὐτὸν ἀπέχῃς, οὐκέτι δοῦλον ἀλλ ὰ ὑπὲρ δοῦλον ἀδελφὸν ἀγαπητόν*. There is a twofold contrast; Onesimus *was* a slave and *is* a brother; he *was* lost for a time and *is* regained for eternity.

In Hebrews we have a notable use of *οἱ αἰῶνες* in i. 2, *δι' οὗ ἐποίησεν τοὺς αἰῶνας*, and xi. 3, *πίστει νοοῦμεν κατηρτίσθαι τοὺς αἰῶνας ῥήματι θεοῦ*. This has been taken as referring to ages or orders of finite beings; Westcott is probably right in supposing it to mean 'the sum of all the periods of time, including all that is manifested

[1] *Cp.* the various readings in Rev. xv. 3, *ὁ βασιλεὺς τῶν ἐθνῶν* or *ἁγίων* or *αἰώνων*.

[2] i. 16; vi. 12; vi. 19 (*τῆς ὄντως* (*αἰωνίου*) *ζωῆς*).

in and through them.' This would be similar to uses of αἰών in the Apocrypha.[1]

Christ is spoken of as exercising His royal and priestly work εἰς τὸν αἰῶνα, εἰς τὸν αἰῶνα τοῦ αἰῶνος, and εἰς τοὺς αἰῶνας.[2]

In vi. 5 we have δυνάμεις τε μέλλοντος αἰῶνος; baptised Christians have 'tasted the powers of the world to come'; the absence of the article 'serves to fix attention on the character of the Age as one hitherto unrealised.'[3]

In ix. 26 we read that Christ appeared ἐπὶ συντελείᾳ τῶν αἰώνων: here, as in St. Matthew, the thought seems to be that of the αἰῶνες of the world drawing to their consummation.

Αἰώνιος is used of σωτηρία (v. 9; *cp.* Isa. xlv. 17), κρίμα (vi. 2), λύτρωσις (ix. 12), κληρονομία (ix. 15), διαθήκη (xiii. 20; *cp.* Isa. lv. 3: the New Covenant of Christ's Blood is contrasted with the temporary Covenant of old); ix. 14 is rather a crux—ὃς (Χριστὸς) διὰ πνεύματος αἰωνίου ἑαυτὸν προσήνεγκεν (on the Cross); whether πνεῦμα refers to the Holy Ghost or to the 'endless life' of Christ Himself, the epithet αἰώνιον

[1] *E.g.* Wisd. xiii. 9; in Heb. xi. 3, it is clear that the physical universe is meant from the words τὸ μὴ ἐκ φαινομένων τὸ βλεπόμενον γεγονέναι (we should surely compare 2 Macc. vii. 28, οὐκ ἐξ ὄντων ἐποίησεν αὐτὰ (heaven and earth) ὁ θεός; the Maccabean influence is strong in the eleventh chapter of Hebrews).

[2] θρόνος (i. 8, from Ps. xlv. 6), ἱερεύς (v. 6, from Ps. cx. 4), ἀρχιερεύς (vi. 20, vii. 24), υἱός (vii. 28), Χριστὸς ὁ αὐτός (xiii. 8). The doxology in xiii. 21 has εἰς τοὺς αἰῶνας τῶν αἰώνων.

[3] Westcott, p. 150; *cp.* ii. 5 (God did not subject to angels, τὴν οἰκουμένην τὴν μέλλουσαν); our phrases 'the world to come' and 'world without end' hover between αἰών and ἡ οἰκουμένη, reminding us that 'world' originally meant 'time'; cp. *As You Like It*, Act i. scene 2:

'Hereafter in a better world than this (*i.e.* at a more favourable time), I shall desire more love and knowledge of you'; and Shakespeare, *Sonnet* 57:

> 'Nor dare I chide the world-without-end hour
> Whilst I, my sovereign, watch the clock for you.'

In the Greek Creed, Begotten 'before all worlds' is πρὸ πάντων τῶν αἰώνων and the life 'of the world to come' is τοῦ μέλλοντος αἰῶνος.

brings out the contrast with the lives of the animals that were totally destroyed in the Old Testament sacrifices.

1 Peter has two quotations from Isa. xl. 8, where the Word of God is spoken of as abiding for ever (εἰς τὸν αἰῶνα, i. 23, i. 25), and εἰς τοὺς αἰῶνας τῶν αἰώνων in two doxologies (iv. 11, v. 11); we are said to have been called by God εἰς τὴν αἰώνιον δόξαν ἐν Χριστῷ (v. 10).

2 Peter and Jude may be taken together. Jude v. 13 (and possibly 2 Pet. ii. 17) has ὁ ζόφος τοῦ σκότους εἰς αἰῶνα τετήρηται; the phrase might of course be translated 'till the day of Judgment' as in v. 6, which refers to the rebellious angels. If so, it is like the Apocalyptists rather than the New Testament in usage (see p. 43).

In the doxology we have the only use of αἰών for 'eternity' in the New Testament: νῦν καὶ εἰς ἡμέραν αἰῶνος (2 Pet. iii. 18). Dr. Bigg, anxious to prove that the phrase is Petrine rather than Platonic, takes the phrase as equivalent to Ecclus. xviii. 10, in which the few years of our lives are spoken of as like drops of water or pebbles 'in the day of eternity.' But in 2 Pet. the genitive is in apposition—'the day which is eternity,' and the εἰς shows that it is thought of as superseding the present Time-order; in Ecclus. αἰών is rather naively regarded as a very long span, one day of which far exceeds the longest human life; there is no real parallel to the philosophical language of the Epistle.

In the doxology (Jude v. 25), δόξα πρὸ παντὸς τοῦ αἰῶνος καὶ νῦν καὶ εἰς πάντας τοὺς αἰῶνας, Dr. Bigg translates the spaced phrase by 'before all eternity.' This seems too paradoxical; more probably the words should be compared to 2 Tim. i. 9: πρὸ χρόνων αἰωνίων; if the precise meaning is pressed it would mean 'before created history.' The R.V. has 'before times eternal.'

Jude also has ζωὴ αἰώνιος (v. 21), and the burning of Sodom and Gomorrah is a δεῖγμα, or type, of the πῦρ αἰώνιον of Gehenna (v. 7).[1]

[1] If δεῖγμα means 'an example to us,' the words would seem to mean that the rebellious cities of the plain were actually burned with the fire of Gehenna.

The Apocalypse is the only book of the New Testament which speaks of a limited Messianic Age, but nothing in its use of *αἰών* or *αἰώνιος* reflects that belief. *εἰς τοὺς αἰῶνας τῶν αἰώνων* is used in the doxology of i. 6, of the life of the Risen Christ (i. 18), of the ascription of glory to God (iv. 9, 10), to the Lamb (v. 13), to God again (vii. 12), of the eternal life of God (x. 6), of the reign of Christ (xi. 15), of the smoke of the torment of the Beast and his followers (xiv. 11) (the reading here is *εἰς αἰῶνας αἰώνων*), again, of the life of God (xv. 7), of the smoke of the torment of Rome (xix. 3), of the torment of the Devil, the Beast, and the false prophet (xx. 10), of the reign of the saints (xxii. 5), where the phrase is probably 'in contrast with the thousand years of the earlier (millennial) visions' (*New Commentary*, p. 704).

Αἰώνιος occurs once—of the angel *ἔχοντα εὐαγγέλιον αἰώνιον εὐαγγελίσαι ἐπὶ τοὺς καθημένους ἐπὶ τῆς γῆς* (xiv. 6). As in Heb. xiii. 20, the contrast is with the temporary Covenant of the Old Testament.[1]

To sum up, we may say *αἰώνιος* could at a pinch always (except perhaps where it is used of God) be translated 'age-long.' But the context (together with the influence of Hellenistic and Hebraic usage) generally inclines the balance towards the sense of 'everlasting.'

Other Words implying Permanence in the New Testament

Adverbs :

ἑκάστοτε, 2 Pet. i. 15, *σπουδάσω δὲ καὶ ἑκάστοτε μετὰ τὴν ἐμὴν ἔξοδον* (of earthly life—at every time after my death they might be able to call these things to remembrance).

ἀεί, of earthly life, *e.g.* Mark xv. 8, *καθὼς ἀεὶ ἐποίει αὐτοῖς* (of release of prisoners at the Passover) ; 2 Cor. iv. 11 : *ἀεὶ γὰρ ἡμεῖς οἱ ζῶντες εἰς θάνατον παραδιδόμεθα.*

[1] It will be remembered that the phrase 'Eternal Gospel' was the watchword of Joachim de Flora and his followers in the thirteenth century ; Papini regards the Veltro of Dante as derived from the letters EVANGELIO ETERNO.

εἰς τὸ διηνεκές, continually; only Hebrews—of Christ as Priest (vii. 3, x. 12), of the priests of the Old Testament (x. 1), of our perfection through Christ (x. 14).

διὰ παντός, continually; Heb. ix. 6, *διὰ παντὸς εἰσίασιν οἱ ἱερεῖς* (to the Tabernacle), once of the life of Heaven—of the angels ever beholding God's face (Matt. xviii. 10).

πάντοτε, usually of earthly life. Our Lord says *ἐμὲ δὲ οὐ πάντοτε ἔχετε* (Matt. xxvi. 11); Luke xviii. 1: *δεῖν πάντοτε προσεύχεσθαι*. But 1 Thess. iv. 17: *πάντοτε* (after Our Lord's Second Coming) *σὺν Κυρίῳ ἐσόμεθα*, and Heb. vii. 25 of Jesus: *πάντοτε ζῶν εἰς τὸ ἐντυγχάνειν ὑπὲρ αὐτῶν*.

Verbs:

μένειν is sometimes used in an eschatological sense, *e.g.* John iii. 36: *ἡ ὀργὴ τοῦ θεοῦ μένει εἰς αὐτόν*; vi. 27: *βρῶσιν μένουσαν εἰς ζωὴν αἰώνιον*; viii. 35: *ὁ υἱὸς μένει εἰς τὸν αἰῶνα*; xii. 34: *ὁ Χριστὸς μένει εἰς τὸν αἰῶνα*; 2 Cor. iii. 11: *τὸ μένον* (the Gospel, as opposed to *τὸ καταργούμενον*—the Law); Heb. vii. 3: *μένει ἱερεὺς εἰς τὸ διηνεκές*; xiii. 14: *οὐ γὰρ ἔχομεν ὧδε μένουσαν πόλιν*.

ἵστημι has now and then such a force, *e.g.* Heb. x. 9: *ἀναιρεῖ τὸ πρῶτον ἵνα τὸ δεύτερον στήσῃ*.

Adjectives:

ἀκατάλυτος (*i.e.* that which cannot be taken to pieces and destroyed), of Our Lord's Life (Heb. vii. 16).

ἀθάνατος does not occur in the New Testament; *ἀθανασία* occurs once of God (1 Tim. vi. 16, *ὁ μόνος ἔχων ἀθανασίαν*, *i.e.* of His own right) and twice of the Christian believer, but of a future state (1 Cor. xv. 53, 54) (*ἐνδύσασθαι*, we put it on).

ἄφθαρτος used of God (Rom. i. 23 and 1 Tim. i. 17, where there is a rejected reading *ἀθανάτῳ*), of the risen Christian (1 Cor. xv. 52), of our *στέφανος* (1 Cor. ix. 25), of our *κληρονομία* (1 Pet. i. 4), of the *σπορά* from which Christians are reborn (1 Pet. i. 23), of the 'apparel of a meek and quiet spirit' (1 Pet. iii. 4).

ἀφθαρσία is used of human immortality in 1 Cor. xv. 42,

50, 53, 54 (alternative for ἀθανασία), 2 Tim. i. 10; of moral purity in Tit. ii. 7 and Eph. vi. 24.

ἄσβεστος is used of the fire of Divine judgment in Matt. iii. 12, Mark ix. 43, Luke iii. 17.

ἀσάλευτος is used of the Kingdom of Christ in Heb. xii. 28.

Patristic Use

The philosophical Fathers use αἰών for eternity as Plato did; so St. Clement of Alexandria: ὅ γ' αἰὼν τοῦ χρόνου τὸ μέλλον καὶ τὸ ἐνεστώς, αὐτὰρ δὴ καὶ τὸ παρῳχηκὸς ἀκαριαίως συνίστησι (*Strom.* i. 13). So St. Gregory of Nazianzen: αἰὼν γὰρ οὔτε χρόνος οὔτε χρόνου τι μέρος· οὐδὲ γὰρ μετρητόν· ἀλλ' ὅπερ ἡμῖν ὁ χρόνος ἡλίου φορᾷ μετρούμενος, τοῦτο τοῖς ἀϊδίοις (in the eternal sphere) αἰών, τὸ συμπαρεκτεινόμενον (stretched out altogether alongside) τοῖς οὖσιν, οἷόν τι χρονικὸν κίνημα καὶ διάστημα (*Orat.* xxxviii. 8).

The earlier Fathers are less technical; St. Clement of Rome has ὁ δημιουργὸς καὶ πατὴρ τῶν αἰώνων (*Ad Cor.* i. xxxv. 3), and σὺ βασιλεῦ τῶν αἰώνων and θρόνος αἰώνιος (lxi. 2). Ignatius has αἰῶνες for 'generations of men'; ἐφανερώθη τοῖς αἰῶσιν ('The revelation was made to mankind') (*Ad Eph.*, xix. 2).

The word αἰών has, of course, a very important and technical meaning in Gnostic speculation. The Pauline conception of the Angel-ruler of this Aeon favoured the use of the word for orders of angels; so in the Apostolic Constitutions we have θεὸς ὁ ποιήσας τὰ χερουβὶμ καὶ τὰ σεραφίμ, αἰῶνάς τε καὶ στρατιάς.[1] In Valentinus the Aeons are emanations from God who 'appear in religion as guardian angels or as heavenly doubles of men and women on earth.'[2] A Roman Gnostic says

[1] viii. 12. It goes on, 'powers and authorities, principalities and thrones, archangels and angels and, *after all these*, . . . this visible world.'

[2] Theodotus explained 1 Cor. xv. 29 as meaning that the Aeons are baptised for us men 'dead' in sin (Dr. Bigg, *Origins of Christianity*, p. 136); αἰὼν τέλειος was the Valentinian God; *Iren.* I. I. I., λέγουσι γάρ τινα εἶναι ἐν ἀοράτοις καὶ ἀκατονομάστοις ὑψώμασι τέλειον αἰῶνα προόντα, τοῦτον δὲ καὶ προαρχὴν καὶ προπάτορα καὶ βυθὸν καλοῦσιν.

in the epitaph on his young wife, 'Thou didst hasten to behold the divine visages of the Aeons, the great Angel of the great Council . . . pressing on into the fatherly bosom of the Aeons.' [1]

Αἰώνιος is used in the ordinary sense of eternal or everlasting.

(*c*) Latin Words

In the sense in which *olam* and *αἰώνιος* refer to the past, the Vulgate has 'dierum saeculi' (Isa. lxiii. 11), 'in diebus antiquis' (Amos ix. 11); for 'the ancient wastes,' 'deserta saeculorum' (Isa. lviii. 12), 'deserta a saeculo' (Isa. lxi. 4), 'solitudines veteres' (Ezek. xxvi. 20); in the case of 'the ancient high places,' 'altitudines sempiternae' (Ezek. xxxvi. 2); 'the ancient paths' is 'semita saeculorum' (Job xxii. 15), and 'the ancient gates of Zion' 'portae aeternales' (Ps. xxiv. 7).

'From of old' is 'a saeculo' (Isa. lxiv. 4), 'a principio' (Joel ii. 2), 'ab initio' (Jos. xxiv. 2), 'ex antiquis' (Prov. viii. 23); the 'long dead' is 'mortuos saeculi' (Ps. cxliii. 3), and 'the former things of old' 'prioris saeculi' (Isa. xlvi. 9). 'From everlasting' in Ps. xciii. 2 is 'a saeculo'; in Hab. iii. 6, 'His goings were as of old' is 'ab itineribus aeternitatis eius'—one of the rather rare occurrences of the noun; 'the years of ancient times' is 'annos aeternos' (Ps. lxxvii. 5).

In the sense of 'for ever' we have 'in aeternum' frequently (*e.g.* Deut. xv. 17) and 'in saeculum' (Exod. xxi. 6) both representing *εἰς τὸν αἰῶνα*; in 1 Sam. i. 22 'jugiter' is used for *ἕως αἰῶνος* and 'semper' for *διὰ παντός* in Lev. xxv. 32; in Ps. xxi. 6 *εἰς αἰῶνα αἰῶνος* is 'in saeculum saeculi,' and in Ps. cxxi. 8 *ἕως τοῦ αἰῶνος* is 'usque in saeculum'; we also have 'in sempiternum' (Ezek. xxvi. 21), 'in perpetuum' (Ezek. xxvii. 36) and 'in saecula' (Ps. lxxxi. 15); in Isa. xxxiv. 10 we have the familiar 'in saecula saeculorum' (*cp.* Ps. x. 16, 'in

[1] See Dr. Bigg (*loc. cit.*).

aeternum et in saeculum saeculi') ; in Exod. xv. 18 'in aeternum et ultra.'

As cases of the adjectival use, in Jer. xxiii. 40, 'an everlasting reproach and a perpetual shame' is 'opprobrium sempiternum et ignominiam aeternam'; 'everlasting love' (Jer. xxxi. 3) is 'charitate perpetua.'

As examples of the noun, we have 'his long home' 'domus aeternitatis suae' (Eccles. xii. 5), and in Dan. xii. 3 the remarkable phrase 'quasi stellae in perpetuas aeternitates.'

The liturgical phrases vary as follows :

Ab aeterno A saeculo Ex hoc Nunc A modo	(usque)	In saeculum In aeternum In sempiternum

In the New Testament the Vulgate renderings are not remarkable. *Αἰών* is represented by 'saeculum'; 'for ever' is 'in aeternum, in saecula, in saeculum saeculi, in saecula saeculorum'; *ἡμέρα αἰῶνος* in 2 Pet. is 'dies aeternitatis'; Rom. xvi. 25 preserves the paradox of the Greek in 'temporibus aeternis'; in 2 Tim. i. 9 and Titus i. 2 *πρὸ χρόνων αἰωνίων* is rendered by 'ante tempora saecularia'—a literal translation of *αἰώνιος*.

It is noticeable that 'aevum' does not seem to occur in the Latin of the Old or New Testament, its place being taken by 'saeculum.'[1] As Latin had the separate word 'aeternitas,' aevum hovers between the meanings of saeculum and aeternitas, and can be used by Aquinas to represent the state of the angels and of the blessed, far superior to human time but inferior to the Eternity of God.

[1] It comes in the Apocrypha (Ecclus. i. 1), 'Sapientia est ante aevum,' and in Esdras iii. 4 we have 'Potestas aevorum est apud Te.' (See Lecture III, p. 75.)

APPENDIX II

ON THE INCARNATION—THE RELATION OF THE ETERNAL AND TEMPORAL IN THE COURSE OF THIS WORLD ORDER

I HAD not time in an already overcrowded course of lectures to deal (as I intended) with this problem, but, as the Incarnation is the supreme example of the relation between the eternal and the temporal, any account of that relation must be brought into connection with it. First, I should like to say that any view of Our Lord's Nature must be an *interpretation* ; such a statement would be a platitude, were it not that many people, tired of the burden and heat of theological controversy, have longed to turn back to the vividness and freshness of the Gospel story, to see the Jesus of history as He was, freed from all later developments and dogmatic presuppositions. In a sense, that is possible ; history can be treated as a film, just to be watched (minus the captions which 'explain' what is happening), or as a drama, like the Passion Play at Ober-Ammergau, to be felt simply as a thing of pathos and beauty. But remember that, on that view, *no* questions are to be asked ; to say 'he is sinless,' 'he is a poet, prophet, reformer, an ordinary man like you or me,' these are interpretations. It may be helpful in our meditations just to put ourselves into the attitude of spectators of the Gospel scenes, yet we cannot help going on to ask (as those who wrote the records asked), 'Who is He?'[1] As in the case of Our Lord's own

[1] Thus St. Mark, the earliest record, treats Jesus from the first as the Son of God ; in one of the earliest of St. Peter's sermons (Acts x. 36) it is said : 'He is Lord of all.' The idea that, if we push

parables, we first follow the story and then we ask, 'What does it mean?'[1] I am aware, of course, that we all are afraid of spoiling the freshness of the story and the reality of that gracious Figure by dry metaphysical schemata; we ask, What is there really in common between the story of the Passion and the Chalcedonian formulae? The story makes one grand impression of unity and simplicity; Chalcedon seems to separate and divide—to posit two stages and actors—the earthly and the heavenly.

True, but does not all analysis do the same? Psychology uses technical terms, which exasperate the ordinary man. So you would be justifiably annoyed if (during some intensely moving situation at the cinema) your next-door neighbour insisted on explaining the mechanism of the films, or criticised the dressing and lighting. We have to take things to pieces; only we must not suppose that things are more real and valuable when they are lying there, broken up into their component parts.

Thus people who affect a great love of the simple, the concrete, the historical,[2] tell us that whatever theories may be held, Our Lord was a completely real human Person, unified and whole, if ever Man was. Of course this is true; the simplicity and directness of Our Lord's actions are most striking; whatever Our Lord is or does, He is or does it completely, with all Himself. Our emotions are shallow, our convictions are hesitating, our actions are wavering, because our nature is imperfect

far enough, we shall find an untheological Christianity is a myth; to use Dr. Glover's phrase, people would not have troubled to write down the story of the 'Jesus of History' if they had not already known 'Jesus in the experience of men.'

[1] The trouble arises from the fact that *ideally* there should be two different ways of reading the Gospels; first, to form an interpretation, and secondly, to apply that interpretation, and the second should follow the first. Actually, of course, they cannot be separated; A says: 'My *general* impression of the Gospels leads me to interpret this text thus,' and B says: 'No, if you dealt with the text honestly, you would *alter* your general impression.'

[2] As a matter of fact, historical facts are never simple; it is theories that are simple.

and divided, and so we do things half-heartedly. Our Lord was never like that; if He was glad, He 'exulted in spirit'[1]; if He was sad, He 'wept'[2]; if He was angry, the shop-keepers in the Temple fled before Him.[3]

But it is a solecism to suppose that by saying Jesus was just a perfect Man, or a very good Man, we get rid of all the elements of mystery, when we recall how mysterious and complex the psychology of genius is, and most of all in Him, Who, at the least, was one of the world's greatest geniuses.[4] Perfection of human nature such as Jesus possessed implies a relationship with God which (even if He were only Man) is infinitely mysterious and miraculous, if only because it is unique.[5]

With the Unitarian theory that Jesus was just a very good Man I am not here concerned, not only because I do not believe it, but also because it would be without special significance for our problem; the birth of Christ would be merely a fact of creation, such as we were considering in the seventh lecture.

I pass on to say a few words on the Kenotic theory, though it is now, I think, rightly out of fashion; it is based on a rather literal interpretation of Phil. ii. 7, which it takes as meaning that the Son of God laid aside His Divine Nature when He was born at Bethlehem and resumed it at the Resurrection.[6]

[1] Luke x. 21. [2] John xi. 35.

[3] John ii. 15.

[4] After all, there is no other person who can be imagined as having persuaded his followers to identify him with the God of Monotheism; no one else was likely to be 'mistaken for God.'

[5] I am always surprised how easily certain critics suppose it a lucky accident that such a Man was born just at that time and never before or since.

[6] *ἑαυτὸν ἐκένωσεν*: 'He made Himself of no reputation' (A.V.); 'He emptied Himself' (R.V.). The verb *κενόω* everywhere else is used in the metaphorical sense of emptying of value and meaning (*πίστις*, Rom. iv. 14; *ὁ σταυρός*, 1 Cor. i. 17; *καύχημά μου*, 1 Cor. ix. 15). It seems hard to take it literally here, and there is something to be said for the Authorised rendering.

The objections seem to be threefold :

First, God cannot cease to be God [1] ; the theory that the Second Person of the Trinity could cease His Divine functions without affecting those of the other Two seems highly tritheistic and to regard the Holy Trinity as a kind of partnership ; on the other hand, it is essential to the Christian theory of redemption that the words and acts of Jesus should be the words and acts of God.

Secondly, it is a false view that Deity is as it were a full vessel, by emptying which we arrive at Humanity as a kind of residuum, as if God minus so much equals Man. Humanity is infinitely inferior to God, but it is different in quality as well as quantity.

Thirdly, it is a temporal illusion to suppose that the Second Person of the Holy Trinity suddenly became humble or performed a totally new act of humiliation when He became Man. He is always humble, always the Servant in Creation as well as in redemption ; if Christ is the Humility of God,[2] He is so always, whether on the Throne or in the manger ; the Incarnation is the translation in human language of an *eternal* fact.

Rejecting, therefore, the view that Jesus had only a human nature, we pass on to the view that His Divine and human natures are the same fact seen under two different aspects. Canon Raven says : 'Scholars have lately begun to realise . . . that our faith is in the One Person Who is at once and always both human and divine ; that the Life of Jesus can be described both as a story of Manhood and as a manifestation of Godhead ; that the

[1] Kenosis is the reverse of Adoptionism ; in one case, Man ceases to be Man and becomes God ; in the other, God ceases to be God and becomes Man. It is difficult to see how the Eternal can 'become' the temporal ; 'Was made Man' does not = 'was changed into Man.'

[2] We might call Christ 'the aspect of God as serving,' if the word 'aspect' were not so impersonal ; cp. *The Ring and the Book* (*Caponsacchi*) :

> 'To learn not only by a comet's rush
> But a rose's birth,—not by the grandeur, God—
> But the comfort, Christ.'

two natures represent the two points of view from which one and the same Being can be studied. . . . The two stories . . . will each include all the facts and will each be equally true—though they will be couched in totally different language, and the second (the Divine) can only be told in full when we learn the speech of eternity.' [1]

In a large sense this is true, but from our immediate point of view it needs a little precision. It is true indeed that God and Man are not opposites.[2] Man is made in God's image; he is (in the old phrase) 'capax Dei.' The Godlike in Man and the human heart of God can and do co-operate. All human actions done by Grace have their divine and human histories—not different as if Man did one part and God another, but the same under two aspects. We can speak of God's acts through St. Francis or of St. Francis' acts by the Grace of God; yet we know that God and St. Francis are not 'the same person.'

For, even in the case of the greatest saints, there is much that does not overlap; infinite tracts of the Divine Life do not belong to St. Francis and there is in him a personality which, in the last resort, is not God.

In Christ the overlapping is complete; all God is in Jesus; all Jesus is God. That is one side of the paradox, but there is another side. Jesus is wholly Divine and yet that Divinity is only revealed under the limitations of human nature; on the other hand, God is wholly Man, yet that Manhood is only possible because it is more than human.

Christ could only reveal such aspects of God as could be represented on the human stage; He could not reveal Omniscience or Omnipotence. On the other hand, Christ was only Man because He was more; human nature could not, in its fallen state, have revealed the

[1] *Creator Spirit*, p. 79.

[2] *Cp.* Myers' famous line,

'Jesu, divinest when Thou most art Man,'

and Traherne (*Meditations*, p. 66), 'God never shewed Himself more a God than when He appeared man.'

Divine glory ; God Himself had to save humanity from within, by making the very heart of it His own.

Thus Christ's Divine Nature *appears* as if it were less than Divine, and His Human Nature as if it were more than human.[1]

That is what justifies the Chalcedonian distinction between the two Natures ; though the fullness of Deity is in Jesus the Man, it is not limited to His earthly life. The Godhead we see in Jesus is revealed in other ways—in the natural world as the Logos, in the spiritual world as the Light of men.[2]

Thus the two Natures of Christ correspond to the eternal and the temporal ; the temporal process of His Life perfectly imitates the Eternal,[3] but it adds nothing to it and takes nothing from it. It makes and can make no change in the Divine Nature.

But all this heightens the difficulty about the word 'Person' ; are we not, in effect, saying that one Person was born at Bethlehem and another Person was at the same time ruling the universe ?

[1] Hence one can see that the Arian idea of a demi-god, far more than man but less than God, might seem to satisfy the appearances.

[2] Any view that the Divine Nature of the Son was *wholly* concentrated in the Humanity of Jesus seems to me tritheistic ; it disconnects the Son from the Father and the Holy Spirit ; but I would subscribe humbly to Dr. Gore's words, 'Within the sphere and limit of His mortal life He appears as restricted by human conditions ; and we thankfully accept this . . . without attempting to relate it to what lies outside our possibilities of knowledge' (*Belief in Christ*, p. 226).

[3] We must remember that, in a large sense, the phrase 'the temporal process of Christ's life' includes the work of the Logos in Creation as well as the Life of the Ascended Christ in His Church ; the Days of His Flesh sum up and express in the most perfect form His past action as Logos (so St. John says, 'He was the Light (in) the world (and then) He was made flesh') ; also Christ's life on earth gives the meaning and direction of His future activities through the Spirit. (*Cp.* the Archbishop of York, *Faith and Life*, p. 28, 'What is offered (in the Life of Jesus) is not the goal of History, but the direction in which History should move, and the power which should carry it forward.')

The idea of a person is by no means an easy or obvious one; the word may be used in the most trivial and insignificant manner ('Another person has just entered the room') or it may be applied to such subtle and complicated conceptions as the 'corporate personality' of the State or of a group within the State.

We should notice a tendency in orthodox theology to hesitate about the use of the word 'Person,' in connection *both* with Christ's Divine *and* His Human Nature. In the case of the Divine Nature, though the Church uses the word Person, she is very conscious that it is inadequate; 'person' implies too easily a sense of real distinction and has to be corrected by the doctrine of περιχώρησις, according to which the Father and the Holy Spirit take part in what the Son does in a manner that could not be predicated of human persons. In the case of His Human Nature, Christ was not just 'a man,' one of the countless multitude of created beings. The underlying personality of His humanity is the Divine Logos, and His Human Nature is meant to include that of all humanity.[1] Theologians have too hastily spoken of Jesus as 'impersonal'; 'omnipersonal' would have been a better word. No one denies that He was one of the 'strongest personalities' that ever lived; the question is whether He was not much more as well—whether when He says, 'Come unto Me,' when He feeds us with Himself, when He is 'in' every man as that man's truest self, so that St. Paul can call the Church His Body, it is not obvious that His relation to us is never that of 'just another person.'[2]

[1] 'The Son of God did not assume a man's person unto His own, but a man's nature to His own Person . . . the Son of God took not to Himself a man's person, but the nature only of a man' (Hooker, Bk. 5. c. 52. 3).

[2] Many phrases have been used to describe the relation of Christ to us. St. Paul calls Him the New Adam, the Head of the Church. Others have called Him the representative Man or, like Dr. Moberly, the Platonic Idea of Man; we best realise this in our Sacramental communion; we do not receive a man, but the perfection of human nature—the Incarnate Logos of Humanity.

In fact, just in so far as we use the word 'person' in the sense of what *separates* from others, we make the word inapplicable to Christ. His Divine Nature transcends all barriers within the Godhead; His Human Nature penetrates all consciousness; His human life is a field of mediation between the Life of God and the life of humanity; it is (so to speak) open at both ends, towards God and towards Man; as St. Paul says to his Corinthian converts, 'Ye are Christ's, and Christ is God's' (1 Cor. iii. 23).

The Eternal Logos dwells in all men; all men's lives are meant to be the temporal μίμησις of the Logos, but whereas we, each of us, can only imitate it partially, reflecting it in our own little facets, Christ in His human life imitates the whole Logos perfectly, because He is that Logos. This means far more than that He was a very good man; it means that in Him, and because He was divine, a new humanity is created.[1] That is why we call Him the Universal Christ.

As to the question, What was the relation in Jesus between His Divine and His Human Nature?—for example, Did He know He was God?—it is probably far beyond us. The psychological question must be distinguished from the metaphysical; whether Jesus knew He was God is a question separate from whether He was God.

It is natural, of course, that strong objection should be felt to any idea that Jesus acted sometimes in His Divine and sometimes in His Human Nature. Such a theory might seem to make the Incarnation intermittent, so that Jesus would not be continuously human.[2] The general

[1] When we say we are 're-created' in Jesus we mean that, just as at the first creation the high destiny of Man was in the mind of the creative Logos, so our Christian excellences are already in Christ. I am sure that for us the New Testament conception of Redemption as a 'new creation' is the most helpful of all.

[2] *Cp.* the story of the incarnation of Rāma in Andrew's *Renaissance in India*, pp. 99, 100. 'His mother says, "Though we know that the whole universe is present in each hair of thy body, yet here thou

impression we get from the Gospels is that He lived and fought and conquered by a human faith in God, but if we say that He had no consciousness of Deity till after His Resurrection, we find difficulty in accounting for the Synoptic sayings about the Sonship, the return to judge the world and the words of Institution at the Eucharist, and of course (if we accept the witness of the Fourth Gospel) such utterances as 'I and the Father are one,' 'Before Abraham was, I am.' He felt, as all saints have felt, His utter dependence upon God; He felt, as only sinless Man could feel, unclouded intimacy with God; may He not have felt dimly, and at great moments, that identity in Him of human and divine which is now fully realised in His heavenly life? [1]

The Divine Person must be carefully distinguished from the Divine Nature. The Divine Person was always and at every moment operative in the humanity of Jesus; the Human Life could not have been lived without it, but the Divine Nature (that is, the glory and power of Deity) was under self-restraint—a better word for our purpose than 'emptying.' What is restrained is not destroyed; the Godhead is most fully active in Christ's humanity, but there are aspects of the Divine glory—the manifestation of Christ in Nature, in every human soul, at the right hand of the Father—which in the sphere of His human life seem to have been in abeyance. That is really all we can say.

art, sweetly dreaming in my arms." The Lord Rāma smiled at her adoration and was about to set in motion the magic that dazzles the crowd, so that the mother might have pride in her son. But, just as he began to do so, she cried hurriedly, "My soul is terrified at these marvels; disperse them from my sight; let me see thee as my baby child again, in play and sport, for that is my greatest joy." She spoke and he obeyed his mother, and at once returning to his infant form, began as a child to cry.'

[1] Yet even such a consciousness would be by means of a *human* faith; in all these questions, are we not haunted too much by old ideas of the contrast between God and Man? Even if Jesus did know that He was God, would His humility, His self-identification with our sorrows and struggles, be really *less*?

To sum up, we must distinguish carefully (*a*) the Eternal attributes of the Son of God as the Second Person of the Holy Trinity—(His Divine Nature); they are no more affected by the Incarnation than by Creation; God acts in the life of Jesus, as He acts in the lives of all human beings; only, the whole of God's action is able to work there, because (so to speak) there is no separate and independent personality to limit it ('A higher gift than Grace . . . God's Presence and His very Self'); (*b*) the Human Nature of Christ—in part like all human lives, a piece of the Time process, and therefore distinguishable from (however closely united to) the unchanging and eternal Being; (*c*) the cosmic functions of the Logos—such as the government of the universe and the indwelling in every human soul. We can say *either* that they were suspended during His earthly life, *or* that they were consciously exercised by Our Lord during His life (a difficult view), *or* that the Divine Nature, though wholly present to and limited by the Human Nature, could also in some unimaginable way be still exercised throughout the universe (the presence of the Logos in Christ being somehow the crown and completion of His Presence with all things), *or* (perhaps the best answer) that we do not know.

I conclude with a few words on two questions:

(1) How are we to conceive of the Divine Nature of Christ as 'acting'? (2) How are we to conceive of His Human Nature as limited and restrained?

(1) If the Person of Jesus is eternal and divine, how can we say, 'He came down from Heaven'? or (if that be regarded as too figurative) how can we say that He walked and ate and taught? Can we predicate of it any action in Time?

We are all ready enough to admit that, when in the Old Testament we read of God repenting, being appeased, of His anger, His sorrow, His weariness, it does not mean a real alteration of mood. He may seem to change His plans, but He never changes His mind; He may seem to do what He has not done before ; He never does what He has not thought of before ; or (to adopt the formula we have been using) God is not in Time but sustains and directs the Time process from His Eternity.

His action then is not in Time ; He does not grow older or wiser [1] ; He does not do this or that as if He had a history ; His own eternal Perfection, itself unchanging, by being what it is, not by doing anything, influences the Time process, which is a fragmentary representation of His Being.

Does God then 'do nothing'? No ; He is the very Source of all activity ; for all that happens is from His Infinite Life ; only it is a type of activity that is changeless, because it is full and complete ; He does not *do*, He *is*, which is far better.[2] He is outside all Space and Time ; so He is able to make any place or moment the special vehicle of His revelation ; so it is in the Sacraments ; so it was in the Incarnation.

Therefore it was that the Divine and changeless Nature of Our Lord ruled the changing Human Nature, which responded freely and joyously—not as if it *could* have rebelled, for that would have been to split His Person into two.[3]

(2) Therefore when we come to the second question, the limitations of His Human Nature, it is hard to suppose that in His temptations Christ was 'free to fall.'

Could the Divine purpose of redemption really have hung in suspense while Jesus reflected in the desert? Surely the 'temptation' only means that the ideas came

[1] Whatever theory of the Incarnation we hold, we should find it hard to say that God learned the alphabet for the first time at Nazareth.

[2] So a holy man may profoundly influence a situation not by doing anything in particular but just by being what he is.

[3] Just as a person deeply in love serves willingly and freely, without any sense of a possible alternative (the 'service which is perfect freedom').

into His mind and were rejected the moment they were seen to be against God's Will.

Advocates of the 'fully human Christ' reply, that unless Jesus could have fallen, He did not win a *real* victory over *real* temptations, and therefore was not a *real* Man like us. I have reiterated the epithet 'real,' for I think it is there we tend to go wrong. A victory is not less 'real' because the disposition of the general made it infallible. Temptation is not less 'real' because we feel sure to overcome.[1] A man is not less 'real' because he scorns and puts resolutely away the suggestions of evil.[2]

In the sphere of His earthly life, Christ's Divine Nature was restrained by a persistent act of will,[3] which for us is best represented by the translation of Divine attributes into human terms, just as a wise man might lay aside his knowledge in order to see things again through the eyes of children.

We have suggested that the Divine attribute of holiness is translated into terms of free but not fallible goodness; what are we to say of capacity for suffering? It was present in Christ's human nature; what element in the Divine Nature does it 'translate'?

This is a loud and ancient controversy, and it would be beyond the scale of this Appendix to do more than make a general remark upon it.

Our ideas of joy and suffering tend to be emotional; as Plato taught in the Tenth Book of the *Republic*, pleasure

[1] It is a fallacy to suppose that the strain of temptation comes from the feeling 'I might fail'; on the contrary, as Dr. Moberly says in a different context, the fact that we have yielded and might yield to evil again blunts the horror of sin; only the sinless One has held out to the end and can feel the full horror of it.

[2] People who want a Christ 'like us' should really wish that He had sinned just a little, or that He should have felt at least a temporary inclination to evil; they forget that, in any case, His temptations were not, like ours, to what is mean and bad; they were temptations that only the Son of God could have.

[3] *Cp.* St. John x. 18, 'No man taketh (My life) from Me, but I lay it down of Myself.'

and pain get their vividness from contrast and transition. Pleasure has always a reference to pain avoided or overcome ; pain is sharpened by the memory of a pleasure missed or lost. There can be no such experience in the Divine Being, which cannot pass from states of enjoyment to states of sadness ; it does not follow that with Plato we should regard the Divine felicity as a calm beyond pleasure and pain.

Thomas Traherne (*Meditations*, pp. 27–29) makes an important attack upon the Greek theory of *ἀταραξία* ; he quotes the saying of Socrates that 'the gods needed nothing, at all, and they were most like them that least needed,' and he comments : 'The heathen deities wanted nothing and were therefore unhappy, for they had no being. But the Lord God of Israel, the Living and True God, was from all Eternity, and from all Eternity wanted like a God. He wanted the communication of His divine essence, and persons to enjoy it. He wanted Worlds, He wanted Spectators, He wanted Joys, He wanted Treasures. He wanted, yet He wanted not, for He had them.'

The paradox lies in the closing play on words. God wished for all these things, but He did not 'want' them, in the sense of 'being without' them ; they were all there in the treasury of His perfection ; all human desire (Plato tells us in the *Phaedrus*) has an element of pain, for it is 'in want' of its object ; but in God's Eternity, Desire and Satisfaction are simultaneous ; so Traherne goes on (*ibid.*, pp. 30, 31), 'He is infinitely Glorious, because all His wants and supplies are at the same time in His Nature from Eternity. He had, and from Eternity He was without, all His Treasures. . . . Being Eternal and Immutable, (He) enjoyeth all His wants and treasures together. . . . His wants always delight Him ; His treasures never cloy Him.'

In the world of His Creation He desires the redemption of His people and the coming of His Kingdom, but the desire is free from the uncertainty and depression of human suffering. God, Who sees the end in the beginning, sees beyond the struggle the triumph when He shall be all in all ; He is ' patient because He is eternal.' [1]

In the human nature of Our Lord we have human suffering coloured, as ours is, by the limitations and perhaps by the uncertainty of human nature [2] ; but of the Divine Nature we cannot admit any suffering like that ; all we can say is that the Love of God has in it a readiness to suffer which is expressed in the actual sufferings of the Cross ; the Divine ' sympathy ' is not so much an entering into our sufferings as an infusion of His joy.

[1] The admission of possible contingency cannot cloud the certainty of the Divine triumph at the last. We are all impressed with the sincerity and pathos of Studdert Kennedy's plea that God (like us) is ' up against ' evil, and that His life is a perpetual Cross. But it seems to me the foundation of sound metaphysics that not only is the Power which rules the universe Love, but also that the Love which rules the universe is Power.

[2] The cry from the Cross (' Why hast Thou forsaken Me ? ') may be an example of such uncertainty, but the passage in Heb. xii. 2 suggests that the suffering was dominated by a joy that sprang from faith : *ἀντὶ τῆς προκειμένης αὐτῷ χαρᾶς* (clearly, from the context, ' set before Him ' by *faith*) *ὑπέμεινεν σταυρόν, αἰσχύνης καταφρονήσας*. *Cp.* Dr. Rogers (*Atheism and Theism*, p. 27), ' As long as we can bear (suffering), it may be a joy. Men on the football field enjoy things against which they would strike if compelled, or paid, to endure them. They climb mountains to give themselves trouble. . . . The pain is little till it hinders them or masters them.'

INDEX OF AUTHORS

INDEX OF SUBJECTS

Printed in England at The Ballantyne Press *by*
Spottiswoode, Ballantyne & Co. Ltd.
Colchester, London & Eton